MANAGING MONEY & FINANCE

Managing Money & Finance

Geoffrey P E Clarkson

Bryan J Elliott

Gower Press

First published in Britain by Gower Press Limited
140 Great Portland Street, London W1N 5TA
1969

Second impression 1969

SBN 7161 0016 9

TO ELEANOR AND DOROTHY

Set in 11 on 12 point Imprint and printed by
The Camelot Press Ltd.,
London and Southampton

CONTENTS

Acknowledgements *xi*

1 FINANCIAL DECISION MAKING 1
Money and finance—Financial manager—Planning and control—Financial management—Structure of the book—Topics covered

PART I: MANAGING MONEY, CASH, AND NEAR CASH

2 MONEY, CASH, AND NEAR CASH 19
Money—Cash—Nearness to cash and liquidity—Solvency—Working capital—Liquidity, solvency, and working capital ratios—Example of working capital flows—Timing of flows—Flow of funds—Product-cash cycle—Example of a new product

3 MANAGING CASH 35
Depositing receipts—Operating liquidity—Operating solvency—Initial cash balance—Sales, receipts, and expenditures—Projected cash flows—Cash budget

4 SHORT-TERM MONEY MARKETS 54
The City—Bill of exchange—Fine, bank, and other bills—Discount market—Market for Government securities—Other financial services—Summary

5 MANAGING SHORT-TERM MONEY FLOWS 69
Prelude to planning—Planning the money flows—Creating a money flow plan—The plan in detail—Summary and conclusions

Part II: MANAGING WORKING CAPITAL AND FIXED ASSETS

6 Working capital 89

Current assets—Current liabilities—Short-term liabilities—Deferred current liabilities—Level of current liabilities—Some working capital measures

7 Managing working capital 105

Long-term considerations—Short-term considerations—Managing current assets—Cost of credit sales—Financing accounts receivable—Managing stocks—Managing current liabilities

8 Managing fixed assets 124

Fixed assets—Long-term investments—Operational assets—Fixed assets and the capital structure—Managing tangible fixed assets—Volume decision—Ownership decision—Effects of taxation—Managing intangible fixed assets

Part III: MANAGING THE CAPITAL STRUCTURE

9 Capital structure 147

Ordinary shares–accounting classifications—Preference shares—Reserves—Capital debt—Debentures—Loans—Bills of sale and mortgages—Assessing the capital structure—Capital gearing and leverage ratios—Cost of capital

10 Managing the capital structure 168

Level of capital debt—Preference shares and break even analysis—Retained earnings policies—Managing earnings—Dividend policies—Rights issues—Price/earnings multiples

Part IV: MANAGING THE CORPORATE STRUCTURE

11 Corporate structure 191

Partnership, close, and public companies—Economic considerations—Corporate structure—Ownership and control

12 MANAGING THE CORPORATE STRUCTURE 208

Managing debt—Managing taxation—Small firms—Large firms—Managing ownership and control—Managing close companies—Managing partnerships

13 MERGERS AND TAKEOVERS 226

Definition of mergers and takeovers—Value of a company—What to take over—Characteristics of takeover situations—How to take over—How to avoid a takeover

APPENDICES

1 PRESENT VALUE OF £1 238

2 PRESENT VALUE OF £1 PER ANNUM 246

Index 253

FIGURES AND TABLES

Figures

1	Product–cash cycle	33
2	Money market: principal flow of bills	66

Tables

1:1	Expected net income from two projects	5
1:2	Present value of income streams from two projects	6
2:1	Balance sheets	26
2:2	Working capital positions before and after completion of order	27
2:3	Quarterly balance sheets	30
2:4	Sources and uses of cash for first and second quarters	31
3:1	Cost a day of not depositing receipts	37
3:2	Company balance sheets	44
3:3	Projected sources and uses of funds (to year end)	45
3:4	Projected sales and receipts	46
3:5	Projected cash flows	48
3:6	Cash budget	50
3:7	Projected operating data	50
4:1	Quotation of money market rates (*Financial Times*, 14 May 1968)	67
4:2	Some money market instruments and investments	68
5:1	Weekly cash projection	72
5:2	Daily cash projection—special periods only	73
5:3	Weekly additions (subtractions) to excess cash	77
5:4	Time divisions of money available (required)	80

6:1 Raw material stock ages 101
6:2 Comparison of average ages 103
6:3 Accounts receivable ages 103
6:4 Accounts receivable ages 104
7:1 Examples of net working capitals 106
7:2 Net cash value of receivables 110
7:3 Receivable balances and cash flows compared 112
7:4 Average age of receivables to be purchased 117
7:5 Value of receivables investment 118
7:6 Age classification of die castings 120
8:1 Outline of balance sheet structure 131
8:2 Balance sheets 134
8:3 Comparative analysis 135
8:4 Lease or buy asset balances for Efficiency Company 137
9:1 Capital structure for two firms 158
9:2 Capital structure for two firms 165
9:3 Weighted average cost of capital 166
10:1 Efficiency Company balance sheet 171
11:1 Tax payments for a close company 205
12:1 Tax and retained earnings for close company (£20 000) 214
12:2 Tax and retained earnings for partnership (£20 000) 214
12:3 Tax and retained earnings for close company (£40 000) 216
12:4 Tax and retained earnings for partnership (£40 000) 216
12:5 Efficiency Company balance sheet 218
12:6 Efficiency Company, résumé of financial statistics 219
12:7 Tax and retained earnings for close company (£500 000) 220
12:8 Tax and retained earnings for public company (£500 000) 220
12:9 Ownership and control of earnings of Efficiency Company 222

ACKNOWLEDGEMENTS

The authors gratefully acknowledge their debt to the Manchester Business School and its students, both graduate and managerial, for their continued interest and frequent stimulation in matters financial. Dr Elliott would like to express his appreciation to the Social Science Research Council for their financial support.

To our wives we owe a special debt of gratitude for their tolerance and encouragement of our efforts. Finally we should like to thank Miss Wynne Waterworth for the unenviable task of producing vast quantities of accurate typing.

Geoffrey P E Clarkson
Bryan J Elliott

ONE

FINANCIAL DECISION MAKING

The management of money and finance is a vital part of all business enterprise. Manufacturing, trading, and marketing may be a firm's more visible activities, but without adequate financing they cannot be carried out. Many firms consider themselves to be in business to manufacture or trade, a few regard themselves as marketing organisations. We suggest that they are also in business to make and use money. The successful enterprise will regard itself as a complex which is in business to manufacture and trade, to market and to finance. Each facet of the total activity is interdependent, yet each has its own particular needs, skills, and expertise in order to function effectively. This volume is directed to the skills and expertise required by an organisation that is financially efficient.

This first chapter is an introduction to the book. It is a guide to the reader who may wish to pursue selected interests. Both money and finance are important ingredients of industrial enterprise, but some readers may see their interests lying more in one area than the other.

This chapter begins with a discussion of the role of money and finance and their relationship to financial managers, accountants, investors, and others who take part in the world of finance. We recommend that this section be read with some care. It will help the reader to identify his own position with regard to money and finance as well as introducing him to the main theme of the book.

The next part presents an outline of the book's structure. Though the entire contents will be of general interest, particular chapters will have special relevance to certain readers. It is intended that this guide to the book will permit the general reader to pick out his main interests and the specialist to ignore those topics with which he is already familiar.

The final section of this chapter contains a more detailed description of some of the important topics covered. Hence, these two final sections provide a detailed map to this book and to the activity of managing money and finance.

Money and finance

Profit is a reward for a successful business venture. These earnings are the funds from which dividends are paid to yield a suitable return on the risk money provided by investors. Earnings have an even more important part to play in a business enterprise. They are the source from which a firm finances its growth. Growth in earnings is the highest objective of financial management since a steady rise in earnings entails an equivalent growth in the value of the venture. Company share prices, the worth of proprietor and partnership firms and all capitalised values depend largely upon the generation and growth of earnings from the activities of the enterprise. Profit, earnings, and growth, no matter how prized, are unobtainable without appropriate finance. Hence, the management of finance is a very necessary part of the management of earnings and growth.

To manage an enterprise successfully, a firm must pay detailed attention to financial decision processes. Business finance is not concerned merely with legal and accountancy approaches to financial documents, instruments, and records. These are essential facets of financial operations but are passive services which the financial manager must use. The active management of finance is dedicated to the operations themselves and decision making is the activity of operations.

Financial decision making concerns every phase of a company's operations where the flow of funds and the generation of profit are involved. A firm which is consciously aware of its financial operations can manage its earnings in the same manner and with the same efficiency as it would wish to apply to the production and sale of its goods and services. Active financial decision making leads to positive control of the inflow and outflow of funds. This book is concerned with the management of a firm's finance and describes in detail a number of the more important issues and decision procedures.

To illustrate these remarks, consider a firm which is principally concerned with manufacturing and selling its products. It has never bothered too much with the financial side of its operations. Its attitude to the management of these operations can be described as passive. The firm is doing quite well, when it receives a substantial new order for one of its products. Raw materials are ordered and received and the main plant is put to work at maximum capacity. Suddenly, the managers discover that they are running out of funds. To meet this new order they have spent all their surplus cash on raw materials, wages, and production. To bridge the gap they need a loan, but their overdraft is already fully extended and their bank manager is not able to raise the limit. Money must be raised and it is available at a price. It is the price they have to pay that counts, and it is this price that reflects their lack of financial management. In contrast, a company with an active sense of financial management would have foreseen the need for additional funds. Control of the funds flow is part of their daily life and whenever shortages are predicted they arrange in advance for the credit facilities required. Credit is available from many sources under a variety of interest rates and conditions. Active managers are aware of these opportunities and select among them as circumstances suggest.

Financial manager

In this book we make frequent use of the term "financial manager." By this term we are not necessarily referring to a particular person whether he be the owner, director, or managing director. Though all such individuals play a vital role in a company's affairs, financial managers are those persons who make decisions which directly affect the flow of funds and the generation of profit and earnings. The financial manager may well be the head of a firm when long-term financial policy is being decided. Equally he may be farther down the managerial line making decisions when to pay for the next shipment of stock or whether to take a short-term loan to finance the purchase of some new machinery. Financial management encompasses a company's activities and the financial manager is any person who at a given moment is making a decision affecting the firm's financial position.

In a single proprietor or small partnership firm financial decisions will be taken primarily by the owners. In most cases they will take part in, if not control entirely, the host of decisions that make up the total management of their firm. To these owners we address the complete contents of this book. Larger firms will employ management personnel to conduct the daily affairs of the enterprise, leaving the owner/directors free to decide overall strategy and to handle important decisions of policy. For these companies parts of this book are directed at the owners, while the remainder is addressed to those who carry out the day-to-day management of the firm's finances. In very large companies there will be a finance department with a director who has a seat on the board. To these gentlemen we address the whole of this volume as it is their formal responsibility to give advice and to manage all aspects of their company's financial affairs.

Investors, whether large or small, play a vital role in the life of all commercial enterprise. It is they who provide the capital upon which all such activity is based. To judge the risk and value of investments, information and analysis is required. The contents of this book are directed to all investors. It is our belief that a detailed understanding of a firm's financial operations will enable them to invest their money with greater skill and confidence.

Planning and control

Effective financial management is based upon three factors: analysis of past performance, planning for future activities, and control of current activity. Control is achieved by carrying out decisions in accordance with agreed plans. Accordingly, financial planning is of crucial importance. At one level a plan may need to be no more than a statement of intent to expand production facilities at the end of the year. At other levels a plan will include a detailed description of the expected daily flows of funds. In many cases past performance can serve as a most useful guide to future activity. Most financial ratios and measures are easy to compute and once available can serve as the base line from which to measure improvements. Without plans, control is difficult to achieve or maintain as there are no standards by which performance can be judged. In addition, when the unexpected occurs there is no ready way of adjusting to or compensating for the events that have taken place. Plans are at the heart of all financial management and this volume presents a number of simple techniques to assist in the task of formulating effective plans.

Year	*Project 1*	*Project 2*
1	£2000	£1000
2	1600	1000
3	1400	1400
4	1000	1600
5	1000	2000
Total	£7000	£7000

TABLE 1:1 EXPECTED NET INCOME FROM TWO PROJECTS

For example, suppose that a project is to be undertaken and estimates are made of the net inflows of funds that will result. Suppose further that there are two possible ways of managing the project. The first produces a stream of income given above in Table 1:1 under the heading Project 1. The second is expected to produce the income listed under Project 2. Both projects will produce income for five years and both appear to generate the same total income. A financial manager will want to choose the one that yields the highest return. This return must be related to the point in time that the decision is taken. In short, to choose between these two projects the time value of money must be considered. Suppose this company considers their own cost of money to be equivalent to an interest rate of 10 per cent per year. In order to compare the two projects the income in each year will have to be discounted back to the present day at a rate of 10 per cent per year. £2000 received at the end of one year is today worth £2000 $\times$ 0.91 = £1820 at a 10 per cent interest rate. Similarly £1600 received at the end of the second year is today worth £1600 $\times$ 0.83 = £1328. The complete set of calculations for the two projects are presented in Table 1:2. As can be readily seen Project 1 has the higher present value and hence is to be preferred to Project 2.

Year	Estimated income Project 1	Estimated income Project 2	*Present value of £1 at 10% at the end of given years*	Present value of Estimated income Project 1	Present value of Estimated income Project 2
1	£2000	£1000	0.91	£1820	£910
2	1600	1000	0.83	1328	830
3	1400	1400	0.75	1050	1050
4	1000	1600	0.68	680	1088
5	1000	2000	0.62	620	1240
Total	£7000	£7000	Total	5498	5118
			Present value	£5498	£5118

TABLE 1:2 PRESENT VALUE OF INCOME STREAMS FROM TWO PROJECTS

Financial planning is responsible for deciding upon the time cost of money to use in the company's financial calculations. A particular interest rate, however, is of no value unless it is used to control the relevant financial decisions. Project 2 might well have been chosen for other than financial reasons until the agreed discount rate was applied. To plan without using the results to effect control is as wasteful of time, money, and effort as to try to control without a plan. Both techniques must be employed if a company is to be efficiently managed. Each subject treated in this book is presented with this dual purpose in mind.

Financial management

The fundamental proposition upon which this volume is based is that increased earnings (profits) are the primary objective of all financial management. Each firm may have a different product and its own way of managing its general affairs, but all firms earn profits by the same process. It is with the financial aspects of this earning process that the subsequent chapters are concerned. If this process is understood and managed effectively, the rate of return from operations can only increase. Our objective, therefore, is to present the methods whereby any firm can increase its earnings.

Financial managers are first and foremost in the service of the business owners. That the financial manager may also be the owner does not detract from the validity of this statement. Every increase in earnings entails an increase in the value of the firm. The market value of a firm is the capitalised value of the expected stream of earnings discounted at some appropriate rate. In a public company the owners are ordinary shareholders. The value of their holdings is determined by the market price of the firm's issued shares, which is in turn influenced by any changes in the rate at which profits are earned and dividends paid. Thus, if the principal objective was stated as that of maximising the shareholders' capital value, this would merely be another way of saying that earnings should be increased as rapidly as possible.

This book is devoted to the problems of increasing earnings. There are many ways of achieving this objective, one of which is to cut down on the outflow of funds. A large and ever-present drain on funds is tax. To reduce the tax burden on a firm is automatically to raise its earnings. Moreover, tax avoidance is an altogether legal as well as lucrative pursuit, and the opportunities available should be carefully studied and considered by all financial managers. The higher the tax rate being charged the more it pays to adjust the company's financing to take advantage of all possible allowances. Interest charges, for example, are allowable against tax. Hence, for a given interest rate the greater the tax rate the less it effectively costs the firm to service debt.

On the other hand, earnings can be increased by employing assets more efficiently. All companies have cash reserves which are maintained in case of emergencies. Cash by itself earns no return and can be put to work at minimal risk and almost immediate availability in time deposits and other short-term investments. To manage a firm's cash it is necessary to examine the way in which it flows in and out. The timing of receipts and payments is the essence of cash management and effort spent in this direction can bring handsome returns. To generate extra cash is one part of the problem, how to invest it is the other. It may be possible to invest for a month or a year or only a week or a day. Whatever the time period there is an investment which suits the need. Hence, to manage a company's cash it is essential to know the range of opportunities available in the open market for short- and long-term money.

Working capital provides another possible vehicle for increasing earnings. Working capital has a tendency to become tied up in assets for long periods of time. Some stocks are seldom used and occupy storage space aside from the cost of the funds they represent. The management of working capital is based on the notion that the more frequently these funds can be turned over the higher will be the total rate of return. Turnover of working capital can be achieved by a number of means. Stocks can be processed, debts can be collected, and creditors settled all with increasing speed. One of the consequences of a faster turnover of working capital is that it takes less funds to finance.

The management of a company's finance is as much a task of finding new sources of funds as it is the effective use of those the firm already employs. Growth inevitably requires additional funds and the financial manager must be prepared to make use of all available supplies. In a world without taxes, debt is both a risk and a cost. Taxes, however, reduce the cost of debt though they do not alleviate the risk. Another aspect of the world of taxes is the allowances for capital depreciation. Major assets such as plant and machinery depreciate in value through use and capital allowances are chargeable against tax. Capital allowances, however, are small compared to the cost of leasing the same fixed assets. Though leasing entails an increase in disbursements, the sale of assets generates extra funds. In addition tax rates reduce the effective cost of a lease since such payments are allowable. The decision whether to lease or buy should be considered with some care as the sale of assets can release much needed capital.

The capital structure as well as the corporate structure are important areas for financial decisions. Partnerships cannot issue preference or ordinary shares and have, as a rule, unlimited liability for their debts. Companies can be public or private according to legal definition and in addition the tax laws define a particular type of company, the close company. The methods available for raising long-term finance depend upon the type of corporate structure employed. In addition, tax rates differ for proprietorships, partnerships, and companies, public and private whether close or not, which in turn affects the cost of each type of capital raised. The type of corporate structure is a decision for the owners to take. Accordingly, the management of the capital structure must be treated within specific contexts. For each structure offers some financial advantages which the effective manager will hasten to use. The objective is to increase earnings.

Additional capital if properly employed will stimulate the desired growth.

Structure of the book

This book is organised around the major theme of how to increase earnings. As there are countless ways in which earnings can be improved, we have limited our attention to those items which, in our opinion, are of greatest importance. Indeed, we have been determinedly selective, and present in the following chapters a sequence of histories, techniques, and examples that describe and portray the more powerful tools of financial management. Our objective is to make a complicated subject easy to understand and to operate within. To assist in this endeavour we have included whenever appropriate a number of tables and detailed examples to emphasise the steps to take. It is our deepest hope that readers will not only be able to comprehend what we have written but also will be able to perceive how to apply immediately these methods of analysis and control. Financial management is a skill. To perfect a skill, practice and good technique are required. In the chapters that follow we present the techniques with examples to attest to their value. It is up to the reader to improve his skill by applying these techniques in the conduct of his firm's financial affairs.

The book is divided into four main sections. Part 1 deals with the management of money, cash, and near cash, the most liquid assets of a firm. To manage money and cash it is necessary to know the role it plays both in the firm and in the community as a whole. Cash flows in and out of a company as part of its normal operations. An acute shortage of cash can lead to insolvency and a resulting loss of control. An excess idle reserve is a waste of earning power. To balance these extremes, control must be exercised over the internal flow of cash. Since excesses and shortages will always occur in any enterprise, cash planning must include a working relation with external sources of supply and avenues for use. The City and its money market is the largest supplier and user of cash and a knowledge of its operations is vital for effective cash management.

Part 2 is directed at the management of working capital and fixed assets. Though cash and near cash are part of a firm's working capital they are sufficiently important to be treated separately in Part 1. Part 2, therefore, focuses on the management of the remaining current assets and liabilities. Once again the emphasis is placed on how to manage working capital to increase earnings. Liabilities are sources of funds and must be managed well if they are to continue to supply a firm with this type of capital. Current and fixed assets can be managed so that they earn handsome returns. Funds invested in current assets ought to be turned over as rapidly as a firm's operations will allow. Fixed assets are examined in relation to the tax effects of leasing or owning the same item. The net effect of write-offs permitted by capital allowances may affect earnings less favourably than leasing under certain conditions. All firms have current and fixed assets and their management is of great importance to the enterprise's financial health.

Part 3 is concerned with the management of a company's capital structure. Capital structures are constructed from mixtures of ordinary and preference shares, capital and revenue reserves, debentures and other forms of long-term debt. The management of this structure is a process of deciding how and under what conditions to issue particular securities. Voting ordinary shares represent a company's equity. Debentures represent a long-term debt. Gearing can assist earnings, and it is management's job to ensure that an appropriate level of debt is maintained. To manage a capital structure it is also necessary to decide on long-term policies with respect to dividends and the reinvestment of earnings. Dividends can be paid in cash or scrip and earnings can be distributed or retained. Each firm may have a different view on what is best for them, but there are a number of techniques that can be used to improve this decision-making process.

Part 4 treats the problem of managing the corporate structure. A growth in earnings implies a growth in the firm. Specific corporate structures are suited to particular stages in the development of a small proprietorship into a large public company. The corporate structure also places restrictions on and offers opportunities for raising particular types of long-term capital. The degree of ownership and the level of tax are both directly related to the corporate structure. Single proprietorships and partnerships are wholly owned by individuals and are taxed as such. Close companies whether public or private are taxed first as corporations and again, in part, as individuals since the voting equity is controlled by a few persons. Other public and private companies have widespread ownership and are taxed solely as corporations. The decision on corporate structure is the owners' prerogative, but it should not be taken without due consideration of the financial issues involved. Growth can be achieved by retention of earnings, raising additional capital, and takeovers. Whatever route is chosen there is a corporate structure or sequence of such structures that are best suited to immediate and long-term goals.

Each section of the book is divided into a number of chapters. Except for Chapters 8 and 13 they are arranged in a sequence of pairs. The first chapter describes and presents all terms and tools of analysis relevant to the topic at hand. In the second chapter these concepts and techniques are applied to specific examples to demonstrate how they can be employed. Thus, for example, readers who are already familiar with the relations among money, cash, and near cash, the relevance of liquidity and solvency and the importance of cash flows to a company's financial management, can ignore Chapter 2. Chapter 3 applies these techniques and ratios to the problems of cash management and hence is of more general interest. Similarly, those who are acquainted with the workings of the City and are aware of the investment opportunities provided by the money market can pass by Chapter 4 and examine Chapter 5 where a detailed analysis of a money flow and investment plan is provided. A simple guide to the ordering and contents of the chapters is as follows: all chapter titles which begin with the term "managing" are active demonstrators of techniques. The remainder describe the background, issues involved, terms used, and the methods of analysis best suited to tackle the problem at hand.

Financial management is a combination of knowledge and decision-making technique. Readers are urged to make use of the material presented in the order and manner that suits them best. This book can be treated as a reference guide or a bedside companion. Our purpose is to stimulate the generation of earnings.

Topics covered

Money, cash and near cash are the most liquid of all company assets. Cash as a form of money gives pleasure to hold but earns no return. Without a supply of cash a business cannot operate.

How does cash flow through a firm's operations and what are the measures of the efficiency with which cash is employed? How does a firm generate the cash it needs? What are the sources and where is it spent? How much cash is required? If a new product is being developed what is the cycle of the cash flows? These are some of the questions dealt with in Chapter 2.

Funds are received by firms in many forms. One of the most important is the cheques presented by customers for goods and services sold by the firm. Such receipts are collected, entered into the books, and deposited by the firm at its bank. How long does this process take? What does it cost per day if these cheques are not deposited at once? What is the operating liquidity of a firm? What rate of turnover in cash ought it to strive to achieve? How is cash controlled and how is the operating solvency of a firm measured? Cash is controlled by an analysis and projection of the cash flows. A statement of these flows becomes a cash budget which in turn is used to control actual performance. Detailed answers with examples are provided to these problems in Chapter 3.

Active management of a firm's cash flows will produce temporary cash surpluses as well as shortages. Hence, to manage cash effectively it is as necessary to know how to invest the excess as it is to be able to find extra funds when they are required. The greatest source and consumer of cash is the short-term money market. The money market is part of the City which in turn consists of a variety of financial institutions. What are these institutions and how do they operate? What financial services do they provide and how may a firm make use of them? How do funds flow through the City? Chapter 4 describes these institutions, the money market and the financial opportunities the City provides. In addition a detailed list is provided of the types of instruments and investments readily available in the money market.

The management of cash entails strict control of short-term money flows. Control is achieved by projecting expected receipts and payments and by maintaining a balance of cash flows based on these estimates. Cash management requires a detailed knowledge of a company's funds flows. Chapter 5 describes and illustrates these management techniques by providing an example of a cash and investment programme for a particular firm.

All firms have current assets as well as current liabilities and most companies endeavour to keep the volume of these liabilities well below that of the balance of current assets. To control these proportions, ratios of current assets to current liabilities and liquid assets to current liabilities are commonly used. To make the best use of available working capital financial managers must do more than balance assets and liabilities. Chapter 6 presents a number of analytic tools which can be used to manage the growth of working capital. Debts are settled with cash, hence earnings are the basis for a decision on what level of current liabilities a company can afford. Individual balance sheet items can be turned over with greater or lesser speed. What is the average age of trade debts, stocks and accounts receivable? Given this information what can be done to manage these balances to improve the working capital position? This chapter is concerned with the analysis of these items and describes with examples the techniques to employ.

The management of working capital is a major task for financial managers. If sales and production are to expand, working capital must grow proportionately. How can a growth in working capital be financed? What can be done to increase the turnover of cash in current assets? What volume of current liabilities should be maintained? Chapter 7 focuses on these problems and presents a number of solutions. For most firms the principal current assets are stock and trade accounts receivable. Both present particular opportunities and problems. They can be used as security for loans or as the basis for an investment programme. Trade receivables can be factored for cash or purchased as an investment. Their collection period can be managed, being reduced by offering discounts for prompt payment. Cash discounts can be earned by negotiating discounts with suppliers or by delaying payment if discounts are refused. An adequate supply of working capital is vital to the financial health of a firm. Chapter 7 provides a set of techniques that can be used to generate and manage the required working capital funds.

Plant, machinery, land, and premises represents the bulk of most companies' fixed assets. Fixed assets are an investment and the majority depreciate in value. The management of fixed assets is an exercise in long-term investment management. Does the investment earn an adequate net return? How can the rate of return be increased? Which assets appreciate in value? What are the factors to determine when deciding whether to lease or buy? The management of fixed assets is in part determined by tax considerations. Capital allowances are smaller than lease payments, and both can be deducted from revenue before tax is assessed. The differential can be managed to the advantage of the firm's finance. Intangible assets such as goodwill, research and development, and market research can be built up out of allowable expenses. Chapter 8 describes the main characteristics of fixed assets and presents solutions to the problem of how to manage these investments.

The capital structure of a company can be composed of a variety of ordinary and preference shares, capital and revenue reserves, and a range of instruments representing capital debt. Chapter 9 describes each of these types of capital and the contractual obligations they represent. An analysis of a company's capital structure will include a reference to its gearing and the amount of leverage. These concepts and ratios are discussed and techniques are presented for assessing the capital structure as a whole. The cost of a particular type of long-term capital depends upon a number of factors, one of which is tax. What determines the cost of ordinary shares? What is the relation between the cost of capital debt and preference shares? What is the cost of the total supply of capital to a firm? Chapter 9 focuses on these questions and presents the analytic tools required to guide management in its decisions on capital structure.

Gearing and leverage ratios provide a static measure of the quantity of fixed interest securities in the capital structure. But the interest on debts as well as the loans themselves are paid out of earnings. Hence, the volume of long-term debt a company can afford depends upon their earning capacity. Chapter 10 presents a method for determining the level of debt a company can afford. Taxation is an important factor when considering the issuing or redemption of preference shares or debentures. Dividends must be determined when ordinary shares are discussed. Since earnings and the retention of earnings are vital to the growth of a firm, what does it cost the company to distribute cash dividends? If growth in earnings is the primary objective what dividend and retained earnings policies should be pursued? Share prices respond to earnings and dividend policies. In addition the market price represents some price-to-earnings multiple. Share prices will rise more rapidly if this earnings multiple can be raised. Chapter 10 is devoted to these aspects of the management of the capital structure.

Business is conducted within a legal framework known as corporate structure. Whether a firm operates as a single proprietorship, a partnership, a private or public company close or not, the manner in which it conducts its affairs is in part governed by its legal form. The rights and obligations of ownership, the liability for the firm's debts, and the level of tax applied to earnings are all defined by the corporate form. What corporate structure suits the requirements of different types of enterprises? What are the advantages and disadvantages of each structure? How does the corporate form affect the power to borrow? What is the cost of raising funds from the general investing public and at what risk to ownership and control can such capital sums be purchased? Chapter 11 describes the range of corporate structures and provides the analytic framework within which policy decisions can be made.

The choice of a corporate structure is not a decision that has to be taken once and for all. An enterprise may start as a single proprietorship and as it grows alter its form to that of a partnership. A partnership may become a private or public company and be further classed as close. What factors affect this decision process? What are the tax and financial advantages of the possible alternatives? Chapter 12 is concerned with the management of the corporate structure and presents a detailed analysis of the decision problem. Ownership, control, and taxation are at the very heart of the choice of corporate structure and a sequence of examples is provided to illustrate the crucial points.

Companies can expand by internal growth alone or by acquiring others by takeover. What are the factors to consider when searching for a firm to take over? Alternatively, the question could be phrased, how should a firm behave if it wishes to be taken over? What are the advantages to the owners of a takeover and what are the costs? Not every company welcomes the prospect of being bought out by another. Hence, it is equally important to know how to manage the affairs of a firm faced with being taken over. Chapter 13 describes the takeover process and presents the principal factors to consider. Since firms with earnings that can be readily increased are attractive as takeover situations, that chapter serves as summary to the book as well as a guide to the world of takeover decisions.

This brief introduction to the contents of the book should serve as a guide to the reader seeking an effective answer to a specific problem. However, the book also builds a rounded picture of the activities which constitute efficient financial management. The conduct of financial operations is as much an attitude of mind on the part of those concerned with the total management of the firm as it is a technical activity. Consequently the book should be read in its entirety if a favourable attitude is seen as a desirable attribute for anyone interested in making money and creating wealth.

Part One

MANAGING MONEY, CASH, AND NEAR CASH

2	Money, Cash, and Near Cash	19
3	Managing Cash	35
4	Short-term Money Markets	54
5	Managing Short-term Money Flows	69

TWO

MONEY, CASH AND NEAR CASH

Money

Money is many things to many people. Some view it as the gold, silver, or semi-precious metal with which coins are made. Others regard money as wealth. In all cases it is the agent by which prices are measured and goods are exchanged. Possession of money can become an objective in itself, for money has a number of desirable properties. As legal tender it is used to settle accounts and contractual obligations. As an asset it is not subject to investment risk as long as its purchasing power remains unchanged. During periods of inflation, for example, the relative value of money decreases in proportion to the amount prices have risen. As a stock of potential buying power it often gives as much pleasure to hold as it does to use.

Money as notes and coinage has little or no intrinsic value. It is our acceptance of money as a medium of exchange that elevates it above the brass, copper, silver alloy, or paper of which it is made. To accept money as a medium of exchange bestows real value upon it. Money is a store of potential wealth, a potential which cannot be realised until it is put to work. It is at work when it is being spent and is earning a return. When idle it generates no income.

Money is an entity around which all business activity revolves. Firms use money to purchase a variety of goods and services from which saleable products are created. When sold these products generate revenue which is the essential end product of the commercial process—money. In this process the objective of a business enterprise is to ensure that revenue exceeds cost. This difference is the company's earnings on its investment of money.

Money can be considered to be idle when it exists on current account, in the firm's safes, cash boxes, and as petty cash. As far as the firm is concerned, money is a very scarce resource and should not be kept idle. Firms compete with each other for access to this scarce resource. Those which offer the greatest incentives will find the largest supplies. An enterprise which earns profits, grows, uses its resources efficiently, and actively pursues its objectives is most likely to offer the incentives which ensure an adequate supply of money.

Cash

Cash is a particular form of money. It is defined as ready money, a term which implies activity. It is indeed ready for many purposes. As legal tender, it is completely negotiable and is used to settle contractual obligations. It is equally ready to be managed in order to earn a profit and increase itself. Too often it is held idle in massive amounts to meet unexpected emergencies. It is ready but the firm has not put it to work.

Cash is a major product of a firm's activities. It is used to finance production and is received as revenue from the sale of goods and services. It is held as petty cash throughout a company and, in varying amounts, in company safes. The sum total of such amounts, often quite small individually, can be substantial. It may well represent a significant proportion of current assets. The total amount of cash in hand can be determined, at the principal accounting dates, by an examination of the company balance sheet. Balance sheet cash indicates the sum of money deposited on current account as well as all cash held at the company. It specifies the amount of the resource that is being kept idle. Savings and other varieties of time deposits are not included since such deposits yield a return and take time to convert to cash. In addition, the balance sheet entry does not include customers' cheques and drafts which have not yet been cleared by the bank and entered on a company's account. Though the balance sheet gives an accurate reading of the cash in hand at a particular date, this information can be misleading. All cash balances are subject to "window dressing" operations and do not necessarily reflect the normal working level of cash.

Nearness to cash and liquidity

All assets can be sold at some price and within a certain period of time. This sale or market price is the current exchange rate for that asset. Not all assets are equally saleable at short notice. Many cannot be encashed at all except at a large discount. It can be seen, therefore, that assets vary with respect to the time and effort required to sell them. This time and effort is a measure of their *liquidity* or *nearness to cash.*

For our purposes near cash will be taken to be all assets that can be readily converted to cash. For example, the price of an ordinary share purchased through the stock exchange may rise or fall over time. Whatever its price it has high liquidity since it can easily be turned into cash. On the other hand, assets such as land, factories, offices, or homes, have low liquidity. For even though these assets may appreciate in value it takes time and effort to sell them. In effect, near cash represents those assets which have high liquidity.

It is possible to define near cash in terms of the discount or cost of conversion to cash. Since price risk is inherent in the evaluation of liquidity, the rise or fall in value could be used as an index of nearness to cash. In our opinion time is more important than cost, particularly since historical costs are sunk and are not relevant to current and future decisions. However, both time and price risk are important and it is management's task to achieve an efficient balance between them.

Cash, by itself, earns no return. Hence, nearness to cash can be taken as a measure of idleness. Since nearness to cash is a measure of liquidity, liquidity entails idleness. As a result financial managers ought to avoid treating liquidity as a major objective. It is a fact of financial life that the nearer an investment is to cash the lower is its rate of return. Rates of return reflect the degree of risk involved, and to earn sensible profits risks must be taken. Risk implies a threat to wealth and a conflict arises between profitability and safety. Financial management is the management and control of risk taking. It is up to each firm to decide for itself on the appropriate balance to maintain.

The pursuit of liquidity can lead a firm into an unsatisfactory position. The usual outcome is a tendency to hold a large proportion of current assets in cash and near cash. Not only is this poor management of scarce resources, but it also leads to a direct loss of earning power. Earnings from cash are zero. Earnings from near cash are, at best, not much more than half that to be obtained in business operations. Consequently, large cash and near cash balances are expensive to hold. None the less, many firms keep sums of cash in hand that far exceed their monthly requirements. When pressed for an explanation some reply that they are saving for a major capital investment. Others state that they can never tell when an investment opportunity will arise or a takeover be proposed. To be prepared they must have a lot of cash in hand. Such arguments may appear to be persuasive but their commercial sense is poor. An enterprise is in business to generate earnings, and idle funds detract from this endeavour. It is not good enough to say, "but our job is to make motor cars, not money." There is no reason why a firm cannot try to do both. The essence of the operation is the efficient use of money, one aspect of which is the control of cash.

The theme of liquidity runs through the opening sections of this book where liquidity refers to the state of an asset's nearness to cash. Cash is the most liquid of all assets. Nearness to cash has been defined in terms of the time and effort needed to sell an asset. Hence, the liquidity of all assets can be judged in terms of their nearness to cash. Allied to the condition of liquidity is the special case of solvency. Liquidity and solvency are both vital to the financial health of a firm. Liquidity exists when quantities of the scarce resource, cash, are readily available or are easily obtainable within a short period of time. Too much liquidity is a misuse of money. Too little leads to severe cash problems which can result in an inability to be able to settle debts when due.

Solvency

Solvency represents the time state of liquidity. To be solvent entails an ability to meet debt payments on due date by having money available in the form of cash, near cash, or credit. It is not necessary to be liquid to be solvent. It is only necessary to be able to become sufficiently liquid should the need arise.

The ability to become liquid is a function of time and the state of assets in relation to cash. If too high a proportion of assets exist in a state far removed from cash a problem of solvency can arise. To be unable to generate cash when required creates the risk of insolvency and is known as overtrading. Firms which overtrade cause apprehension in the minds of their creditors. This can lead them to demand immediate payment of their debts. If sufficient cash cannot be obtained, the firm may be declared technically insolvent.

Technical and legal insolvency. Technical insolvency, as distinct from legal insolvency, occurs when a firm has sufficient assets to meet all financial obligations but not enough time to convert those assets into cash. Legal insolvency is a condition of permanent cash shortage no matter how much time is provided. The cash that could be realised from a firm's assets is less than the immediate demands of its creditors. Clearly, both states of insolvency are to be avoided. It is financial management's task to maintain the liquid and solvent positions so that the company is always able to perform its commercial activities. This is a difficult task to accomplish for the line between idleness and overtrading is indeed narrow.

Working capital

The liquidity and solvency of a firm are closely related to its working capital position.

Gross working capital. This is the sum total of all current assets.

Current assets. These consist of all stocks, including finished goods, goods in process and raw materials; accounts receivable (debtors); short-term investments (near cash); and cash.

Net working capital. This is the amount by which current assets are in excess of current liabilities.

Current liabilities. These are a firm's debts which must be settled within the following twelve months. They represent goods delivered, services rendered, and the remaining credit obligations of the firm. They may require early settlement, or involve an interest charge which can vary from zero in the case of net monthly accounts due, to bank charge rates on overdrafts. Current liabilities represent the total amount of short-term debt. They are the cheaper forms of debt but involve the highest insolvency risks. For current liabilities have due dates for payment and cash must be found to settle these accounts.

It is the function of financial management to fund the company debt at lowest cost consistent with acceptable risk. This is readily evident when the net working capital position is examined. Since net working capital is the net value of current assets this balance must be totally financed from long-term sources. Thus, the management of current assets and current liabilities is an important part of financial management.

Liquidity, solvency, and working capital ratios

The usual way to measure a firm's liquidity is to divide the current assets (gross working capital) by the current liabilities to get the current or 2 to 1 ratio:

$$\text{current ratio} = \frac{\text{current assets}}{\text{current liabilities}}$$

This ratio, sometimes called the working capital ratio, provides a rough measure of the safety afforded the firm's short-term creditors. For, in the event of a technical liquidation, current assets are more likely to yield a higher percentage of their real value than are fixed assets. Short-term lenders regard current assets as the ultimate source for the repayment of their loans. Consequently, the higher the current ratio the greater is their feeling of security.

The working capital ratio is frequently misleading and often has little value as a tool for financial management. To calculate the ratio, figures are taken from a balance sheet. These numbers reflect the past activities of the firm. Though it may comfort a manager to know that his current ratio was in satisfactory form two months ago, he knows nothing about its present state. Not only do balance sheets always represent the past, but they are also summary statements of the accounts. They do not include information on timing, particularly with reference to the periods within which the current liabilities become due. A firm could have a current ratio of 4 to 1 at the time of its audit, but if its current assets were primarily made up of goods in process and most of its current liabilities were due at the end of the current month it might face a severe shortage of cash. On the other hand a firm which acted as an agent buying and selling finished goods could have a low current ratio and be in a sound liquidity position.

One way of coping with the inadequacies of the current ratio is to consider the firm's liquid assets in relation to its current liabilities. Liquid assets consist of cash, accounts receivable (debtors) from which an allowance for bad debts should be made, and such investments and securities as can be realised without difficulty (near cash). Dividing liquid assets by current liabilities gives the quick or liquid ratio:

$$\text{quick ratio} = \frac{\text{liquid assets}}{\text{current liabilities}}$$

This ratio has significance if the timing between the receipts generated by the liquid assets and payments falling due is in suitable balance. If timings are balanced, liquid assets and current liabilities should be managed so that the quick ratio is approximately equal to 1. If it is less than one, liquid assets no longer cover the payments due, while if the value is much greater than one, scarce resources are being wasted by being kept idle in a needlessly liquid condition. Despite the refinement provided by the use of liquid assets neither ratio deals with the immediate present. In addition both ignore the flow of cash through the firm's accounts, a flow which is of prime importance to its operating liquidity and solvency.

The fundamental problem posed in the management of net and gross working capital can best be illustrated by examining the effects on a firm of an increase in sales. To fill new orders extra units must be produced. Extra production requires additional raw materials, labour, and overhead expenses. Even after the sale is effected an interval of time will elapse before payment is received. Throughout the manufacturing, selling and delivery period the firm's activities have to be financed. Though the effects of this financing will eventually be reflected in the current and quick ratios, it is the pattern and timing of the expenditures and receipts that generates the firm's current liquidity and solvency.

Example of working capital flows

Consider the consequences of the following sequence of events on the much simplified balance sheets of two firms, Liquidity Company Limited and Efficiency Company Limited, whose starting balances are given in Table 2:1. Both firms receive an order for £500 000 of goods. The order itself has no effect on working capital, it merely becomes an entry in the order book. Suppose each firm has sufficient productive capacity available to handle the order. It has to buy £100 000 of raw materials. These materials are purchased on terms of net cash monthly. Gross working capital grows immediately by £100 000. This increase in gross working capital is financed by the supplier who is not paid until the month's end.

The raw material begins its passage through the manufacturing process. In consequence a direct wage bill of £100 000 is incurred. By the time the goods are completed labour and overheads have risen to a total of £200 000. To produce orders firms have had to find £300 000 to pay wages, overheads, and suppliers' bills.

Suppose both firms borrowed these funds from their respective

Liquidity Company				
Net worth	£3500	Fixed assets		£2500
Current liabilities	500	Current assets:		
		Liquid assets	1000	
		Other assets	500	1500
Total	£4000	Total		£4000

Efficiency Company				
Net worth	£1800	Fixed assets		£1300
Current liabilities	1200	Current assets:		
		Liquid assets	1200	
		Other assets	500	1700
Total	£3000	Total		£3000

TABLE 2:1 BALANCE SHEETS (ALL FIGURES IN £'000S)

banks by extending their overdrafts. Current assets rise by £300 000 and current liabilities show a corresponding increase. Notice that these transactions have not affected the net working capital position. What has decreased is the current and quick ratios. This is readily seen in Table 2:2. Both companies are now noticeably less liquid. Though the Efficiency Company was and is in the weaker financial position, the Liquidity Company has incurred a proportionately greater reduction in its current liquidity. Now consider the effects of completing the sales transactions. The order is delivered and an invoice sent out for £500 000 on terms of net cash monthly. The stock of finished goods has been turned into account receivable (debtors) which are valued at the sales price, presuming no bad debts. The value of liquid assets rises immediately by £200 000. Current liquidity improves when judged by the ratio test, but a cash shortage remains until the debtor's account is settled.

Liquidity Company		
	Before	*After*
Liquid assets	£1000	£1000
Other assets	500	800
Current assets	1500	1800
Current liabilities	500	800
Net working capital	1000	1000
Current ratio	3 to 1	2.2 to 1
Quick ratio	2 to 1	1.25 to 1

Efficiency Company		
Liquid assets	£1200	£1200
Other assets	500	800
Current assets	1700	2000
Current liabilities	1200	1500
Net working capital	500	500
Current ratio	1.4 to 1	1.3 to 1
Quick ratio	1 to 1	0.8 to 1

TABLE 2:2 WORKING CAPITAL POSITIONS BEFORE AND AFTER COMPLETION OF ORDER

Timing of flows

The pattern of payments and receipts which are a part of all business operations depicts the occasions when financing is required. The purchase of materials generates trade accounts payable (creditors), and the manufacturing process creates labour and overhead expenses all of which have to be paid at regular but independent times. Stocks of goods in process and finished goods have to be handled, stored, and shipped. Each operation incurs additional expense that has to be paid as it becomes due. Finished goods, which have been sold, are then delivered usually on credit terms. Credit sales generate trade accounts receivable (debtors). It is at this point that cash shortages reach their peak. Firms face a variety of cash demands, including tax payments, all with individual timings. As a rule they have only one major source of cash revenue—credit sales with yet another timing.

The management of the cash flows is crucial to the financial life of an enterprise. It may be necessary, as well as desirable, to finance such payments by short-term borrowing. Such borrowings must be planned. It is as foolish to borrow money and not use it as it is to discover a sudden need that can only be met by an immediate increase in overdraft. Banks, like other lenders, dislike lending at short notice. They also have their cash flow problems. Further, when a company needs cash urgently the risk of insolvency is at its highest, and willing lenders become scarce as the risk increases. Many profitable firms have gone bankrupt because they ran out of cash. Solvency can always be maintained by holding large amounts of cash, but excessive cash implies a high level of net working capital. Net working capital is financed from long-term sources, and it is obviously expensive to finance excess cash holdings from long-term funds. A more effective manager will determine the minimum cash required, will study the pattern of receipts and payments, and will plan both his short-term borrowings and investments such that the firm is neither wasting its funds nor running unnecessary risks. He will manage money and finance so that it is neither idle nor overtraded.

Flow of funds

The pattern of payments and receipts noted above is a simple instance of the flow of funds through a firm's activities. These flows are usually audited on specific dates such as the end of each month, quarter, or year. Over such intervals of time the total net flows consist of a balance of all cash transactions. Receipts from sales, for example, are balanced against the funds used in the generation of those sales. Similarly, cash borrowed during the period is offset by payments made on the debt.

Total net cash flows are calculated by comparing balance sheet entries for consecutive time periods. In Table 2:3 a simplified statement of a company's balances at the end of each of three consecutive quarters is listed. In addition there are two columns which note the increases or decreases in assets and liabilities that took place during each period. The changes in assets and liabilities are important, for they identify the cash transfers that have been made. A decrease in an asset's value implies that a corresponding increase in cash has been generated from this asset. Alternatively, an increase in asset value means that additional funds were invested in it and implies a net decrease in cash. A decrease in cash can also be achieved by reducing liabilities, while any increase in liabilities or net worth (shareholders' equity) means an increase in funds. These sources and uses of cash can be summarised as follows:

Sources of cash	*Uses of cash*
Decrease in assets	Increase in assets
Increase in liabilities	Decrease in liabilities
Increase in net worth	Decrease in net worth

A summary of the sources and uses of cash can be constructed for the first two quarters from the data in Table 2:3. The summary is shown in Table 2:4. It provides a detailed picture of the flow of funds through the company's operations. During the first quarter cash was generated by negotiating an increase in the bank overdraft, by taking a substantial increase in trade credit, by mortgaging some new machinery, and by adding £29 000 of net profit after taxes and dividends to retained earnings. Most of these funds were used to build up current assets in the form of stocks and accounts receivable (credit sales), and to buy the new machinery which was immediately mortgaged. During the second quarter this pattern of sources and uses is reversed. In Table 2:4 most of the items which appear as sources in the first quarter are listed as uses in the second and vice versa. Funds are generated by reducing the value of current assets and are applied to the reduction of current liabilities.

From the flow of cash depicted in Table 2:4 it is possible to make certain inferences about the company's financial behaviour throughout the two quarters. First of all the company began the year by increasing both stocks and sales. Either sales have a seasonal pattern or the firm has launched a new sales campaign. The effect of increasing sales on current assets and cash flows has already been partially described in the analysis of the activities of the Liquidity and Efficiency Companies (see Table 2:2). It was

	Fourth quarter	*First quarter*	*Increase (decrease)*	*Second quarter*	*Increase (decrease)*
Net worth					
Ordinary shares	220 000	220 000		220 000	
Retained earnings	275 000	293 000	18 000	316 000	23 000
Total	495 000	513 000		536 000	
Long-term liabilities					
Debentures	180 000	180 000		180 000	
Mortgages	90 000	100 000	10 000	100 000	
Total	270 000	280 000		280 000	
Current liabilities					
Bank overdraft	33 000	85 000	52 000	29 000	(56 000)
Accounts payable	95 000	145 000	50 000	112 000	(33 000)
Sundry creditors	17 000	8 000	(9 000)	13 000	5 000
Total	145 000	238 000		154 000	
Fixed assets					
Buildings and property	230 000	227 000	(3 000)	224 000	(3 000)
Machinery	320 000	340 000	20 000	340 000	
Total	550 000	567 000		564 000	
Current assets					
Stock	230 000	268 000	38 000	245 000	(23 000)
Accounts receivable	105 000	150 000	45 000	130 000	(20 000)
Cash	25 000	46 000	21 000	31 000	(15 000)
Total	360 000	464 000		406 000	

TABLE 2:3 QUARTERLY BALANCE SHEETS

First quarter			
Sources		*Uses*	
Retained earnings	£18 000	Sundry creditors	£9 000
Mortgages	10 000	Machinery	20 000
Bank overdraft	52 000	Stocks	38 000
Accounts payable	50 000	Accounts receivable	45 000
Buildings and property	3 000	Cash	21 000
	£133 000		£133 000

Second quarter			
Sources		*Uses*	
Retained earnings	£23 000	Bank overdraft	£56 000
Sundry creditors	5 000	Accounts payable	33 000
Building and property	3 000		
Stocks	23 000		
Accounts receivable	20 000		
Cash	15 000		
	£89 000		£89 000

TABLE 2:4 SOURCES AND USES OF CASH FOR FIRST AND SECOND QUARTERS

noted that a growth in sales needs to be supported by a corresponding growth in raw materials, goods in process and finished goods, and accounts receivable (credit sales). All these activities require cash, and it can be seen from Table 2:4 that the company chose to finance such growth by borrowing from their bank and their suppliers, by mortgaging some new machinery and by making an adequate profit. By the end of the second quarter either the sales drive had come to an end or the company produces seasonal items. During the second quarter most of the cash generated by reducing current assets was used to pay off current liabilities. One can infer that the company was working itself back to a level of sales and production based on its experience of demand in the fourth quarter of the previous year.

Produce–cash cycle

An equally important aspect of working capital behaviour is to understand how cash flows are related to the life cycle of individual products. This life cycle begins when a firm decides to develop a new product. Development costs may be large or small but inevitably they require cash payments. In addition to design and development costs, the firm may incur market test costs. Some reorganisation of the manufacturing process may be required if the tests indicate that the item should be produced. In addition various engineering and other costs will be incurred in setting up a production line. Raw materials must then be purchased and labour and overhead expenses be applied in order to create stocks of partially and completely finished products. During this latter stage some form of sales campaign must be launched. Finally, if sales are generated, delivery can begin once the product is ready.

The design, development, marketing, and production may represent years of time and effort. Whatever the time period, the cash flows during this part of a product's life cycle are negative. It is not until some weeks after the first delivery has been made that the first cash revenue is received. For many products, particularly those requiring advanced technology, the research and development phase occupies a number of years. Testing and refining prototypes can add many more months as faults are discovered and improvements are made. Manufacturing and marketing also take time. Throughout these years the firm has to finance the product from revenue and money sources to which the new product is not yet contributing. To control these expenses, firms frequently set up a research and development department with its own budget. This department then becomes responsible for initiating studies and helping to make marketing and production decisions which identify and create a profitable addition to the product line. Research and development is expensive and is successful only when a new product sells sufficiently well to earn a suitable share of company profit. No product, however, earns cash returns while it is being developed. All such development must be financed, perhaps by an advance sale of rights, perhaps by government grant or from internal funds. The required volume of funds and the timing of outlays must be estimated. Whatever the source, the necessary money must be obtained or the new product cannot be developed, let alone brought to the market to earn profits.

Example of a new product

Let us examine the behaviour of cash revenue for a product that is launched successfully. At first, the cash revenue will be small. As sales and deliveries build up, cash receipts will rise rapidly. It is frequently the case, however, that the cash costs of generating those sales and effecting the deliveries will rise faster than the receipts from filling the orders. The net result is an extended period of cash shortage that will not be relieved until the rate of growth of sales tapers off. A rapid growth in sales can eventually be very profitable, but it always causes a heavy drain on cash.

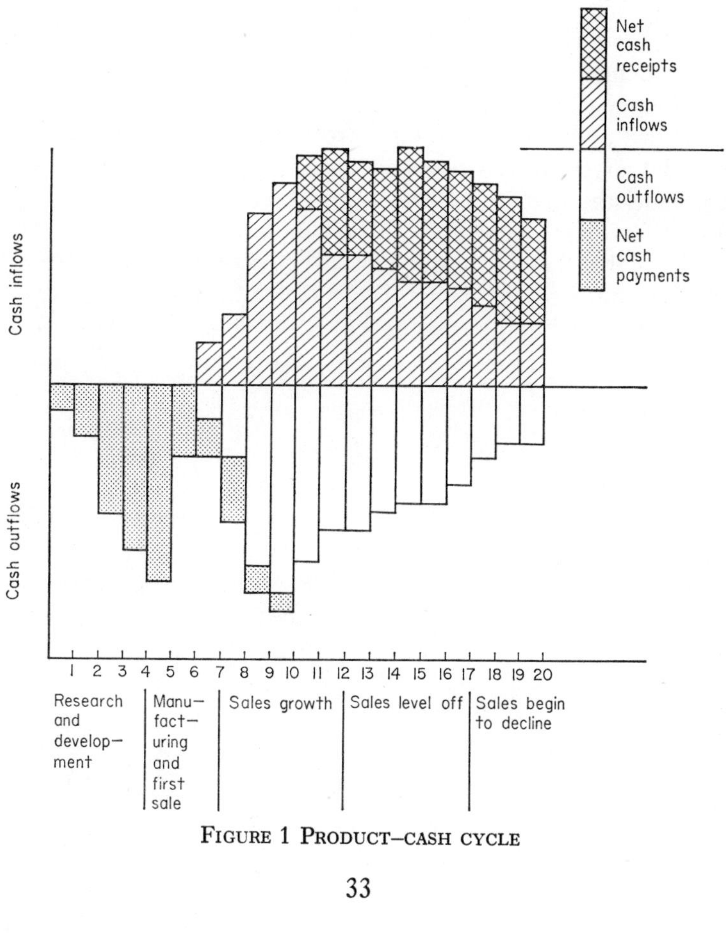

FIGURE 1 PRODUCT–CASH CYCLE

Figure 1 provides a graphic illustration of the cash cycle for a successful new product. If the intervals on the horizontal axis represent quarters, the first net cash receipts are not received until two and a half years after the first expenses are incurred. This timing schedule is representative of many products. There are some products which can be brought to the market more rapidly, just as there are others for which the intervals of time in the cash cycle are measured in years. Whatever the duration of the cash outflows it is important to notice that large net cash receipts begin when the rate of growth in sales slows down. The greatest net inflow of cash occurs when manufacturing expenses decline and the product can be sold mainly from stock. This is the period when growth in sales is declining. It may well signify that the useful life of the product is coming to an end.

The net cash inflows that are generated during the later stages of a product's life can be, and frequently are, used to finance the development of new products. When companies make the statement that 80 per cent of their current sales comes from products that did not exist five years ago and that this pattern is expected to continue, the massive cash flow problems these firms encounter are self-evident. That such firms continue to survive is strong evidence that these cash problems can be managed and controlled. It is the purpose of Chapter 3 to indicate the management techniques required to effect control over the flow of funds.

THREE

MANAGING CASH

Cash is both an essential input and a major product of a company's operations. As an input, it is important to know whether the quantity available on given dates is sufficient to meet requirements. A shortage may incur unnecessary costs and involve unnecessary risks. When viewed as a product, the reinvestment problem becomes important. Too much idle cash is a waste of scarce resources. Accordingly, methods of cash management should be tied to the operating data of the firm. There are a number of such management techniques available, the more important of which will be presented and discussed in this chapter. Whatever tools are used, it must never be forgotten that the management of cash is one of the major activities facing a commercial enterprise. A firm may be making a product which outsells its competitors. In addition it may be immensely profitable, but unless its cash is well managed these earnings might never be realised. Many a company has foundered for lack of cash, and the number of technical insolvencies recorded in the financial press is a warning to all financial managers. A far greater number of firms waste a surprising proportion of their resources by holding excessive amounts of cash. Cash management is vital to the welfare of a business and an efficient financial manager is worth a good deal more than his weight in gold.

The previous chapter dealt with money, cash, and near cash and the problems of liquidity and solvency. To recognise that a problem exists is an excellent basis from which to proceed. Solutions, however, do not appear out of thin air. Effective management requires as close an attention to detail, as it does to strategic planning and operational control. This chapter is concerned with the management of cash. Hence, it first presents methods for use in the analysis of the behaviour of cash in a commercial enterprise. It is directed at certain important questions. How much is too much when it is suggested that firms have too much cash in hand? What cash reserve is required in a variety of circumstances? Once understood, the behaviour of cash can be anticipated and control can be effected by suitable planning. If it is known that a certain sum must be paid out at the end of a period, steps can be taken to ensure that the money is available at the required time. Like the control of stocks or the manufacturing process, control of cash is readily possible once its behaviour over time is known. The second part of this chapter deals with this cash process and presents some simple techniques for its efficient management.

Depositing receipts

The total amount of cash available to a firm for the settlement of its accounts includes all funds on current account at the bank as well as all notes and coin held as petty cash and in safes at the company premises. Readily available cash does not include customer's cheques and drafts that have not been deposited and entered on the account at the bank. Many firms collect all cheques, drafts, and other receipts once a week or at most twice a week. These receipts are entered into the company's accounts and are then taken to the bank. For a firm with an annual sales turnover of over £10 000 000 the cost of not depositing receipts immediately can rise to impressive levels. In Table 3:1 the cost per day of not depositing receipts is shown for a range of turnover running from £1 000 000 to £1 000 000 000 a year. These costs are calculated as is described below.

Annual sales are divided by the number of working or selling days in the year (approximately 250 days).

This yields the average sales for each working day. A firm with £1 million annual turnover sells an average of £4000 a day. A sale does not necessarily indicate a corresponding receipt, except in the case of sale for cash, until the lapse of a period of time. The receipt of payment after an invoice has become due is further liable to delay. Over time such delays tend to even out in the case of companies whose accounts either are rendered on a daily basis or receive a regular pattern of payments throughout the month.

Annual sales turnover	*£1000000*	*£10 000 000*	*£100 000 000*	*£500 000 000*	*£1 000 000 000*
Average daily sales	4 000	40 000	400 000	2 000 000	4 000 000
Average daily receipts	4 000	40 000	400 000	2 000 000	4 000 000
Cost per day =.0002% per £ of receipts	£0.80	£8.0	£80	£400	£800
Cost of banking only twice a week	£3.60	£36	£360	£1 800	£3 600
Cost of banking only once a week	£12.00	£120	£1 200	£6 000	£12 000

TABLE 3:1 COST A DAY OF NOT DEPOSITING RECEIPTS

A regular pattern may result from such encouragements as discounts for cash or settlement within a strictly limited period. Other firms experience a regular pattern of a large influx of payments over a short period at the beginning of the month in response to accounts rendered and again delays become regularised. The subsequent remarks are addressed to companies which experience a regular pattern of receipts on a daily basis, though the relevant costs can readily be calculated for any pattern of receipts. Where accounts are rendered and settled monthly the cost per day of not depositing those funds can be computed from the daily rate given, for example, in Table 3:1. The opportunity to incur this cost occurs only every month, but it is no less worthy of attention since the total sum involved is correspondingly larger.

If sales do not vary a great deal from month to month, then the receipts received per day will be equal, on the average, to the volume of sales per day. Clearly, this will not be true if some accounts are never settled. To simplify the example we have assumed that doubtful accounts can be ignored and that sales volume is relatively steady from month to month so that average daily sales and receipts can be fairly represented by dividing total sales by the number of working days.

The cost per day of holding cheques and drafts can be either an opportunity or a real cost. The cost is real if the firm uses an overdraft to pay bills which could otherwise have been met by the deposited receipts. For a firm with no overdraft there is no actual cost of not depositing. But the opportunity cost is determined by what it could have earned on those receipts by placing them in, for example, the short-term money market. Chapters 4 and 5 are concerned with this market. In the former case, the cost is determined by taking the interest rate charged by the bank on overdrafts and converting it into a daily rate. In Table 3:1 we have taken the overdraft rate to be 8 per cent a year which reduces to roughly 0.02 of 1 per cent a day. The rate per day applicable to opportunity cost will be identical to the rate that can be earned by investing in the money market for a day. Like the interest rate on overdrafts the money market rates change from time to time and for illustrative purposes only we have chosen to use the single rate of 8 per cent a year or 0.02 of 1 per cent a day. Though this may appear to be a trifling amount, notice the sums of money it implies. For the smallest firm in Table 3:1 it represents a mere £0.80 a day which would appear to be hardly enough to pay the cost of a clerk to enter the receipts in the accounts and deposit them at the bank. However, if not deposited these sums accumulate. If such a firm deposits funds only once a week the cost is £12 on average.

The timing of deposits can be determined from a calculation which balances the cost of not depositing against the clerical costs of depositing. The larger the volume of receipts the greater the cost. A firm with daily receipts of two million pounds incurs cost of roughly £400 a day which accumulates, on average, to £6000 by the end of the week. Clearly, large firms consist of many smaller units, each of which may be autonomous with respect to its sales and receipts. If each unit is small and only receives a few thousand pounds a day, then a twice or once weekly schedule of deposits may be acceptable. Larger firms must be more careful as the cost of not depositing can rapidly exceed the clerical expense involved.

Operating liquidity

Cash in current assets, sales, and total cash handled. In the previous chapter, two measures of liquidity were introduced, the current and the liquid ratios. The former is the relation between current assets and current liabilities while the latter is the ratio between liquid assets and current liabilities. Both ratios are measures of a firm's general short-term liquidity. Both are based upon balance sheet data which record the state of the asset and liability balances at the end of the previous quarter, six months, or year. Neither provide management with more than an overall picture of the company's current liquidity, although they do provide an indication of the company's short-term credit worthiness.

Cash management requires more precise tools. A current ratio of 4 to 1 does not signify how much cash to hold or sell nor does a liquid ratio of 2 to 1 provide a much better indication, both merely indicate excess liquidity. To appreciate the amount of excess, a manager requires more detailed information than offered by these ratios. As a first step to obtain such information a manager must determine the amount of cash needed to support the firm's operations. One simple way to measure the efficiency with which cash is being employed is to calculate the ratio of the cash balance to that of total current assets (gross working capital). Current assets represent gross working capital:

$$\text{cash in current assets} = \frac{\text{cash balance}}{\text{current assets}}$$

which in turn reflect the short-term operations of business. A cash ratio based on these assets provides an index of current operations. Moreover, if handled properly it can be used to determine the minimum level of cash to maintain.

Suppose, for example, that for a particular firm the opening cash balance is £19 000 and that current assets total to £225 000. The ratio of cash to current assets is £19 000 divided by £225 000 which, expressed as a percentage, is approximately 8 per cent. For this company at that moment in its history cash represents 8 per cent of its gross working capital. A higher ratio, say 20 per cent, would indicate a large volume of cash and a corresponding high level of liquidity. It would also suggest that management was not bothering to manage its cash and was wasting its resources. There is an opportunity cost, of holding idle cash reserves, which grows to substantial proportions when the quantity of cash held is large.

As a further example, consider the Liquidity and Efficiency Companies mentioned in the previous chapter. The Liquidity Company has current assets of £1 500 000 while those of the

Efficiency Company stand at £1 700 000 and current and liquid ratios of the former are much higher than those of the latter (Table 2:1). The cash balances for these two companies are £255 000 and £51 000 respectively. These balances mean that cash represents 17 per cent of the current assets of the Liquidity Company and 3 per cent of those of the Efficiency Company. We had observed that the Liquidity Company was more liquid than the Efficiency Company, but it is now clear that Liquidity Company is burdened with a gross misuse of cash. This is not to say that it is not possible to justify a high ratio of cash to current assets. Special circumstances can and do exist. They are seldom encountered in a normal commercial enterprise and, as a result, a large cash to current asset ratio can be taken as a sign of poor cash management. The circumstances which require large cash balances are likely to be indicated well in advance and sound financial management will ensure a suitable supply without recourse to excessive permanent cash balances.

If there were one universal standard for this cash ratio, management's task would be considerably reduced. Unfortunately, there is no one best value since each industry has its own pattern of cash payments, receipts, and requirements. A working guide can be created by comparing average values over time for cash to current assets among firms in the same industry. The industry average is only a first step in the process, for an efficient firm should want to be better than average. Within a specific company a more detailed check can be made by inspecting past balance sheets and by discovering the actual cash to current asset ratio that the firm had been using. Experiments should then be carried out testing the effects of various reductions in cash balances on the firm's operations. The objective is to find the lowest value of the ratio with which the company can operate successfully—a level of cash that balances the risk of running out with the cost of an idle surplus.

The ratio of cash to current assets is a measure of the efficiency of cash management which is based on a company's gross working capital. Another equally useful way to judge the amount of cash required is to examine the volume of sales per period in relation to the opening cash balance of the period. The ratio of sales per period to cash balance measures the number of times the initial cash balance is turned over during the particular month, quarter, half-year, or year.

$$\text{turnover of cash in sales} = \frac{\text{sales per period}}{\text{initial cash balance}}$$

Turnover of cash in sales is a measure of the velocity with which cash moves through a firm's operations. For most firms sales are the chief source of revenue, then the higher the velocity of cash movement the lower the amount of cash required to finance the company's activities. For example, if sales for the quarter are £180 000 and the average rate of turnover of cash in sales is 9.5 times, the cash balance required at the beginning of the quarter is £19 000. Alternatively, if the manufacturing process is such that the rate of turnover of cash is low, the initial cash balance will have to be larger. Quarterly sales of £180 000 with a turnover rate of five times would imply an opening cash balance of £36 000.

The rate of turnover of cash in sales is a measure of efficiency in the use of cash as well as a measure of a company's liquidity. The Liquidity Company has £225 000 in cash at the beginning of the year and expects to sell £1 000 000 worth of goods in the first quarter. If these sales occur as forecast this firm will have turned over its opening cash balance less than four times during that quarter. The Efficiency Company on the other hand, expects to sell goods valued at £900 000 during the same period. It has £51 000 in cash at the start of the year and, if the forecast sales are achieved, it will have turned its opening cash balance over more than seventeen times. The higher the rate of cash turnover, the greater the efficiency of cash usage. A company which can increase the velocity of cash passing through its operations can expand its sales volume without adding extra cash. Alternatively it can decrease the amount of cash in hand if sales are not growing. In either event, the cost of maintaining cash relative to sales falls, and the lower the cost the greater will be the profit on those sales.

Efficiency of cash usage and a firm's liquidity are clearly related. For a given level of sales, a high rate of turnover implies a small cash balance. Cash balances are a part of the firm's liquid assets and are used to judge its liquidity. Although a low level of liquidity is frequently viewed with some concern, low liquidity is a result of an efficient use of resources. If the Liquidity and Efficiency Companies belong to the same industry and manufactrue a roughly comparable product mix, then the latter firm is making more effective use of its available resources. The Liquidity Company has more cash available and a higher liquidity rating, but whatever their respective profit figures, the Efficiency Company is earning more for each £1 of cash invested. Once again, there is no one universal standard with which to measure turnover of cash in sales. Each firm must decide by experiment the minimum cash balance it must maintain. A useful guide from which to experiment is the industry average. However, most managers will not be satisfied with average performance. In an industry where the average turnover of cash in sales is around ten times some firms will operate effectively with a turnover in excess of fifteen times.

So far, two measures have been proposed as aids to managing cash at the operating level; the cash balance with respect either to current assets or to sales. Total cash flows, however, are produced by the entire operations of the firm and to judge their behaviour a third and final measure is required. It is necessary to relate the opening cash balance to the total cash flow handled during a given period. The ratio of total cash handled to the opening balance is a measure of the rate of turnover of cash in the total cash flow generated by the firm:

$$\text{turnover of cash in total cash} = \frac{\text{total cash handled}}{\text{opening cash balance}}$$

The total cash handled within a given period is the sum of the sources and uses of cash during that interval. In Table 2:4 sources and uses of cash were listed for the first and second quarters of a particular firm. During the first quarter these totalled £266 000. The cash balance at the beginning of the quarter was £25 000, therefore the rate of turnover of cash during this quarter was £266 000/£25 000 = 10.4 times. Since the sources and uses of cash encompass the firm's entire activities, this ratio can be used to gear the level of cash balance to the company's total operations. Once again an average for the given industry should be subjected to experimentation to discover a satisfactory value for a particular firm. Though a value of ten times may suit many companies it must never be forgotten that these analytical tools are intended to serve. To be of real service they must satisfy operating requirements.

Operating solvency

Control of cash flows. Efficiency and liqudity are two aspects of a three-cornered problem. To complete the picture one must include the operating solvency of the firm. There is no point in increasing efficiency if solvency is ignored and the company runs out of cash. To ensure solvency a firm must have enough cash to meet accounts when they are due. The management of solvency is an exercise in the timing and balancing of the firm's cash receipts and payments—the firm's total cash flows.

To control cash flows it is first necessary to have a plan of the company's expected operations over the relevant future interval of time. Such a plan will include a forecast of sales as well as a set of the projected company balance sheet and profit and loss statements. These plans reflect management's expectations with respect to their company's activities. Plans lead to effective control when they are used as the basis for operations. If plans and budgets are pushed to one side as interesting exercises not to be confused with the real work of managing, then it would be better to forget about them altogether. For plans like any other administrative tool render no useful service unless employed.

A projection of the total cash flows is the master plan from which the daily balance of receipts and payments is eventually derived. To project the total cash flows, two consecutive balance sheets are compared; the balance sheet of the previous period and the projected balance sheet compiled for the relevant future period. To illustrate this process, suppose we are dealing with the same firm whose balance sheets are listed in Table 2:4. In addition, suppose that we are now at the end of the second quarter and we wish to plan for the cash flows for the remainder of the year. We have the projected balance sheet for the year end at hand as well as the balances for the end of the second quarter. These figures are shown in Table 3:2 together with a list of the projected increases and decreases in assets and liabilities that are expected to occur by the end of the year. These increases and decreases are the basis for the projected sources and uses of funds statement which appears in Table 3:3.

The projected sources and uses of funds is a base from which to plan cash flows. Some firms may prefer to begin with a projection of sales, and the operations pertinent to generate those sales. A more complete analysis starts with the total set of activities which includes additions to buildings and machinery as well as the projected increase in undistributed profits to be added to retained earnings. By so doing it can be seen from Table 3:3 that this firm expects its main sources of funds to come from additions to retained earnings, bank overdraft, and accounts payable and reductions in stocks and its cash balance. During this six-month

	Second quarter	*Projected year end*	*Increase (decrease)*
Net worth			
Ordinary shares	220 000	220 000	
Retained earnings	316 000	351 000	35 000
	536 000	571 000	
Long-term liabilities			
Debentures	180 000	180 000	
Mortgages	100 000	70 000	(30 000)
	280 000	250 000	
Current liabilities			
Bank overdraft	29 000	57 000	28 000
Accounts payable	112 000	141 000	29 000
Sundry creditors	13 000	6 000	(7 000)
	154 000	204 000	
Fixed assets			
Buildings and property	224 000	256 000	32 000
Machinery	340 000	380 000	40 000
	564 000	636 000	
Current assets			
Stocks	245 000	216 000	(29 000)
Accounts receivable	130 000	150 000	20 000
Cash	31 000	23 000	(8 000)
	406 000	389 000	

TABLE 3:2 COMPANY BALANCE SHEETS

period it expects to use these funds to pay off some mortgages, decrease the balance owing sundry creditors, and make additions to its buildings, property, machinery, and accounts receivable.

Sources		*Uses*	
Retained earnings	£35 000	Mortgages	£30 000
Bank overdraft	28 000	Sundry creditors	7 000
Accounts payable	29 000	Buildings and property	32 000
Stocks	29 000	Machinery	40 000
Cash	8 000	Accounts receivable	20 000
	£129 000		£129 000

TABLE 3:3 PROJECTED SOURCES AND USES OF FUNDS (TO YEAR END)

Initial cash balance

The first question such a projection of cash flows can answer is whether the initial cash balance is adequate. The total cash to be handled during this period is the sum of the sources and uses which equals £129 000 × 2 = £258 000 and the opening cash balance is £31 000. Thus, the ratio of total cash handled to opening cash balance is given by £258 000/£31 000 = 8.3 times. This firm turns over its cash, on average, 10 times a period so that the balance of £31 000 appears more than adequate when judged by this measure. A further check on the cash balance is then made by taking the projected sales for the period, which are £480 000, and determining the number of times the cash balance is expected to be turned over in these sales. The rate of turnover of cash in sales is given by £480 000/£31 000 = 15.5 times. Since the firm averages a turnover of cash in sales of 9 times per quarter, this rate would project to roughly 18 times a half year. Once again it would appear that the opening balance of £31 000 is slightly in excess of requirements. A final check is made by computing for the end of the second quarter, the ratio between cash and current assets, £31 000/£406 000, which expressed as a percentage is 7.5 per cent. Although not excessive there is more cash in hand than required and it can be seen that management is aware of this problem by examining the ratio of cash to that of the current assets which are expected at the end of the year. Here the ratio is £23 000/389 000 which is equal to 5.9 per cent, a somewhat lower and more reasonable value.

Sales, receipts, and expenditures

Once the opening cash balance has been checked it is time to turn to an examination of the firm's main source of cash revenue—the flow of cash receipts. It has already been noted that the firm has projected its sales for the coming six months at a volume of £480 000. Not all sales made during this period will be turned into cash receipts for all the customers are invoiced net cash monthly. In addition allowance must be made for doubtful accounts and bad debts. The result is that only a proportion of sales made this month will turn up as cash receipts next month, and an estimate of cash revenues must take this factor into account. For the coming six months sales and receipts are projected in Table 3:4. In this table allowance has been made for late payment by showing sales made in one month being collected over the next two. No allowance has been included for doubtful accounts. One way to treat them is to set up a reserve for doubtful accounts into which a small percentage of the estimated cash receipts is placed. When such accounts prove to be uncollectable the appropriate alterations are made. To keep the example simple such adjustments have been ignored, so that one can take the total sales receipts to be given by the last line in the table.

	July	*August*	*Sept*	*Oct*	*Nov*	*Dec*	*Total*
Net sales:	£68 000	£81 000	£91 000	£83 000	£89 000	£68 000	£480 000
Receipts:							
JULY	48 000	42 000	8 000				
AUGUST		23 000	49 000	9 000			
SEPT			25 000	61 000	5 000		
OCT				19 000	57 000	7 000	
NOV					19 000	63 000	
DEC						18 000	
Total sales receipts	£48 000	£65 000	£82 000	£89 000	£81 000	£88 000	£453 000

TABLE 3:4 PROJECTED SALES AND RECEIPTS

Once total sales receipts have been estimated it is necessary to examine the expenditures that have to be made to generate those receipts. To sell an item of finished goods raw materials must be purchased and labour and overhead expenses applied. Raw materials are purchased on short-term credit which gives rise to the accounts payable entry on the balance sheet. In many cases, discounts from the full price can be negotiated in return for prompt payment, so that purchases and their corresponding payments must be examined with some care. A schedule of purchases is drawn up to complement the projected monthly sales, and from this list of purchases a schedule of payments is constructed similar to that given for receipts in Table 3:4. Monthly disbursements for direct labour, factory overhead, marketing and administrative expenses must also be accounted for. These expenses occur in predictable amounts and at regular intervals, so that schedules containing these disbursements can be readily drawn up.

To complete the cash flow analysis all interest, dividend, and tax payments must be listed as they are expected to come due. In addition any income whether from the expected sale of some asset or the revenue on an investment must not be forgotten. Such income should be listed on a separate schedule so that it can be added to the receipts from sales to provide the firm's total cash inflow.

Projected cash flows

A projection of the cash flows for a given time period is constructed by taking the total projected cash receipts for each month and subtracting from these sums the total expected cash payments. The result is a statement of the cash gain or loss for each month. In the previous section detailed data was provided on the cash receipts from sales. In Table 3:5 other income plus all cash payments are listed as they would appear in the bottom line of their own detailed schedule which would be similar in form to that of sales and receipts in Table 3:4. Dividends, interest, and tax payments, have been combined, to simplify matters, along with mortgage repayments and other disbursements into the category called other expenses. In a more detailed statement of the projected cash flows each of these items would be a separate entry and would have its own supporting schedule.

	July	*Aug*	*Sept*	*Oct*	*Nov*	*Dec*	*Total*
Revenue:	£	£	£	£	£	£	£
Sales receipts	48 000	65 000	82 000	89 000	81 000	88 000	453 000
Other income	1 000			1 300			2 300
TOTAL RECEIPTS	49 000	65 000	82 000	90 300	81 000	88 000	455 300
Payments:							
Raw materials	36 000	45 000	30 000	24 000	31 000	32 000	198 000
Wages and salaries	21 000	25 000	28 000	29 000	27 000	29 000	159 000
Other expenses	13 000	14 000	14 000	15 300	15 000	35 000	106 300
TOTAL PAYMENTS	70 000	84 000	72 000	68 300	73 000	96 000	463 300
NET CASH GAIN (LOSS)	(21000)	(19 000)	10 000	22000	8 000	(8 000)	(8 000)

TABLE 3:5 PROJECTED CASH FLOWS

As can be seen from these data, this company expects its sales receipts to grow quite rapidly during July, August, and September. It can be inferred that they have either launched a new sales drive or that their sales vary with the season. In either event, notice the effect of the increase in sales on the cash flows. During July and August the cost of manufacturing the additional orders exceeds the revenues received, for it takes time before sales are turned into cash receipts. In September cash revenue begins to exceed cash payments and this net inflow is maintained until December when the cash flow turns negative once more. The net cash loss in December is a function of the sudden increase in other expenses, which in this case is accounted for by tax and dividend payments which are expected to be paid in that month.

Cash budget

The cash flows projected in Table 3:5 are a direct result of the forecasted activities of the firm over the next six months. The most general statement of the expected cash flows is contained in the projected year and balance sheet from which the sources and uses of funds are derived. The projection of the cash flows, however, is only one part of the total cash planning. For there is little to be gained by projecting activities which cannot be successfully managed.

The second part of the planning process is to take the projected cash flows and determine whether financing can be arranged to satisfy the fluctuating cash balances. For example, in July and August a total cash drain of £40 000 is projected. If the firm is to make and sell the goods as expected it must raise the required amount of cash. The cash drain as noted in Table 3:5 is not the total amount of cash required. At the beginning of the period there is a cash balance, in this case some £31 000. Thus, by the end of July when the cash outflow has reached £21 000 the cash balance will stand at £10 000. During August this cash balance would completely disappear as the firm absorbed the expected cash drain of £19 000. If a zero cash balance did not present undue hazards a cash budget could be made up in this manner, by taking the initial cash balance as the starting-point and adding and subtracting the cash flows as they occur. The risk involved by having a zero balance is usually more than most firms wish to incur. Accordingly, a sum of money is specified as the minimum cash balance to be maintained on account at all times. Clearly, this amount should be as small as possible since it represents totally idle funds. The amount to hold can be determined as a proportion of current assets or of sales. In either case a minimum cash balance of 2–3 per cent of sales or of current assets should be enough to accommodate most firms' cash requirements.

A cash budget can now be constructed. For each month the net cash gain or loss is taken from the statement of projected cash flows. To this figure one adds the initial cash balance for that month which may be positive or negative. The agreed minimum cash balance is then deducted from this figure to give the closing cash balance for the month. As will be readily apparent, the closing balance may be positive or negative, but in all cases it specifies the total expected cash requirements of the firm.

To clarify this process an example of a cash budget is provided in Table 3:6. The net cash gains or losses are taken from the cash flows projected in Table 3:5. The opening cash balance of £31 000 is found on the balance sheet for the end of the second quarter which is listed in Table 3:2. The minimum cash balance is taken by this firm to be £10 000, a sum which is always deducted from the ending cash balance to yield the total excess or required cash for that month.

	July	*Aug*	*Sept*	*Oct*	*Nov*	*Dec*
	£	£	£	£	£	£
Net cash gain (Loss)	(21 000)	(19 000)	10 000	22 000	8 000	(8 000)
Initial cash	31 000	10 000	(9 000)	1 000	23 000	31 000
Ending cash	10 000	(9 000)	1 000	23 000	31 000	23 000
Minimum cash balance	10 000	10 000	10 000	10 000	10 000	10 000
Excess (required) cash	0	(19 000)	(9 000)	13 000	21 000	13 000

TABLE 3:6 CASH BUDGET

There are several points worth noting in this example. First of all, cash flows bear little direct relation to profits. This company expects to add £35 000 to retained earnings at the end of this six-month period. This implies a net profit from operations before interest, taxes, and dividends of £86 400 as can be seen from Table 3:7. A net operating profit of £86 400 on expected sales of £480 000 is an operating margin of 18 per cent. This profit will be earned whether the total cash flows are positive or negative as long as they are allowed for. Without forethought all such profits are endangered by the risk of insolvency. If a cash plan and budget

Expected sales	£480 000
Profit from operations	86 400
Profit as a per cent of sales = 480 000/86 400 = 18%	
FLOW OF FUNDS DERIVED FROM OPERATING DATA	
Profit from operations (source)	£86 400
Interest payments on all debt (use)	8 000
Net profit before tax	78 400
Tax payments (use)	31 400
Net profit after tax	47 000
Dividend payments (use)	12 000
Retained earnings (net source)	35 000

TABLE 3:7 PROJECTED OPERATING DATA

were not drawn up this company could arrive at the end of July with £10 000 in cash hoping somehow to get by. By early August it would be evident that the cash supply was running out and something would have to be done. Various measures could be taken. One can always try to expand an overdraft, sell off any short-term investments, accounts receivable, or even fixed assets. Haste in such matters is seldom advisable and is frequently costly. Under such conditions a company faces the possibility of not being able to raise sufficient cash by the required time which inevitably leads to a loss of credit standing and the likelihood of technical insolvency.

A second point to note is that the cash budget is the master plan for controlling a firm's cash flows. If the total cash requirements are more than the firm can handle one must return to the projected cash flows to see whether the timing on certain disbursements can be altered. Cash budgeting is an exercise in the co-ordination of cash receipts and payments and the smoother the flow, the less liable are the balances likely to fluctuate and the less the strain on the company's financial resources. Once a satisfactory pattern of balances has been worked out, the cash budget is used as the basis for a financial plan to accommodate the expected cash flows. Such a plan must include arrangements for raising cash when needed as well as investing it when a surplus occurs. If, as in Table 3:6, £10 000 represents a workable minimum balance, then by the time an excess of £13 000 is in hand in October these funds ought to be put to work. If the cash requirements of August and September were financed by an extension of the overdraft, the excess cash can be used to reduce it. Similarly, if short-term investments were sold to generate cash, new investments can be made as soon as surpluses are in hand. Whatever the plan, the management of cash means that financial managers must pay attention at all times to the firm's cash requirements. In this example cash flows are presented and analysed month by month. The more detailed the analysis the more readily the flows can be planned and controlled. Accordingly, a monthly projection can be broken down into weeks and the weeks into working days. Such detail is not superfluous. It is the very essence of good cash management. It is certain that such detail exists in the day to day accounting system of the firm. It is usually serving little useful purpose. To use such detail in the preparation of cash flow projections and cash budgets is an exercise in creating information of immense value.

A third point of interest is that the example used here is of a company which expects to expand in sales during the first three months of this half-year. From Table 3:5 it can be seen that the growth in sales will have tapered off by the end of September. A drop in the rate of growth in sales implies a rise in positive cash flows, for cash receipts begin to exceed cash disbursements. Surplus cash is not generated until October, but the net cash flow is already positive in September as is indicated in Table 3:5. Since the sales pattern appears to be seasonal this firm can count on a cycle of negative and positive cash flows. The financing of cash requirements, therefore, is a short-term problem and should be met by a financial plan that deals in short-term funds. Short-term funds are generated by manipulating current assets and liabilities. Excess cash can be used to invest in more assets or pay off some liabilities. Under some conditions financial managers prefer to provide the necessary cash by buying and selling short-term investments. The cash budget then becomes a guide to the timing of his sales and purchases, and the next two chapters are devoted to a description of the short-term money market and the ways in which such investments can be made and managed.

Since excess cash is generated when sales stop expanding it may well be asked what happens to a company that adopts a policy of continuous growth. Clearly, if sales grow from month to month the firm will face a long period of large, negative cash flows. In the previous chapter the cash cycle of a single product was discussed. If sales growth is generated by a repeated introduction of new products, the positive cash flows from the old and dying items can be used to finance the expansion of the new. Despite such balancings of cash flows, an expanding firm requires increasing amounts of cash to finance its growth. Since overdrafts cannot be extended indefinitely more permanent financing must be undertaken. If each month in the projected cash budget indicates a negative balance this is a signal to the financial manager to consider additional long-term finance. Net working capital (current assets minus current liabilities), it will be remembered, represents the amount of current assets financed from long-term sources. A growth in sales implies a corresponding growth in current assets. These assets must be financed, and if the growth is permanent a proportion of the financing ought to come from long-term funds.

The decision to finance increases in working capital by short- or long-term funds is of prime importance to a company's financial health. Many a firm has been driven into insolvency by financing long-term projects out of short-term funds. Alternatively, there are a large number of firms who, fearful of such risks waste quantities of scarce resources by financing the bulk of their short-term needs out of long-term funds. An effective financial manager will avoid both of these extremes. The next two chapters plus Parts 2 and 3 of this book are devoted to the many aspects of these crucial financial decisions.

FOUR

SHORT-TERM MONEY MARKETS

Tradition distinguishes two types of markets: the money market and the capital market. Cash and near cash are part of a company's working capital and as such represent a portion of the total capital employed. Money, as cash, is also the standard by which the price of all assets whether current or fixed are valued. Though it may appear superfluous to distinguish between capital and money, a distinction does exist and serves a useful purpose within the financial community. The roots of this tradition lie at the foundation of finance which originated with regular trading in all types of trade instruments.

Economists and accountants differentiate between money and capital on the basis of time. They use the term "money market" to describe the demand and supply of all short-term finance (investments and loans). Long-term liabilities such as mortgages, debentures, fixed interest stock and ordinary shares are lumped together under the aegis of the "capital market." The financial institutions which make up the "City" have a slightly different view of what constitutes the money and capital markets. The former is used to distinguish the very short-term loans made within the system, the lending and relending of funds among banks, discount houses, and merchant banks. The latter term describes the whole range of borrowing and lending within the financial community.

The major theme that lies behind the definitions of the professions and business practice is the concept of a willing buyer and a willing seller. It is in this context that a market is involved at all, and the ways in which such a market is subdivided are largely irrelevant. For the purposes of this book the distinctions drawn by the economists and accountants will be used, since the element of time is an important ingredient of efficient financial management. Consequently, the term "money market" will include the limited technical interpretation given to the internal transactions of the financial institutions and will be discussed in this technical sense as well as in its more general context as part of the entire short-term market for funds. In order to describe the workings of the money markets it will be instructive to begin from the viewpoint of the financial institutions. For a knowledge of the workings of this system is essential if potential buyers and sellers are to make effective use of the available opportunities.

The City

The financial institutions which constitute the British system, known as the City, have grown from modest beginnings in the seventeenth century. The present-day expertise and mystique are the result of the mechanisms, procedures, and traditions which have been devised throughout the intervening centuries to facilitate the development of trade. This growth and evolution has led to a tightly interwoven, introspective, and efficient organisation of institutions whose day-to-day activities frequently appear to be totally mysterious and often constitute a barrier to the very people the system was designed to serve. As a result the City has become the subject of much political odium and has been accused of being a self-perpetuating oligarchy whose purpose is to master rather than serve. It is a requisite of sound financial management that the City be viewed as a major source and outlet for funds. To utilise these financial institutions fully it is necessary to understand their activities, and a brief review of their historical development is a sensible way to begin. Brevity, in this case, is essential, as it is beyond the scope of this chapter to present a more detailed history of the City and its many activities since those of insurance, commodities, foreign exchange and gold, and shipping as a capital market are only of passing interest to short-term funds.

The official money market consists of the twelve discount houses of the London Discount Market Association, the seventeen merchant banks which constitute the Accepting Houses Committee, the commercial banks (joint stock banks) which are members of the British Bankers Association, and the Bank of England. Since the foundations of a rudimentary money market in the late seventeenth century, failures, mergers, and takeovers have changed the constitution of the market without materially altering either its functions or its methods. Some of the present members trace their origins directly to the earliest period and are, as a result, well entrenched and steeped in tradition. Such traditions do not detract from the value of their specialised knowledge and expertise. Vast sums of money are handled every day by small staffs, and good profits are made on minute margins. The whole system is built on confidence where confidence is reflected in having a "good name" just as much as it is in the working principle that a gentleman's word is as good as his bond. Without mutual confidence between buyer and seller the money market would cease to function. Accordingly, it is not surprising to find that the City is an essentially closed shop much given to running by its old boy network. For these are its mechanisms for building and maintaining the confidence—so vitally required in the conduct of its affairs.

Bill of exchange

The modern financial system like its predecessors depends for its existence and profit on the fact that money tomorrow is always worth less than money today. This time rate of money is of fundamental importance to trade. It takes time for a seller to deliver goods to a buyer and further time to present and collect the accounts due. Without a system which permits fluctuations in cash flows to be smoothed, the seller can be faced with liquidity problems while waiting for the settlement of account. It was this need to protect liquidity which created the *Bill of Exchange.* Money lending in the sense of casual usury and pawnbroking had been practised for many centuries before the foundation of rational money markets. Such casual borrowing soon proved inadequate to meet the requirements of the rapidly expanding trade of the post-medieval period. Financial centres were first established in the active commercial cities since each depended upon the other's growth and success. The trading merchants supplied finance to each other whenever possible. The cash surpluses of one covered the shortages of another to maintain the liquidity of a group. Eventually, the demand for cash became so great that the larger and more prosperous merchants were able to expand their financial activity to such an extent that they ceased trading in their usual merchandise. These merchants became general suppliers of cash credit to a whole host of traders large and small. As their financial activities grew, centres were established which were not specifically linked to major merchanting. Bruges, Lyon, and Antwerp were early financial centres, followed by Amsterdam and, finally, London.

In the seventeenth century the main investment used to finance trade was the bill of exchange. The primary function of the bill was to enable the seller to obtain cash as soon as necessary after the dispatch of goods and certainly before their receipt, by the buyer. Similarly, it enabled the purchaser to defer payment at least until receipt of the goods and when necessary until resale had been effected. To finance these bills of exchange risk money was required from a third party, and the financer naturally required a commission for this service. To avoid the accusation of usury, which was subject to strict control and severe penalties for abuse, many devices were created to ensure an adequate commission. The more important of these devices was the system of discounting. Discounting was defended as a fair method of coping with the risk inherent in the process of lending money on a bill stated in one currency for repayment in another, since exchange rates were subject to rapid fluctuations.

A modern bill of exchange is a negotiable instrument defined and legalised by the Act of 1882. It is an unconditional order in writing addressed by one person to another, signed by the person giving it, requiring the person to whom it is addressed, to pay on demand or at a fixed or determinable future time, a sum certain in money to or to the order of a specified person or to bearer. It involves both a credit transaction and a transaction in currency.

In the seventeenth century the bill was drawn by minor trading merchants on important major merchants of unquestioned financial standing. Once the bill had been endorsed by the major merchant (accepted), the responsibility for settlement was guaranteed and the bill could be used to finance trade. Possession of a bill of exchange was almost as good as holding cash, since the bill could ultimately be exchanged for cash. It was not until bills became fully negotiable that they attained their present status and the virtual liquidity of cash. The use of inland bills (legalised in 1967) which removed the uncertainty of currency exchange rates, the legalisation of negotiability (1882), and the establishment of the discount market, all prepared the way for the modern money market where borrower and lender meet to match their short-term needs.

Fine, bank, and other bills

There are a variety of bills of exchange in common use. Some are less liquid than others and attract corresponding discounts in the market. All may be considered as sources and uses of short-term funds.

All bills fall into two categories, "period" and "sight." *Period bills* mature for payment after a specified time usually three months (strictly ninety or ninety-one days), but many are drawn for as little as thirty days, to as much as six months (nine months in the case of specialised trade bills). The discount rates applicable to the most common periods are regularly quoted in the financial press. *Sight bills* differ from period bills only in respect of their maturity. A sight bill becomes due on demand when presented to the drawee. With the single exception of maturity, period and sight bills are identical.

A bill of exchange attains the status of *bank bill* after it has been accepted by a London bank or an accepting house of unquestioned standing. It is also called a *fine bank bill* to signify that it commands the lowest (finest) rate of discount in the market. A fine bank bill requires the drawer to have an unquestioned name and the acceptor to be a member of the Accepting Houses Committee or a London clearing bank. It is also usual to have the bill endorsed by a member of the London Discount Market Association. There are a few other variations of the bill of exchange which merit fine rates. One such is an *agency bill* accepted by London branches of certain Overseas Banks of high standing. Another variant is the *trade bill* drawn by one trader on another where both traders have excellent reputations and when a member of the London Discount Market Association is willing to endorse the bill.

In general, agency bills and trade bills are quoted at a higher rate of discount than fine bills. As an investment they offer a higher return for time to maturity with a greater risk and lower liquidity. Fine bills ensure immediate liquidity on presentation to the market, for local banks will cash such instruments with little delay or cost. Other bills may take several days to negotiate since there is a limit to the volume of such bills that can be handled.

The working of the London Discount Market depends upon the support of the lender of last resort. The Bank of England will accept fine bills (it will also accept *treasury bills* and *short-dated government securities* which will be discussed later in the chapter). It will not accept trade bills unless endorsed by a bank or discount house. Furthermore the Bank requires two good names on a bill, one of which must be a British acceptor. *Foreign domicile bills* which are drawn on overseas institutions are not eligible paper. In consequence they cannot be sold on the discount market. London banks will accept commissions to collect on such bills and will often make advances against the collateral. If the foreign institution enjoys the confidence of a London bank it is possible to have the instrument endorsed by that bank. The endorsed bill then becomes eligible for sale.

The names used to describe the various bills in the preceding paragraphs all relate to the status of the instrument. Various degrees of liquidity and security are implied and different ranges of discount are involved. Two other names are used to describe bills of exchange. These names refer to the content of the goods which the bill is being used to finance. The *documentary bill* is used to describe all bills, whatever their status, which involve the movement of goods. All the documents involved in the sale form part of the package. *Finance bills* do not usually involve goods, although they are often used to finance stock. They are really a method of advancing general credit. In general a finance bill attracts a higher rate of discount than a corresponding documentary bill, the primary security being the confidence and trust placed in the two good names on the instrument.

Discount market

Each one of the many types of modern bill serves a specific requirement. All have certain essential elements in common. They are drawn on an established, respected house of unquestioned financial reputation. The good name of such an accepting house is the one feature which guarantees the liquidity of the bill.

Consequently the bill does not become a negotiable instrument until it is endorsed by the drawee who thereby acknowledges, in writing on the face of the bill, his liability for settlement at maturity. Once accepted, the bill becomes eligible for sale. The normal method of sale is for the trader to attach the delivery notes and invoices of the goods to the bill, and to sell the package to a local banker. Such is the intensity of activity in the bill market that a specialised system has evolved to handle these financial transactions. This system is the London Discount Market.

When a bill is sold on the London market the sale price is below the face value. The process of selling below face value is known as discounting, and these discounts are determined in negotiation with the discount houses. The discount is an interest rate designed to cover the cost of time before the bill matures and is liquidated. Discount rates are expressed as rates per cent per annum and are a function of the outstanding time to maturity. Such bills represent investments and as such are renegotiable. The discount houses borrow most of their short-term money from within the money market but do borrow from outside sources such as industrial concerns. The bulk of these funds are placed on call at a low interest rate, and if drawn for seven days or more a higher rate is charged. Discount houses purchase bills of exchange and other non-commercial investments such as government paper, treasury bills, and gilt edged securities with lives to maturity of up to five years (*shorts*). Local authority bonds are also bought although their liquidity does not approach that of government paper. In recent times, the bill of exchange has declined in relative importance due to the rise in lending by bank overdraft. None the less, the discount houses conduct a substantial volume of business. It is obvious that the discount houses are matching the cash requirements of very short-term lenders with those of longer-term borrowers. In normal commercial practice this would be a potentially disastrous situation. To cope with this threat to their liquidity discount houses have recourse to the Bank of England as lender of last resort. The Bank of England will rediscount all bills held by the discount houses provided that they contain two good names, one of which must be a British acceptance house. Local Authority Bonds are not acceptable. The minimum rediscount rate is known as bank rate and is always above the normal discount market rate. Bank rate thus acts as a control mechanism on the amount of liquidity available to the whole financial market. Discount houses will only incur the loss inherent in borrowing at bank rate when all other funds have been absorbed. As a result discount houses incur capital losses when banks and other lenders call in their very short-term money and a cash shortage exists. Conversely, when cash surpluses are available and banks and other lenders are seeking to invest their cash reserves discount houses earn good profits.

Most bills of exchange and all treasury bills are considered to be "eligible papers" (acceptable for rediscounting) by the Bank of England. The Bank is therefore willing to rediscount most bills held by the discount houses. With the relative decline in holdings of bills of exchange and the rapid growth in holdings of treasury bills and short dated securities, the Bank has tended to act more as a money lender rather than as an acceptor of bills for rediscounting.

The discount houses provide an active market in every kind of bill. Packages of such bills are usually sold to banks in round amounts of £100 000 and upwards. The buyer is able to specify the institutional content of the package and the ranges of maturity dates. Such packages are also available as investments to other institutions including industrial firms. As an investment they form part of the overnight and time market. Being virtually as liquid as cash they can be held to maturity or resold at a discount which permits the seller to realise the interest due to him for the period the investment was held. This return to the investor is subject to the discount house being paid a fraction of a per cent in the rate (usually 0.125 per cent) to cover services and bill endorsement. (It will doubtless be realised that the overnight and time markets have wider connotations than those described above and these will be discussed in due course.) When a package is sold, the discount house endorses each bill and assumes the responsibility for payment at maturity in the event of any default. Accordingly, bills have a double guarantee (triple if the reputation of the drawer is included) and are virtually as liquid as cash. Such bills can be used by third parties to finance their own trading and are often converted to letters of credit.

It can readily be seen that the official money market constitutes a system for trading in financial paper where the value of the paper handled exceeds by several times the actual amount of cash invested. As a result the money market is an important source of liquidity. Since it is designed to match the needs of very short-term lenders with those of borrowers of money for similar and slightly longer periods, it provides both with a source of funds and an opportunity for investment which can and should be exploited by the financial management of industrial and commercial concerns.

Market for government securities

Chapter 5 deals with the expertise needed to utilise the services and opportunities of the money market. This chapter is concerned with a description of that market and to complete the picture additional aspects of the short-term money market must be examined.

If the bill of exchange can be considered to be responsible for the establishment of money markets then the rise in the power and activities of governments can be held to be responsible for its spread into a wider service. Government departments incur liabilities which require cash settlement. These cash demands seldom coincide with the inward flow of cash from tax and other fiscal sources. Consequently government departments must find the requisite funds, and they do so by borrowing from each other and from the general public. They borrow from each other by means of the *tap of treasury bills* and from the public by means of gilt edged securities. The Bank of England is responsible for the management of government paper (the national debt), but by tradition the government broker is the senior partner of an old, established stockbroking firm (Mullen's & Company) and makes all deals on the Stock Exchange on behalf of government agencies.

It was originally intended that the national debt, largely incurred in the pursuance of major wars, should be liquidated over time. It has long been obvious that such an aim is specious. The security of government paper rests on the ability of the market to perpetuate this debt by issuing replacement paper. The money market is a large investor in surplus treasury bills and issued securities and it should be noted that this paper is also available as an investment for the surplus cash of individuals and industrial concerns. By tradition, the short-term money market in government securities is limited to those stocks with lives of less than five years to maturity. All long-dated stocks eventually become shorts and merit attention as short-term investments for excess cash.

Treasury bills are issued to meet the short-term requirements of the treasury. They are issued through the tap to government departments which have surplus cash in hand and by weekly tenders to the official money market. At present, the weekly tenders are taken by the discount houses and banks who are purchasing for their own investment requirements. Banks, however, can acquire treasury bills by tender for industrial concerns wishing to make such an investment. Treasury bills carry a lower rate of interest than commercial bills but are slightly more liquid.

Government securities are bought and sold on the gilt edged market. They are necessarily less liquid than either treasury bills or commercial bills since both a willing buyer and a willing seller has to be found. The government broker assists the market by buying and selling such reserve quantities as are necessary to prevent erratic fluctuations in prices. Prices do reflect the many factors which affect investors' confidence in the economic well-being of a country and they are liable to change from day to day. The shorter the time to maturity in a government security, the more stable is its price and the greater is liquidity. This stability is in part due to the government broker who usually takes the opportunity to buy-in as much available stock as possible before redemption date. His objectives are to reduce the volume of work at redemption date and to ensure an orderly market. Thus, although the liquidity of any government security is a function of its redemption date, the existence of an orderly market ensures a practical liquidity which is little short of the treasury and commercial bills. Sales of government securities are made for cash (as distinct from sales of ordinary shares which are sold for account) and their liquidity is therefore a function of bank clearance time, a matter of some three days in present conditions.

Other financial services

In addition to its specialised activities in the money market, the City provides a host of other services which are available to the public. Both the commercial and the merchant banks provide normal banking facilities. They accept deposits on current account which earn no interest. Current accounts provide banks with zero charge cash surpluses, but these funds have maximum liquidity to the depositor and are subject to immediate recall. Banks invest a large proportion of these deposits in the money market and in overdrafts. Indeed they maintain a cash surplus of only 8 per cent of total deposits of all kinds or some 15 per cent of current accounts. Cash in excess of this necessary minimum is invested at call in the discount market and is employed to maintain a balance within the banking system by being lent overnight at minute interest rates.

In addition to accepting deposits on current account banks attract deposits repayable at notice. Such time deposits are usually subject to a minimum notice of seven days and attract a very low rate of interest. As an investment the deposit account has a degree of liquidity not shared by other time deposits and interest bearing assets. For, in practice, banks allow balances to be transferred from deposit to current account with at most a small interest penalty. A third type of deposit is the savings account. This is designed for small savings and only a limited amount is accepted at savings interest rate, any excess being granted deposit rate.

These banking activities constitute an important set of sources and uses of cash funds, all of which are available to the financial manager. One common source of finance is the bank overdraft. An overdraft is a flexible source of funds that is reasonably inexpensive to maintain in normal economic circumstances. It suffers from two disadvantages. In theory it is only on loan at call, although bankers seldom exercise this right. Secondly, an overdraft is subject to an interest rate that depends, in turn, upon the bank rate. Since the bank rate fluctuates as a result of various political and economic pressures, the financial manager has no control over the rate charged on overdrafts. Another source of funds is provided by the finance houses who are suppliers of hire purchase and credit finance. They offer finance facilities to the industrial concern in the form of credit for the purchase of such items as vehicles and machinery. In turn, they also accept deposits either on call or subject to notice. The larger finance houses usually require a minimum deposit of £500 or more, but many accept deposits without any limit. Since the major houses are owned and backed by the commercial and merchant banks these deposits represent a highly liquid investment. Building societies and insurance companies offer yet another market for funds. Both offer mortgage facilities on property and accept deposits of limited size. In the case of the building societies deposits are limited to £5000, a legal constraint which stems from their preferential treatment in regard to tax assessment.

Summary

The flow of funds through the money market is presented in schematic form in Figure 2. Short-dated government stock is not included in this flow since these securities are directly available to everyone.

Every forward movement of a monetary instrument entails a flow of cash in the reverse direction. To begin with, acceptance houses take a small commission, by negotiation with the instigator of a commercial bill (the drawer), to cover their services as acceptors. As the accepted bill moves through the system it acquires added status by being endorsed by other signatures. An accepted bill is a negotiable instrument with a high liquidity and fine bills are virtually as liquid as cash. All bills carry an interest rate to maturity, and as such are an attractive investment. Accepted bills can be sold (discounted) in the discount market the seller receiving cash in return less a commission to the discount house. This commission is known as the discount and represents the time value of money. An accepted and discounted bill (a fine bill if the acceptor or discounter has a special status) is a totally negotiable instrument. It is available as a short-term investment to banks, institutions, industrial concerns and individuals. Thus, the cash requirements of many firms, particularly exporters, can be met without their having to wait for payment from their overseas customers.

The specialised market in treasury bills is also depicted in Figure 2. Treasury bills meet the cash needs of government departments by creating a flow of short-term funds to smooth the fluctuations in fiscal appropriations. Once again, the surplus cash of the financial community is efficiently and profitably applied to satisfy borrowing requirements. Treasury bills are the most liquid short-term investment and command the lowest discount rates. They are a totally secure investment and are encashable without notice.

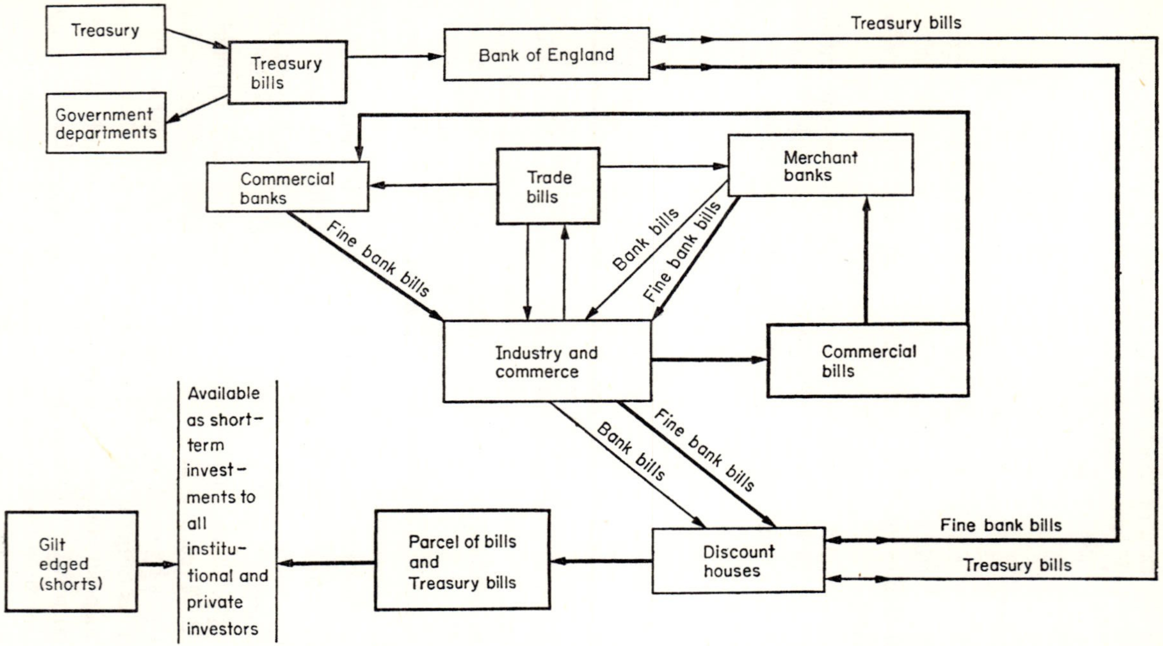

FIGURE 2 MONEY MARKET: PRINCIPAL FLOW OF BILLS

The money market cannot operate successfully without a large and continuous turnover in short-term funds. The market lends and borrows money on call and at notice (seven days or more) at competitive rates of interest. In recent years there has been a chronic shortage of cash and assistance has been required from the authorities. Consequently, the market has sought new funds and continental investors have taken advantage of the available investment opportunities. A source of cash which could relieve this shortage is at present tied up in the idle reserves of many businesses. The next chapter is concerned with the management of a firm's short-term funds and as a result presents methods by which such funds can be made available and invested in the money market. An indication of the return on investment offered by the money market is provided in Table 4:1. These quotations of rates are published regularly in the financial press. Finally, Table 4:2 contains a list of the range of instruments and investments that are available in the money market.

Bank rate $7\frac{1}{2}\%$ *(21 March 1968)*

Loans		*Bank bills*			*Trade bills*		
Overnight call money	7 day notice	2 and 3 months	4 months	6 months	3 months	4 months	9 months
$5\frac{7}{8}$–$7\frac{1}{8}$	$5\frac{3}{4}$–$7\frac{1}{8}$	$7\frac{3}{8}$–$7\frac{7}{16}$	$7\frac{3}{8}$–$7\frac{7}{16}$	$7\frac{3}{8}$–$7\frac{7}{16}$	$8\frac{1}{2}$–9	$8\frac{1}{2}$–$9\frac{1}{4}$	$8\frac{3}{4}$–$9\frac{1}{2}$

LOCAL AUTHORITY BONDS

Notice	*Rate*
2 days	$8\frac{1}{2}$–$8\frac{5}{8}$
7 days	$8\frac{5}{8}$–$8\frac{3}{4}$
30 days	$8\frac{1}{2}$–$8\frac{5}{8}$
90 days	$8\frac{3}{8}$–$8\frac{1}{2}$
6 months	$8\frac{1}{8}$–$8\frac{1}{4}$

FINANCE HOUSES

Deposit time	*Rate*
3 months	$8\frac{1}{2}$–$8\frac{7}{8}$
6 months	$8\frac{1}{2}$–$8\frac{5}{8}$

TABLE 4:1 QUOTATION OF MONEY MARKET RATES
(*Financial Times*, 14 May 1968)

Instrument	*Lot size*	*Period to maturity*	*Discount (interest) rate*	*Liquidity*
Treasury bills	£100 000–£1 000 000 (split lots available from banks at slightly lower rates)	Dated by month Usually 91 days	$7\frac{1}{64}$	Highest
Fine bank bills		1–30 days	$7\frac{1}{2}$–$7\frac{9}{16}$	Very high
		31–90 days	$7\frac{3}{8}$–$7\frac{7}{16}$	
		6 months	$7\frac{1}{2}$–$7\frac{7}{16}$	
Fine agency bills		31–90 days	$7\frac{1}{2}$–$7\frac{9}{16}$	Very high
		6 months	$7\frac{9}{16}$–$7\frac{5}{8}$	
Fine trade bills	Mixed lots of £100 000 to £1 000 000. Purchaser has the right to state the content of the mixture.	3 months	$8\frac{1}{2}$–9	Very high
		4 months	$8\frac{1}{2}$–$9\frac{1}{4}$	
		9 months	$8\frac{3}{4}$–$9\frac{1}{2}$	
Bank bills		1–30 days	9–10	High
		31–90 days	$9\frac{1}{4}$–$10\frac{1}{4}$	
		6 months	$10\frac{1}{2}$–11	
Agency bills		31–90 days	9–$9\frac{1}{2}$	Good
		6 months	$9\frac{3}{4}$–10	
Trade bills		3 months 4 months 9 months	By negotiation	Medium
DEPOSITS				
Commercial bank	Usually no lower limit	Call money	Nil	Highest
		7 days	5	High
Merchant bank	Sometimes a minimum of £500	Call money	$5\frac{7}{8}$–$7\frac{1}{8}$	Highest
		7 days	$5\frac{3}{4}$–$7\frac{1}{8}$	High
Finance house	Sometimes a minimum of £500	3 months	$8\frac{1}{2}$–$8\frac{7}{8}$	
		6 months	$8\frac{1}{2}$–$8\frac{5}{8}$	Good
Building society	£5–£5000	1 month Notice	$7\frac{3}{4}$ (gross)	Low
STOCKS AND BONDS				
Gilt edge	Nominal £100	1 day–5 years	$6\frac{1}{8}$–$7\frac{7}{16}$	Good
Local authority	£100	2 days–5 years	$7\frac{3}{4}$–$8\frac{3}{4}$	Low

TABLE 4:2 SOME MONEY MARKET INSTRUMENTS AND INVESTMENTS
The discounts quoted refer to documentary bills. In all cases finance paper will carry higher rates. Finance house deposits and local authority bonds can usually be liquidated by arrangement at short notice. This process always involves a capital loss penalty.

FIVE

MANAGING SHORT-TERM MONEY FLOWS

The management of a company's short-term money flows has two important aspects; the first is to maintain a high level of liquidity with a minimum of risk; the second is to generate additional income by investing idle funds when available or paying off loans when they are no longer needed. These aspects require a skill in financial management that is not developed in the ordinary course of events. On the one hand it entails viewing the money market as a ready source of short-term loans and on the other as providing a wide variety of short-term investments for a company's surplus cash. In addition, cash must be seen as both a major product of, and an essential input to, a firm's operations, so that cash flows are examined in detail. All commercial enterprise is faced with the recurring need to satisfy cash demands followed by a requirement to find suitable investments for temporary cash surpluses. This cycle of cash flows must be managed and managed well if the firm's financial health is to be maintained, and the money market offers unique services to assist the manager in this task.

In Chapter 3 a projection of the cash flows and a cash budget were presented as tools by which a company's cash can be managed and controlled. Cash flows become a firm's money flows when the results of the cash budget are used to plan and control the borrowing and lending of short-term funds. It is the timing and balancing of the cash demands posed by this budget that constitutes the core of money flow management. When cash shortages are expected, funds must be borrowed or investments sold. When excesses are available they must be invested or used to pay off outstanding loans. In all cases the objective is to coordinate these movements of money. Co-ordination needs analysis and planning and this chapter is devoted to a description of the techniques required to achieve effective control of a company's short-term money flows.

Prelude to planning

Detailed cash flows. Table 3:5 of Chapter 3 presents a six-month projection of a particular company's expected cash flows. The projection is presented on a monthly basis with each item in the table representing a net balance for the month. Though such a projection can serve as the basis for a monthly cash budget it does not contain the detail required for a money flow analysis. To generate the required plan, a manager must bear in mind that the short-term money market offers loans and investment opportunities for periods as short as overnight and at call, to as long as months or even years. In addition, it is necessary to remember that interest rates are a direct function of the time until maturity and that liquidity moves in the opposite direction. For example, a penalty must be paid to obtain cash from a time deposit within the usual notice period.

Given the wide variety of investments and loans available the monthly cash flow and cash budget (Tables 3:5 and 3:6, respectively) are clearly inadequate. In general, it is necessary to expand the monthly analysis to include the expected weekly transactions, for the cash budget only projects total cash shortages and surpluses. The greater detail of a projected week by week analysis indicates the type of loan or investment required.

An example of a projection of weekly cash flows is provided in Table 5:1. The data in this table are a more detailed representation of the firm's expected cash flows shown in Table 3:5. An examination of these weekly data reveals that the company expects a pattern of receipts in response to sales which produces a heavy cash inflow in the first week of the month and few receipts during the remaining weeks. In contrast to this inflow, the firm has three major patterns of payments. Each week it pays a wage bill and once a month it pays for its raw materials and supplies. Since discounts are sometimes offered for quick payment, this firm makes a point of receiving raw materials during the last week of the month and makes payment within the required three days. Finally, the company has to make a number of specialised payments that include mortgage repayments, rent, and hire purchase instalments which are made on a fixed day of the month. Such are the peculiarities of leasing agreements that the payment dates are usually specified as the first or last day of the month. Further regular payments have to be made at longer intervals, such as rates, electricity, gas and dividends, the timing of which can be predicted with accuracy.

The regularity with which contracts set the first or last day of the month for the settlement of instalment payments has serious implications for financial management. It requires that special attention be given to these outflows in the cash flow analysis. For example, compare the flows shown in Tables 3:6 and 5:1. The cash budget (Table 3:6) shows that an extra £19 000 will be required in August. The weekly projection (Table 5:1), on the other hand, indicates a maximum cash shortage of £24 000 between 25 August and 8 September. Notice as well that the cash budget predicts a cash shortage of £10 000 for September. It can be seen from the detailed data that payments are to be made in the first few days of September before any receipts have arrived. This additional shortage is not apparent from the budget. Fortunately, the cash budget is not always in error and in fact it is a better indicator of cash requirements at the end of September and October. The weeks ending on 6 October and 3 November both allow for a balancing of large payments made at the beginning of these weeks with corresponding receipts at the end.

In normal practice a weekly analysis of the cash flows should prove to be an adequate basis from which to make investment plans. Since many payments and receipts are concentrated into the few days covering the end of one month and the beginning of the next special attention must be given to these periods. It could be argued that a daily analysis ought to be made throughout, but in our opinion such detail is usually unnecessary. The only exception is the end of month period noted above and an example of the supplementary detail which can be provided for these occasions is provided in Table 5:2. Projections of cash flows are made to indicate the total amounts of surplus or required cash available within given manageable intervals. Only when payment times are inflexible must allowance be made.

It should be noted that neither the monthly cash budget nor

the weekly projection of cash flows gave sufficient detail at certain periods. None the less, the minimum cash reserve of £10 000 was more than adequate to cover any discrepancy. Indeed, by attending to the detailed flows in Table 5:2 it would be possible to reduce the level of idle cash held in emergency reserve. This extra amount could be invested with the highest possible liquidity to protect the firm against unforeseen demands.

		Receipts		*Payments*			
Week ending	*Cash balance*	*Sales*	*Other*	*Raw materials*	*Wages*	*Other*	*Excess (required)*
July 7	66 000	40 000			5000		56 000
14	63 000	4 000	1000		5000	3 000	53 000
21	61 500	4 000			5500		51 500
28	11 000			36 000	5500	9 000	1 000
Aug 4	50 000	50 000			6000	5 000	40 000
11	54 000	10 000			6000		44 000
18	53 000	5 000			6000		43 000
25	47 000				6000		37 000
Sept 1	(14 000)			45 000	6000	10 000	(24 000)
8	50 000	80 000			6000	10 000	40 000
15	46 000	2 000			6000		36 000
22	40 000				6000		30 000
29	4 000			30 000	6000		(6 000)
Oct 6	69 000	75 000	1300		6000	5 300	59 000
13	73 000	10 000			6000		63 000
20	71 000	4 000			6000		61 000
27	51 000				6000	14 000	41 000
Nov 3	86 000	70 000		24 000	6000	5 000	76 000
10	91 000	11 000			6000		81 000
17	85 000				6000		75 000
24	79 000				6000		69 000
Dec 1	32 000			31 000	6000	10 000	22 000
8	106 000	80 000			6000		96 000
15	74 000	4 000			6000	30 000	64 000
22	72 000	4 000			6000		62 000
29	34 000			32 000	6000		24 000
Jan 4	23 000				6000	5 000	13 000

TABLE 5:1 WEEKLY CASH PROJECTION

NOTE: (*a*) Opening cash balance 1 July is £31 000;(*b*) minimum cash balance throughout is £10 000; (*c*) As of 30 June all payments for materials and services have been completed.

Planning the money flows

The purpose of any plan is to provide advance notice of likely future decisions and to indicate possible courses of action. An investment plan must be used in this manner for, given the variety of available investments, some form of selection technique is essential. In the majority of firms the financial manager will not have sufficient resources of time and equipment to enable him to compare all possible investments each time a cash surplus arises.

				Payments		
Date	*Cash balance*	*Receipts*	*Raw materials*	*Wages*	*Other*	*Excess (required)*
Aug 25	47 000			5000		37 000
28	2 000		45 000			(8 000)
31	(9 000)			1000	10 000	(19 000)
Sept 1	(14 000)			5000		(24 000)
3	36 000	60 000				26 000
29	4 000			5000		(6 000)
30	1 000				3 000	(9 000)
Oct 2	(1 000)				2 000	(11 000)
3	59 000	60 000				49 000
27	51 000			5000		41 000
28	26 000		24 000		1 000	16 000
30	23 000				3 000	13 000
Nov 1	22 000				1 000	12 000
2	21 000			1000		11 000
3	86 000	70 000		5000		76 000

TABLE 5:2 DAILY CASH PROJECTION—SPECIAL PERIODS ONLY

In this case, an investment plan would show him, in advance, the type of instrument to seek at the projected times. The manager can then concentrate on those investments which fall into the desired category and ignore the rest.

A finance department in a large firm might well have the necessary resources to carry out computer simulation exercises designed to select an optimum return on the total cash flow. These exercises would take into account the possibilities of high rates on time deposits without ignoring the encashment penalties and would include comparisons with the other forms of day-to-day investments. This technique is certainly to be recommended to companies with sufficient funds. Interest rates do change rapidly and opportunities to exploit these shifts by switching do occur. Powerful methods of this kind are best employed when used to make choices from the variety of available instruments within a given range. To use such techniques to predict, months in advance, the type of investments upon which to concentrate could appear to be potentially hazardous. Simulations must be based upon estimates of future interest rates and, although expected value criteria are used, such estimates can turn out to be wrong. In order to cope, investment plans must be flexible. If simulation techniques are used complete flexibility is provided since the plan can always be rerun with updated interest rates. Without such technical assistance financial managers must be constantly reminding themselves that projected interest rates may shift and that investment plans must be revised as economic conditions change.

Whatever the degree of sophistication the primary function of investment plans is to serve as an early warning device. A close comparison of alternative investments must be carried out at the time decisions are made, and it may well suit many financial departments to use computational aids only at this decision point. Moreover, an effective investment manager will always check the plan; making whatever adjustments are indicated before taking final decisions. Though these last minute alterations may cause substantial shifts in investment selections, the value of the plan is its capacity to give warning of impending decisions. When used in conjunction with the cash budget, plans concentrate attention on the essentials of the investment decision process. If the firm had unlimited personnel and resources plans would be unnecessary as all calculations could be carried out whenever needed. Few companies are in such a position, and even if they were it could readily be demonstrated that a modicum of planning would lower decision-making costs by an appreciable amount.

A singular advantage of a complete money flow plan is its ability to point out unexpected investment opportunities. If an attractive investment becomes available and it requires more funds than can be provided by the expected excess cash, then the plan will indicate what adjustments can be made to accommodate this purchase. Plans are equally useful when considering the likelihood of cash shortages. Requirements for short-term funds are indicated well in advance and careful inspection of the cash flows will reveal the type and duration of loan to be taken. Lenders are altogether human and are subject to the usual emotions connected with money, liquidity, and solvency. They are reluctant to lend money at very short notice particularly when the borrower does not present sufficient evidence of his ability to repay. A money flow plan is the evidence such a lender would require. Hence, it can be seen that these plans have more than one use. First, they provide management with ample time in which to make the necessary financial arrangements. Secondly, they permit unforseen events to be incorporated as they occur, for plans can always be reworked to accommodate a change in the money flows. Finally, if a decision is taken to borrow more funds, the presentation of the money flow plan is the best method of demonstrating to the lender that the company knows how to manage its financial affairs.

In the last twenty years there has been a relative decline in bill financing. During tight money conditions these bills are used more frequently, but the major recent source of short-term funds has come from bank overdrafts. As a result, bank managers are particularly interested in a company's cash budget and money flow plan. For the manager has his own cash flow decisions to make aside from wanting to give his customers such advice and service as he can. Budgets and money plans also permit the bank manager, particularly in times of tight money, to balance the requirements of one firm with the excesses of another. Thus, full co-operation on the part of the borrower will most likely result in complete satisfaction even under restricted monetary conditions.

Creating a money flow plan

To create an example of a money flow plan let us examine the implications of the cash flows portrayed in Tables 5:1 and 5:2. The first columns in both tables indicate the expected closing cash balances at the end of each week. The last columns show the excess (or required) cash to a minimum idle permanent reserve of £10 000. A list can be constructed from these figures which shows the additions (subtractions) which are made to the cash excess during each week. Such a list is presented in Table 5:3.

Additions (subtractions) to excess cash indicate the type of investment or loan to make. For example, it is clear from Table 5:3 that as of 1 July £21 000 is available for immediate investment. The table also predicts that none of this cash will be required until some time during the week ending on 28 July. A close check on the data in Table 5:1 suggests that the amount should be lowered to £20 000 and that this sum could be invested for twenty-one days to achieve the best interest rate. Now £20 000 invested at, say, 8 per cent for twenty-one days will produce a return of approximately £84. Although this is not a vast sum it is a fair return for a first step in planning. In addition, it must be remembered that the figures in this example are taken from a small firm. Multiply all numbers by a hundred or a thousand and the scale of return available to larger companies can be perceived.

An investment decision must now be made and based on actual quoted rates. Part of the task is to assess the future course of interest rates over the next twenty-eight days. Firms which employ an investment analyst will be able to make such judgements on their own. Other firms would be well advised to seek a specialist's advice either from their stockbroker, bank manager, or other financial contacts. If the assessment indicates that rates will rise, it will probably be more profitable to invest these funds in very short-term deposits, perhaps even call money, to take advantage of the rise. If a fall in rates appears likely then a maximum-term deposit would be best.

At this point in the plan, the manager should consider the possibility of investing the £20 000 for longer than the twenty-one days. To analyse this decision two aspects must be examined. The first concerns a judgement which balances the cost of encashment penalties against any increase in interest rates for a longer term investment. If a favourable balance can be achieved the manager must then look more closely at the expected activity during the week ending on 28 July when £20 000 are expected to be used. To make this assessment, greater detail is required on the flow of payments and receipts. Since the investment decision must be made now and the week in question is less than one month away, it is quite likely that these details will be readily available. It might turn out that the timings on receipts and payments were such that some or all of the £20 000 can be kept invested for the entire twenty-eight days. Analyses of this sort are pertinent to the whole money flow plan. Once interest rates are quoted and the schedule of receipts and payments can be fixed with some assurance, an investment decision can be taken which includes as many as possible of the available opportunities.

Week ending	*Excess (required)*	*Additions (subtractions)*
b/fd	21 000	
July 7	56 000	35 000
14	53 000	(3 000)
21	51 500	(1 500)
28	1 000	(50 500)
Aug 4	40 000	39 000
11	44 000	4 000
18	43 000	(1 000)
25	37 000	(6 000)
Sept 1	(24 000)	(61 000)
8	40 000	64 000
15	36 000	(4 000)
22	30 000	(6 000)
29	(6 000)	(36 000)
Oct 6	59 000	65 000
13	63 000	4 000
20	61 000	(2 000)
22	41 000	(20 000)
Nov 3	76 000	35 000
10	81 000	5 000
17	75 000	(6 000)
24	69 000	(6 000)
Dec 1	22 000	(47 000)
8	96 000	74 000
15	64 000	(32 000)
22	62 000	(2 000)
29	24 000	(38 000)
Jan 4	13 000	(11 000)

TABLE 5:3 WEEKLY ADDITIONS (SUBTRACTIONS) TO EXCESS CASH

The opening statement of the money flow plan would now read: "Invest £20 000 at best rate for a period of twenty-one to twenty-eight days." Since immediate liquidity is not required a Local Authority Bond should be examined. If this decision is made it will leave £1000 available for investment. An examination of Table 5:3 indicates that this £1000 can remain invested until the week ending on 25 August, a two-month period. A small amount, such as £1000, is not usually placed in two-month bills, but can be put into other time deposits.

Once again it should be noted that the company portrayed in Tables 5:1 to 5:3 is only being used for illustrative purposes. It is a small concern with annual turnover of less than £1 000 000. There are many firms with sales of one hundred times this amount and some with five hundred or a thousand times this turnover. An appropriate scaling of the cash flows suggests that many firms have regular opportunities to invest in bills in packages of £100 000 or more—which gives them direct access to the discount market. Firms of this size can take advantage of the going interest rates without having to pay intermediary and split lot commissions. It is as an illustration only, therefore, that the second statement on the investment plan might read: "Invest £1000 either in two-month bank bills or treasury bills to mature on 25 August."

At this stage in the proceedings, the financial manager in a large firm should review the situation. His advisers might know of an investment which lies outside the normal money market. It may be available immediately and require more cash than is currently registered in the surplus account. Or it may not come due for a week at which point there will be additional excess cash to invest. In the first instance it might be sensible to accept the opportunity and meet cash requirements out of overdraft facilities. In the second case, excess cash could be invested on a daily basis until the investment came due. These decisions are made only when interest rates are known and cash surpluses virtually in hand. They do not form a part of the long-term money flow plan itself. The object of this instrument is to enable a manager to take the best decision as and when opportunities arise.

The plan in detail

It is now possible to formulate the bulk of the money flow plan—a plan which will govern future investment activity. The preceding decisions were immediately necessary because this company had a cash surplus at hand from previous operations, a situation common to the experience of many British firms. In addition this decision process was used to illustrate the range of activities and alternatives to be considered. They arise repeatedly within the framework of the money flow plan and need immediate resolution as cash excesses or requirements come due.

To construct the plan of future money flows one final set of figures is required. These are shown in Table 5:4 where the expected additions (subtractions) to the previous cash balance are subdivided into those amounts which are available (required) only for day-to-day investment (loan) and amounts which are available (required) for time deposit (period loan).

The construction of this table involves a major decision as to the objectives of the investment programme. This is management's task and prerogative. When interest rates are high but beginning to fall the objective might be to invest all surplus funds for as long as possible. When interest rates are low a policy of day-to-day investment might be indicated in anticipation of a rise in longer-term rates. It must also be noted that a day-to-day investment policy contains a high degree of flexibility. A time deposit made against a contracted interest rate cannot be altered at will. Moreover, time deposits are vulnerable to a reduction in liquidity if interest rates rise. Thus, the investment policy which governs the structure of the money flow plan must be taken in relation to the present and expected conditions and behaviour of the money market.

The investment plan in Table 5:4 was constructed to take advantage of prevailing conditions which were that two- to six-month investments offered the highest interest rates. Although shorter or longer periods only offered slightly lower rates, small changes in interest rates are quite significant when measured against large sums of money. For example, interest rates for one year or more were 1 to 2 per cent lower than the two- to six-month rate which indicated that the market was anticipating a fall. Call money was also yielding 1 to 2 per cent less which further increased the value of the two- to six-month rates. It must never be forgotten, however, that interest rates can change rapidly and unexpectedly and financial managers must be prepared to update their objectives and plans as often as is required.

Tables 5:2 and 5:4 contain the main details for a money flow plan. Individual managers will have their own style of forms and may well find it an advantage to combine both tables to produce a single set of figures. Whatever style is adopted, these numbers

Week ending	*Plan statement number*	*Additions (subtractions) made during week*	*Surplus to invest* Day to day	*Time deposit*	*Cash required* Day to day	*Period*
b/fd	1	21 000		(1 000) (2 mths)		
				(20 000) (21)		
July						
7	2	35 000	1 500 (7)			
			3 000	30 500 (14)		
14	3	(3 000)				3 000 (21)
21	4	(15 000)				1 500 (14)
28	5	(50 500)			50 500 (7)	
Aug						
4	6	39 000		(36 000) (21)		
				(3 000) (14)		
11	7	4 000	(3 000) (7)			
			(1 000)			
18	8	(1 000)				1 000 (21)
25	9	(6 000)				6 000 (14)
Sept						
1	10	(61 000)			*[24 000]	
					61 000 (7)	
8	11	64 000	(6 000) (7)			
			(4 000)	30 000 (14)		
15	12	(4 000)				4 000 (21)
22	13	(6 000)			*[6 000]	6 000 (14)
29	14	(36 000)		(13 000) (3 mths)	36 000 (7)	
				(9 000) (11 wks)	* [2 000 (3)	
					Sept 30	
Oct				(19 000) (7 wks)	2 000 (1)	
6	15	65 000		(18 000) (14)	Oct 2]	
13	16	4 000	(2 000) (7)			
			(2 000)			
20	17	(2 000)				2 000 (14)
27	18	(20 000)			20 000 (7)	
Nov						
3	19	35 000	1 000 (7)	(28 000) (21)		
				(6 000) (14)		
10	20	5 000	5 000			
17	21	(6 000)				6 000 (21)
24	22	(6 000)				6 000 (14)
Dec						
1	23	(47 000)			47 000 (7)	
8	24	74 000	(2 000) (7)	(2 000) (21)		
			(32 000)	(38 000) (14)		
15	25	(32 000)				32 000 (21)
22	26	(2 000)				2 000 (14)
29	27	(38 000)				38 000 (7)
Jan						
4	28	(11 000)			11 00	

TABLE 5:4 TIME DIVISION OF MONEY AVAILABLE (REQUIRED)
The figure in ( ) brackets represents the time each amount of money is available for investment or required for use. (Expressed in days unless otherwise specified.)

* Required to be financed from sources outside the regular flow of funds.
Detail from Table 5:2.

ought to be translated into instructions for action at the stated times. This translation constitutes a working document for internal circulation and assessment. As an example of a particular style Table 5:4 includes some of the details taken from Table 5:2. This step is important for it draws attention to the need for additional finance requirements which were previously hidden by the positive cash flows occurring during the same week. Once again, whatever style is chosen it must be remembered that these details are necessary and should be suitably recorded and readily available.

The first two statements of the investment plan have already been noted, to wit: "Invest £20 000 at best rate for a period of twenty-one to twenty-eight days; and invest £1000 either in two-month bank bills or treasury bills to mature on 25 August." These decisions were a response to the excess cash present at the beginning of July. Thus the full money flow plan, including these statements, might well read as follows.

1 *Immediate action.* Invest £20 000 at best rate for a period of twenty-one to twenty-eight days. Examine local authority bonds and bills with early maturity.

Invest £1000 for a period of two months. Bills with maturity dates in August would be suitable.

2 *Week ending 7 July.* £30 500 will be available for investment for between fourteen and twenty-one days. Examine local authority deposit rates. Obtain quotations for fine trade bills and other bank bills with the correct maturity. Quotations are to be obtained from our bankers if a split parcel is required and from the market if a whole parcel can be purchased.

£1500 will be available for deposit at seven days' notice.

£3000 will be available for day-to-day lending.

Assess future behaviour of interest rates. If a substantial fall can be expected within a few days, seek a contract deposit at highest rate and arrange for overdraft facilities to cover future needs.

3 *Week ending 14 July.* £3000 will be required for twenty-one days to finance operations. This shortage can be met by calling the day-to-day loans made during the previous week. If these

funds have been put on time deposit arrange for overdraft facilities.

4 *Week ending 21 July*. £1500 will be required for fourteen days. An investment of a like amount was made at seven days' notice two weeks ago. If interest rates are expected to fall leave the investment and check on overdraft facilities. If interest rates are stable or rising notice should be given to time the receipt of these funds with the occurrence of the cash shortage.

5 *Week ending 28 July*. £50 500 will be required for seven days. Two period investments of £20 000 and £30 500 respectively have been made to mature in time to cover this outflow. Check the range of current investments to see if any advantage can be gained by holding or switching these investments and financing the £50 500 from other sources.

The remainder of the plan would follow a similar outline. It is a continuing attempt to match investment decisions to the expected inflows and outflows of cash. Since the money flow plan is a projection, each instruction gives notice of future actions. The longer the period covered the more flexible must be the later instructions. For example, by the time the end of August is reached these statements might well read as follows.

10 *Week ending 1 September*. £61 000 will be required for seven days. Certain investments will be maturing and supply part of this shortage. However, a total of £24 000 will have to be obtained from outside the cash flows. Detailed attention will be required on a daily basis.

From Table 5:2 it can be seen that £8000 must be found on 28 August if the minimum cash reserve of £10 000 is to be maintained. This cash will be needed for six days. A further sum of £11 000 must be found on 31 August for three days. Finally, on 1 September £5000 will be required for two days.

It would appear that day-to-day loans on overdraft will be the best method of providing these funds. Arrangements had better be made well in advance and an appointment with the bank manager booked for early August. Check on interest rate behaviour for if the full £61 000 has to be financed an expected rise in interest rates would suggest that a commercial bill should be arranged. If acceptance commissions and market discount is favourable when compared to overdraft charges, then negotiations should be started to draw up a bill on those credit sales whose receipts are likely to be delayed. (This action refers particularly to export sales and goods serviced by wholesalers on ninety days' credit.) If interest rates are expected to fall then day-to-day financing by overdraft may be more suitable. Both overdrafts and bills require time to organise, so the analysis must be carried out in good time. The acquisition of funds from sources outside the firm's cash flows has special implications for subsequent investment decisions. If shortages are financed on a day-to-day basis, surpluses may well be used to pay off this debt. When compiling a weekly cash flow such as is shown in Tables 5:2 and 5:4 it is usual practice to assume that all loans are taken from day to day and are to be eliminated as soon as receipts are available. In the plan provided above, all external financing has been "repaid" in this manner. If a decision is made to finance the required £24 000 on the whole of the £61 000 shortage by a commercial bill then, an additional surplus of £24 000 will be available for investment at the end of this week. In this event the plan for the next week might read as follows.

11 *Week ending 8 September*. £30 000 will be available for investment for fourteen to twenty-one days. A further sum of £24 000 may become available if a bill of exchange is sold to finance the shortage of the previous week.

£6000 will be available for deposit at seven days' notice.

£4000 will be available to overnight investment.

Similar conditions arise during the week ending on 29 September but a new complication occurs during the following week and it is instructive to examine the plan statement.

15 *Week ending 6 October*. £2000 will be required on 30 September for three days.

£2000 will be required on 2 October for use overnight.

On 3 October a large inflow of funds is expected.

These funds will be available for investment as follows:

£13 000 can be invested for three months or more.

Local authority bonds, trade, bank and treasury bills, or finance house deposits are indicated.

£9000 will be available for up to three months.

Similar investments should be considered, particularly if in conjunction with the £13 000 a complete package can be purchased.

£19 000 will be available for up to two months. Local authority deposits, fine bank bills, and treasury bills would be appropriate.

£18 000 will be available for fourteen to twenty-one days and a suitable time deposit can be used.

Check expected economic behaviour, particularly with respect to interest rates. If rates are rising consider holding all funds in day-to-day investments in anticipation of a rise in longer-term rates. If rates are stable or falling, maximum-term investments should be taken as soon as funds are in hand. Carry out this analysis during the previous two weeks.

Finally, due notice must be taken of all previous investment decisions. Shifts in economic conditions may have altered the cash flows. Update the plan if necessary for prior decisions may be generating larger or smaller cash surpluses.

Summary and conclusions

All plans of money flows are constructed in the manner described above. Styles and formats may vary according to the data processing and accounting system used. Similarly, shifts in emphasis between day-to-day and period investments will occur as economic conditions alter. Whatever the style and objectives, the plan is a working document and must be made available to the relevant staff. For the operating staff is responsible for carrying out the activities noted in the plan and must transcribe all notices of future action into their desk diaries to ensure action is taken when required.

An essential ingredient of sound investment decisions is an awareness of current political and economic events and trends. Changes in these factors affect interest rates and once a shift occurs the money flow plan ought to be updated. All such adjustments must be must be communicated to the operating staff, for effective management of the money flows cannot be achieved without the free and quick passage of relevant information. Though last minute alterations may well be possible they are always expensive to make.

This chapter has described a number of financial instruments that can be used by companies as sources and uses of funds. All of this financial paper is serviced by the money market within which individual houses and banks provide their range of specialities. Large firms with complex cash flows will want to maintain personal contact with a representative of as many elements of this market as possible. The money market operates on confidence and contacts must be developed and maintained to make the best use of the excellent available services. Smaller firms can be equally well served by a single house such as their bankers, commercial or merchant. With the relative decline of bill financing and the growth of overdraft facilities both major groups of the money market have tended to grow together and now offer quite similar services.

The short-term money market is an efficient organisation for the movement of money. To date British industry has not used their services as much as it should. The evidence for this statement is provided by the large volume of idle liquid assets held by British firms. It is in the interest of shareholders, management, and the financial community that these funds be put to work. This is particularly true in times of a credit squeeze and tight money conditions. When cash is in short supply overdrafts become difficult to negotiate. To maintain a high level of business activity, finance must be generated by commercial bills. The money market can only supply its credit and investment services if the volume of money available is moved around the system with sufficient speed. In tight money conditions the Bank of England as lender of last resort can control the ultimate liquidity of the market and hence the level of commercial activity. For industry to hoard cash under such conditions is tantamount to cutting off its own supply of credit. And without enormous amounts of credit a nations' enterprise cannot expand. The answer is to reduce cash reserves to a minimum. Only by such cash management can credit supplies be maintained and multiplied by the money market.

Part Two

MANAGING WORKING CAPITAL AND FIXED ASSETS

6 Working Capital 89

7 Managing Working Capital 105

8 Managing Fixed Assets 124

SIX

WORKING CAPITAL

Working capital is that proportion of a company's total capital which is employed in short-term operations. It is customary to divide working capital into two categories: gross and net. Gross working capital is the sum total of all current assets, while net working capital is the difference between current assets and current liabilities. The former presents the financial problem of how to manage the individual components which comprise the list of current assets. The latter has financial significance for two reasons. The amount of net working capital represents the volume of current assets which are being financed by long-term sources. Though current assets and liabilities are turned over within relatively short periods of time, the net balance of current assets is that proportion which is permanently owned by the company. The second point is that creditors have a particular interest in the net working capital position and regard these assets as the ultimate source of funds for the repayment of their loans.

This chapter and the next are primarily concerned with the techniques and skills required for the efficient management of a firm's working capital. To understand the problems posed for such management it is appropriate to begin by examining the variety of current assets and liabilities and their importance to a firm's operations. Different firms require particular amounts and varieties of both gross and net working capital. It is important that financial management be aware of the relations among the individual items before focusing on the question of their overall management. Various ratios and measures which link current assets and liabilities to day-to-day operations are outlined and discussed. A longer-term view is provided by an analysis of the sources and uses of working capital funds. It is shown that as in the case of cash flows, control is achieved by the use of detailed projections and working plans.

Current assets

Current assets represent funds that are invested in the short-term operations of the firm. Out of all possible investments a company could make, current assets are those which can be expected to be turned over into cash within a twelve-month period. A typical list of such assets would include finished goods stock, goods in progress, raw material stock, accounts receivable (debtors), tax reserve certificates, payments in advance, short-term investments, and cash at bank and in hand. This list is presented in the order in which it is recorded on balance sheets and it should be noticed that they are arranged in ascending order of liquidity. Cash, being the most liquid of all assets is at the end of the list. Stocks, whether in the form of raw materials, work in progress or finished goods, are the least liquid and are recorded at the beginning.

Stocks present many difficult management problems in addition to that of their liquidity. Once again, raw materials have to be processed through the manufacturing operation and there is a long time period between acquisition and eventual sale. A partial exception to this process occurs if the firm also deals in the commodity markets and treats its purchases of raw materials as part of an investment programme in commodities. In all cases some stocks must be processed through the factory and their liquidity involves risks which management must be prepared to accept, if the firm is to make profits. Stocks in all forms require handling and storage. Some varieties suffer spoilage and wastage over time. In addition market prices can change rapidly, as evidenced by the history of copper and other metals. A firm may well be faced with stocks that are falling in value even as they are being manufactured into finished goods. The reverse is also possible. Although investment in the commodity markets is considerably more risky than in that of the money market, a company which requires large amounts of traded raw materials would do well to study the problem in some detail. Whatever the trading possibilities, stocks pose severe cash problems for management. They absorb funds when purchased, while being processed and when held as finished goods awaiting shipment and delivery.

When finished goods are sold, they are shipped to the customer against an invoice. Once an invoice is dispatched, finished goods are transformed into accounts receivable (trade debtors) which enjoy a higher degree of liquidity. The accounts receivable entry on the current asset list represents the sum total of uncollected credit sales. They are the cash claims against the firm's customers for their credit purchases. Some companies make most of their sales for cash and do not have large sums tied up in accounts receivable. Many firms, however, provide some form of credit, such as net cash monthly, and as a result invest substantial sums in receivables.

The management of accounts receivable has posed a number of problems not the least of which is that of doubtful accounts. All businesses suffer bad debts and it is sound financial practice to provide a reserve for doubtful accounts. Such a reserve effectively reduces the value of accounts receivable. Managements' task is to keep bad debts to a minimum by dealing effectively with the host of credit problems involved. The effective net balance of accounts receivable represents a more liquid asset than the investment in stocks, for the time delay to payment is considerably shorter. Despite their liquidity, these trade balances must be managed with care as a rise in credit sales leads directly to an increased investment in accounts receivable which in turn can seriously impair the solvency of a firm.

The remaining classes of current assets have a sufficiently high degree of liquidity to pose only minor liquidity risk. An exception to this statement is funds invested in tax reserve certificates which represent advance payment on taxes. This asset has no liquidity since it can only be used to offset future tax liabilities. Another asset with low liquidity is funds which may have been spent to prepay certain expenses before they become due. The remaining current assets generally have high liquidity and are represented, in most cases, by short-term investments and cash. The management of these liquid assets has been discussed at length in Part 1.

Current liabilities

Current liabilities represent all debts owed by a company which are due for payment within a year. Unlike current assets, whose liquidity can be compared to cash, current liabilities do not have a readily measurable degree of insolvency. Since these debts must be settled with cash, they all represent due cash payments which must be made within a specified time. At the same time, current liabilities, as noted in Chapter 3 can be a source as well as a use of funds. Consequently, a firm's balance sheet entries on current liabilities represent the short-term financing of that company.

Current liabilities can be divided into two categories: those that are generated by the requirements of the company's short-term operations such as trade accounts payable and bank overdrafts; and those that arise as a consequence of long-term financing and external considerations such as interest, dividend, and tax payments.

Short-term liabilities

The most common source of short-term finance is the bank overdraft. Overdrafts are negotiated lines of credit, at call, where the bank reserves the right to alter the rate of interest charged in accordance with changes in bank rate. The upper limit on the credit line is also subject to revision, downward in times of a credit squeeze and upward during periods of easy money conditions. In many cases, firms do not expect to pay off the entire balance of their overdraft within any twelve-month period. Indeed, though an overdraft can be called at short notice and in full by the bank, most companies run what amounts to a permanent debit balance the level of which merely rises and falls with the cash flows from short-term operations. As such, an overdraft is in effect a part of the firm's long-term funds, but since this facility can be cancelled it is as well to treat these funds as though they had to be paid off within the year.

A second major source of short-term funds, and corresponding drain on cash, is the trade accounts payable (creditors). All accounts for raw materials and other merchandise bought for the company's operations have to be settled within relatively short periods of time. Payment terms are negotiated with the suppliers and may include a cash discount for prompt or early payment. Machine tools and other equipment can be purchased on longer credit terms, but in all cases a contract will be negotiated which will specify the timing of the cash disbursements due.

Notes and bills payable represent short-term cash borrowings that are based upon promissory notes. These notes may be unsecured or secured by some of the firm's assets. In all cases, however, their terms, interest rates, methods of repayment, etc, are negotiable up to the signing of the contract. Though smaller firms sometimes borrow funds from their owners or directors (director's loans) most borrowing takes place against notes payable to banks and finance houses.

A further source of funds is the wage and salary withholdings under the PAYE scheme. Whenever wages and salaries are paid the company withholds, from the employees, a percentage of their earnings. These withholdings do not have to be paid to the Inland Revenue immediately upon collection. Payment dates are stipulated in the PAYE regulations. They occur, in practice, thirty to forty days after collection has taken place. Until payment is due, these funds are recorded on the balance sheet as a liability and are an interest free source of funds.

Deferred current liabilities

A certain number of current liabilities arise as a result of a company's long-term commitments. These commitments entail regular cash payments which become due on specified dates. All accruals are deferred payments. They usually take the form of wage, salary, interest, and tax payments that are known to be due within the next accounting period. Dividend payments, declared but as yet undistributed, are also a deferred payment and a current liability until disbursed. Similarly, debenture, or other repayments that are expected to take place within the next accounting period are listed as current liabilities until paid. In effect, these balance sheet entries represent the cash payments a firm has agreed to make, whether to its employees, stock and debenture holders, or tax authorities by specific dates within the near future.

Level of current liabilities

Current liabilities are debts which must be paid in cash within a year. In actual practice, many of the recorded current liabilities will become due for payment on the average, within a period of thirty days. Trade accounts payable and most accruals are usually due by stated dates within the next month. On the other hand, items such as bank overdrafts, notes payable and other negotiated cash debts have an effective long-term payments schedule. Since current liabilities represent cash debts, a firm's solvency depends upon its being able to discharge those debts by the due date.

In Part 1 of this book, a company's cash flows were discussed in detail. It was noted how cash inflows were balanced against debts settlement requirements. Sufficient cash must be available at the requisite times and the attendant management problems were outlined. A further problem, which has to be solved by effective financial management, is the question of volume or level of current debt which a firm can manage and afford. It is right and efficient to analyse the cash flows in minute detail to take advantage of every £1 of cash in the system. It is even more essential to give thought to the total level of current debt. It is as easy to fall into the trap of having more than can be met from the firm's cash inflows as it is to not have enough to finance the firm's operations. A balance must be maintained between the threat of insolvency caused by too much debt and the waste of available resources brought about by having too little.

The appropriate level of current liabilities is frequently judged by comparing it to that of the current assets. The familiar current ratio (see page 24) is used to check that current liabilities have not exceeded 50 per cent of the value of current assets without deliberate management intent. In addition, the quick ratio (see page 25) is used to evaluate the levels of current liabilities against liquid assets. It is commonly believed that the firm is in good financial health if current liabilities do not exceed the level of liquid assets. Both of these ratios are concerned with historic current balances recorded on the accounts at a particular moment in time. Furthermore, these ratios reflect the lender's concern for his money not the company's ability to meet its obligations. The lender rightly wishes to keep his risk within manageable proportions and seeks evidence of the borrowers financial reputation. If the value of current assets is at least twice that of current debt then he feels reassured. He believes that, if the worst happens, his funds will be repaid from the sale of net assets. However, most managers do not anticipate the imminent demise of their firm. Accordingly, they do not expect to have to pay their bills out of the proceeds of a forced sale of their current assets. In short, while the current and quick ratios may well be of significance to the lender, neither are of great use to the financial manager.

Companies pay their bills out of cash earnings. If cash inflows cannot be generated to balance the cash outflows technical insolvency occurs, and the firm ceases to be a going concern. Management's task is to avoid insolvency and it must plan and control the total level of current liabilities. Control is achieved by measuring net current debt against cash earnings and the technique is outlined below.

Net current debt is the difference between current liabilities and liquid assets, where liquid assets are cash, near cash and accounts receivable. Cash earnings can be measured in a number of ways; we shall consider them to be a company's earnings before taxes. Given these two items, a current liquidity measure is defined by:

$$\text{current liquidity} = \frac{\text{net current debt} \times 365}{\text{earnings before tax}}$$

Dividing net current debt by earnings before tax and multiplying by the number of days in a year gives the total number of days required to pay off all current debt out of earnings. If this number of days exceeds 365 then, unless earnings grow, the firm may not be able to meet its current obligations. If the number of days is less than this upper limit, the level of current debt is readily manageable barring any sudden drop in earnings. Such is the essence of control.

There are two important points to note about such a measure of current liquidity. It is a tool by which the upper limit of manageable current liabilities can be determined. Since current liabilities are defined as those debts which are due to be paid within a year, the result of this calculation ought always to be less than 365 days. The second point to note is that this one measure can also be used to determine whether a company is wasting available resources by not having enough current debt. If the calculation should yield a number of days less than 200 then it is clear that additional current finance can be obtained without undue risk. Financial managers must decide on the number of days to maintain in respect of their particular firms operating cash flows. If earnings are rising, a number close to the limit can be safe. If earnings are steady or subject to a fall, a reserve allowance must be made. A number like 250 days might be indicated. Whatever the situation it is management's job to assess the trend of earnings and make the decision on what degree of risk to take.

The following example is presented to clarify the proposition. We have previously considered the cash flows of a company in Chapter 2 (see Table 2:3). The company under consideration has current assets and liabilities at the end of the fourth quarter of:

Current liabilities	£145 000
Current assets	360 000
Liquid assets	130 000

Since the current ratio is greater than 2 to 1 most financial managers would say that this firm is in a sound position with respect to current liquidity. The quick ratio is slightly less than 1 to 1, which indicates that the ability to pay off debt largely resides in the capacity to generate earnings. To calculate this firm's current liquidity we must know its earnings before taxes. Suppose that earnings before taxes for the year were £20 000, then current liquidity would be determined by:

$$\frac{\text{current liabilities} - \text{liquid assets}}{\text{earnings before taxes}} \times 365$$

$$= \frac{145\,000 - 130\,000}{20\,000} \times 365$$

$$= 274 \text{ days}$$

For this supposed level of earnings the firm can pay off all current debt within 274 days which is not unreasonable.

An examination of this year's financial data in Chapters 2 and 3 suggests that the company actually earned £130 000 before tax and not the £20 000 presumed in the illustration. With this volume of earnings the current liquidity measure becomes:

$$\frac{145\,000 - 130\,000}{130\,000} \times 365 \text{ days}$$

$$= 42 \text{ days}$$

In fact all current debt could be paid off within forty-two days. This is a position of great liquidity which indicates that management is not taking advantage of available short-term finance.

All firms require working capital and the smaller the amount of current debt the larger is the volume of working capital that is financed from long-term sources. The company discussed above has a net current debt of £15 000 and annual earnings before tax of £130 000. If management is confident of its ability to generate earnings so that the level is expected at least to be maintained in the coming year, what level of current liabilities ought this firm to carry? The answer depends on a judgement of the number of days to use as a standard. Can the firm operate successfully with a current liquidity of 300 days or should management be more conservative and use 280 days as the criterion? This target is management's decision.

As an example let us suppose a decision is taken on a standard of 280 days and earnings for the year are expected to be £140 000. Net current debt stands at £15 000. The volume of current debt that can be obtained and managed is given by:

$$\frac{15\,000 + \text{new current debt}}{140\,000} \times 365 = 280$$

from which it can be calculated that:
new current debt = £92 500

To satisfy a current liquidity target of 280 days, this firm can afford, and ought to seek out and take on, an additional £92 500 of current debt.

To generate this extra working capital the firm might just extend its overdraft by £92 500. If it did, the current ratio would fall to 360 000/237 500 = 1.5 to 1. Both the bank and the company's other lenders might be unhappy with such a figure and the firm's credit standing might be impaired as a result. However, if current liabilities were expanded because of a planned growth in sales, current assets would grow in proportion to current liabilities. Such proportional increases maintain the balance required by current ratios while permitting the firm to acquire the working capital necessary to finance its growth. Though current ratios must be taken into consideration, earnings are the key to current liquidity.

Some working capital measures

Average age of trade debts. The total level of current liabilities can be determined and managed by using the current liquidity measure described above. An appropriate amount of current liabilities does not solve all working capital problems. The total value may be under control, the individual components may not. A major item of current debt is the volume of credit contained in trade accounts payable. Trade debt represents funds loaned to the company on a short-term basis. It is generated by buying raw materials and other supplies on credit. Although this is a cheap source of funds it is a poor strategy to increase this debt by not paying these accounts when they become due.

One way of checking upon the state of a firm's trade accounts payable is to calculate their average age. The age of an account payable is the time taken from receipt of invoice until payment is made. The average age of all accounts payable is given by:

$$\text{average age} = \frac{B}{TC} \times D$$

where B = balance of trade credit at beginning of period
TC = trade credit purchases to be made during the period
D = number of days in the accounting period

Using the data from Table 3:2 (page 44) the balance of trade credit at the end of the second quarter is £112 000. The trade credit expected to be used during the third quarter is £145 000 and the number of days in the accounting period (a quarter) is 90. Given these figures:

$$\text{average age} = \frac{112\,000}{145\,000} \times 90$$
$$= 69 \text{ days}$$

The average age is sixty-nine days, which is the number of days, on average, that credit purchases go unpaid. By itself this gives an indication of a firm's payment practice. To be of greatest use the average age of accounts payable must be linked to the production and sale cycles.

To balance the flow of cash through the working capital cycle management does not want to be paying money out at a faster rate than it is flowing in. If the average age of trade debts is less than the production and sales cycle, payments are being made more rapidly than the raw materials can be processed and sold. The alternative situation—that is when the production and sales cycle is shorter than the average age—poses a threat to the firm's solvency. In this situation trade debt can build up in ever increasing amounts until a point is reached when it cannot be paid off on the due date. As a result, the average age of the trade debt should be controlled so that it does not exceed that of the production and sales cycle.

In some companies the manufacturing process takes a very long time so that any comparison with the average age of trade debt becomes quite meaningless. In this event, it may be a worth-while financial operation to view the trade purchases which support this manufacturing process as a medium- or even long-term investment problem. It may well prove advisable and profitable to take advantage of the opportunity to create subsidiary operations. Such operations can be diversified and can instigate mergers and takeovers. Activity in the commodity market also constitutes such a diversification in respect of raw material purchases.

In the case of extended manufacturing processes, a more realistic measure than the age of trade debt is required. The average age of the firm's accounts receivable can be used as the standard. If the average age of accounts receivable is less than that of trade credit, the firm is financially healthy. Inflows are being received more rapidly than payments are being made. However, if the average age of accounts receivable exceeds that of those payable, a threat to solvency exists. Demands for cash may well exceed the supply being generated. Action must be taken to correct the situation.

Average age of stocks. Stocks, whether raw material or work in progress, frequently represent a substantial proportion of current assets. Funds invested in these stocks are turned over every time the raw material is processed into finished goods and sold. In the short term, stocks are financed by trade credit. As has just been discussed, the average age of this trade debt ought to be no more than the time it takes to transform these stocks into sales. Accordingly, once such trade credit has been repaid, the company invests its own funds in these stocks. A return on this investment can only be realised as and when finished goods are sold. Hence, it is of great importance to note the average age of stocks. The longer company funds are invested in stocks the smaller the eventual return.

Thc average age of stocks, whether raw material or goods in progress, is a relation between the value of stocks at the beginning of an accounting period and the value of all stock purchases made during that period. Like the average age of trade accounts payable, the age of stocks is calculated as follows:

$$\text{average age of stock} = \frac{S}{P} \times D$$

where S = stock balance at beginning of period
P = purchases of stock during the period
D = number of days in the accounting period

To illustrate the meaning of this calculation, suppose that the stock balance at the beginning of the quarter is £245 000. Purchases during the quarter are expected to amount to £111 000 (see Tables 3:2 and 3:5) and the number of days is 90. Then the average age of stock will be given by:

$$\text{average age of stock} = \frac{245\,000}{111\,000} \times 90$$
$$= 199 \text{ days}$$

That is to say, on the average 199 days purchases of raw materials are invested in the total stock balances.

The balance of stock will be made up partly of finished goods, goods in progress and raw materials. To compute the average age of each of these categories of stock the correct balances must be used. Suppose, for example, that the raw material balance at the beginning of this period was £75 000. Then the average age of raw material stock will be equal to (75 000/111 000) × 90 = 61 days. A sixty-one-day average turn around period for raw material stock is only slightly less than the sixty-nine days taken, on average, by the firm to pay its trade accounts. As such it represents a reasonable balance. For the total figure of 199 days suggests that the manufacturing process takes a long time to complete, and under these conditions it is difficult to turn stocks over with any speed. One point should be particularly noted. If the average age of stocks increases over time the chance of recovering the full cash value of these stocks decreases. As time passes it becomes more and more difficult to collect the full cost of these stocks through the sales price of the finished product.

Age classification (days)	*Date of purchase*	*Amount*	*Percentage each is of total*
0–15	17 June	£15 000	20.0
16–30	11 June	11 000	14.7
31–45	24 May	7 000	9.3
46–60	8 May	22 000	29.4
61–75	17 April	20 000	26.6
		£75 000	100.0

TABLE 6:1 RAW MATERIAL STOCK AGES
(as of 1 July)

A method for determining the rate at which specific categories of raw materials and partly finished goods are moving through the production process is to identify each item by its purchase and completion date. For example, Table 6:1 classifies the raw material stocks on hand at 1 July by fifteen-day intervals of age groupings. As can be seen over half of the current raw materials have been on hand for more than forty-five days. Though this may just indicate that these materials are used in the latter part of the productive process this ageing of stocks would warrant a careful inspection. One way to achieve control over the time factor is to draw up such a table for all stocks every accounting period. A comparison of the percentages in the final column from period to period will indicate immediately whether raw materials, or other stocks, are moving as rapidly as usual through the production cycle.

Average age of receivables. Accounts receivable (trade debtors) are classified among a company's most liquid assets as they represent the major source of cash revenue. This potential revenue is transferred into cash receipts only if the firm's customers pay their bills. Hence, it is extremely important to make sure both that these bills are paid and that they are paid on time. One way of assessing the timing of these payments is to calculate the average age of the accounts receivable. Once again the computation proceeds by dividing the current receivables balance by the expected credit sales for the period and by multiplying the result by the number of days in the accounting period:

$$\text{average age of receivables} = \frac{R}{CS} \times D$$

where R = receivables balance at beginning of the period
CS = credit sales expected during the period
D = number of days in the accounting period

Using the data from Table 3:2 the accounts receivable balance at the end of the second quarter is £130 000. From Table 3:4 total credit sales for the coming quarter are expected to be £240 000. And as there are ninety days in the quarter the average age of receivables is:

$$\text{Average age of receivables} = \frac{130\,000}{240\,000} \times 90$$
$$= 49 \text{ days}$$

The average age of receivables is the same as the average collection period. Clearly, if it takes forty-nine days to collect a particular receipt, age and collection time are synonymous.

The averaging process offers an effective method of comparing the liquidity of current receivable balances with similar items in the past. If the average age increases from period to period, it is evident that increasing amounts of working capital are being tied up in credit sales. It might well be that extended credit terms have been offered in an attempt to increase sales. The effect of these special credit sales will be readily apparent in the age calculation. What management has to decide is whether this increase in invested funds is worth the extra sales. For the greater the average collection period, the smaller is the net return on those credit sales. To remain solvent cash inflows must at least be equal to the outflows. If cash receipts are delayed because of lengthy credit terms the required cash will have to be provided from another source. The lower the average age of receivables the smaller will be the amount of credit sales that must be financed. As an example, consider the average age of receivables for the four quarters of the year for the company whose cash flows were examined in detail in Chapter 3. In Table 6:2 these averages are computed for each quarter and the percentage rates of change noted. It is clear from this table that the average collection period is increasingly independent of changes in the rate of sales.

	First Quarter	*Second Quarter*	*Third Quarter*	*Fourth Quarter*
Credit sales	£218 000	£304 000	£240 000	£240 000
Receivables balance	105 000	150 000	130 000	146 000
Average age (days)	43	44	49	55
Percentage increase (decrease)				
Credit sales		39.4%	(21.0%)	0%
Average age		2.3%	11.4%	12.2%

TABLE 6:2 COMPARISON OF AVERAGE AGES

Although credit sales fell off in the third quarter and remained the same in the fourth, the average collection period increased by over 11 per cent each period. More and more funds are being

Age classification (days)	*Month of sale*	*Value of receivables*	*Percentage each is of total*
1–30	June	£23 000	17.7
31–60	May	48 000	36.9
61–90	April	33 000	25.4
91–120	March	19 000	14.6
121–	Earlier	7 000	5.4
		£130 000	100.0

TABLE 6:3 ACCOUNTS RECEIVABLE AGES
(at 1 July)

invested in accounts receivable without a commensurate increase in credit sales.

To control the quality and liquidity of the receivables balance it is necessary to divide them into categories by age groups. As in the case of stock balances, receivables can be classified by the date at which the sale took place. In Table 6:3 the receivables balance of £130 000 at 1 July is broken down into thirty-day groupings. This analysis shows that roughly 55 per cent of the receivables are less than sixty days old and that 80 per cent are less than ninety days old. A similar analysis of the balance at the beginning of the fourth quarter is given in Table 6:4 and it is clear why the average age of receivables has increased. Though credit sales have remained constant there is a body of uncollected receivables which is becoming ever older and is working its way down the age categories. By 1 October only 35 per cent of the receivables are less than sixty days old and 68 per cent are less than ninety days old. Previously slightly more than 5 per cent were over 120 days due, now over 12 per cent are in this category. Either credit terms have been generally extended or the firm has lost control on a few, particular accounts. Whatever the reason it is clear that the situation needs to be corrected. A firm cannot afford the luxury of financing accounts receivable for ever. Companies require cash inflows with which to pay their own bills. To permit the average age of receivables to grow in this manner, is to subject a firm to an unnecessary risk of insolvency.

Age classification (days)	*Month of sale*	*Value of receivables*	*Percentage each is of total*
1–30	September	£19 000	13.0
31–60	August	33 000	22.6
61–90	July	47 000	32.2
91–120	June	29 000	19.8
121–	Earlier	18 000	12.4
		£146 000	100.0

TABLE 6:4 ACCOUNTS RECEIVABLE AGES
(as of 1 October)

SEVEN

MANAGING CAPITAL WORKING

The management of working capital is concerned with two distinct but interwoven sets of activity: short- and long-term financial operations. The former poses the problem of managing the individual current asset balances which make up the gross working capital position. Long-term working capital management is concerned with providing the volume of net working capital (the difference between current assets and current liabilities) required by the company's current and future activities.

It would be very convenient if it were possible to prescribe the precise amount of gross and net working capital each firm needs. Unfortunately, such is not the case. Manufacturing and merchandising enterprises, to mention but two examples, will invest different proportions of their total available monetary resources in working capital. Furthermore, some businesses will buy their fixed assets such as land, buildings, and machinery while others will lease these items. Each situation creates its own working capital problems that must be decided within the constraints and plans of the individual firm. The object of this chapter, therefore, is not to tell managers what working capital they require. Rather it is to present a number of analytic techniques which will identify the decisions to be made when applied to the data of any firm. It is management's job to make and take decisions. All that technical analysis can do is to identify the decisions that have to be made.

Long-term considerations

The major question posed for the management of long-term working capital is that of how much net working capital to employ.

Net working capital is increased by paying off current liabilities or by a net addition to current assets. It is decreased when there is a net increase in current liabilities or a decrease in current assets. In Table 7:1 an example is provided of two firms both of which have the same net working capital position. Firm *A* has no current liabilities at all and current assets of £20 000, while Firm *B* has a net difference between current assets and liabilities of £20 000. If the question is asked, which firm has the better working capital position, what is the answer? Is it an advantage to have no current debt? Ought it to be a part of long-term financial planning to reduce current liabilities to a minimum?

Firm A			
Net worth Long-term debt	£40 000 8 000	Fixed assets Current assets	£28 000 20 000
Total	£48 000	Total	£48 000
Net working capital = £20 000			

Firm B			
Net worth Long-term debt Current liabilities	£40 000 8 000 10 000	Fixed assets Current assets	£28 000 30 000
Total	£58 000	Total	£58 000
Net working capital = £20 000			

TABLE 7:1 EXAMPLES OF NET WORKING CAPITAL

The answers to these and other similar questions can be readily determined, but only if certain fundamental aspects of financial management are recognised and understood. Primarily, the ability to manage and cope with debt is a function of earnings not assets. Though assets can be mortgaged to raise debt, lenders are frequently concerned about the proportion of assets to debt. Debts are paid out of earnings, however, and it is only in emergencies, the result of bad planning and control, that debts are repaid by the forced sale of assets. If the lender's guide of a quick ratio of 1 to 1 is accepted, then the upper limit of current liabilities is given by the value of the company's liquid assets. The lower limit is to have no current debt at all. Beginning with the balances represented by Firm *A* let us examine the effects on the firm of adding current liabilities.

Suppose that Firm *A* is currently enjoying an annual turnover of £100 000 and is earning on these sales £18 000 before taxes. Liquid assets of £9000 are recorded as part of the £20 000 investment in current assets made by Firm *A*. According to the current liquidity measure described in the previous chapter, earnings of £18 000 can support a level of current debt determined by the following relation:

$$\frac{\text{current liabilities} - \text{liquid assets}}{\text{earnings}} \times 365$$

To use this measure, the financial manager has to decide on the number of days to be set as the company's standard. Suppose 280 days is chosen as the criterion by which the volume of current debt is to be judged. Then Firm *A* could take on current liabilities of:

$$\begin{aligned}\text{current liabilities} &= \frac{(18\ 000)(280)}{365} + 9000 \\ &= £22\ 800\end{aligned}$$

A firm does not just acquire additional debt. If a loan is generated the funds are invested in some asset. Hence, the problem is to combine the knowledge of how much debt to afford with the capacity to make effective use of these funds once they are accepted.

Suppose that management has approved the indications of the calculation and increases current liabilities to a level of £22 800. Clearly, the firm's creditors may become dissatisfied if the quick ratio is consequently allowed to fall below 1 to 1. An obvious answer is to use such additional borrowed funds to increase sales. A growth in sales can only be generated by increasing production which in turn requires additional raw material. By negotiating trade credit to finance stock purchases, overdrafts and other short-term funds will be available to finance the sales campaign. As sales are made, the level of accounts receivable will grow. Control must be exercised to ensure that the average age of these receivables does not also increase.

After a period of time Firm *A* will have absorbed this additional finance. Current assets will have increased by £22 800 so that total assets will now stand at £70 800. Originally, Firm *A* generated sales of £100 000 from total assets of £48 000. In other words, the turnover of total assets in sales = sales/total assets = 2.1 to 1. If the firm maintains this rate of activity, the new level of assets will enable it to sell 70 800 × 2.1 = £148 000 of goods a year. The extra finance of £22 800 has produced additional sales capacity of £48 000. If these sales are made and the profit margin is maintained, annual sales of £148 000 will produce earnings before taxes of £26 600. These earnings can in turn be used to finance additional debt and the cycle begins again. Growth takes place.

To summarise, consider the position of Firm *A* as described above. An increase in current debt of £22 800 has made it possible to:

1. Increase current assets by 110 per cent.
2. Increase total assets by 47 per cent.
3. Increase sales, if turnover ratios are maintained, by 48 per cent.
4. Increase earnings before taxes, if profit margins are maintained, by 27 per cent.
5. Increase its capacity to manage further current debt.

These are highly desirable results. That they can be achieved by taking on current debt is one of the more important aspects of financial management. For the primary objective is to increase a company's earnings and the growth and management of gross working capital is an essential ingredient in this endeavour.

Short-term considerations

The short-term management of current assets is concerned with the efficient use of the balances that exist. Over the longer term, financial planning and control must allow for the growth and related investment in the individual items of current assets. Daily and weekly operations, however, are conducted within the framework laid down by the long-term plan. It is the task of short-term asset management to manage current balances as effectively as possible. Since liquid assets are vital to a firm's solvency we shall begin with the management of these assets. Cash and short-term investment have already been described in previous chapters so that the remaining liquid asset, accounts receivable, is the only one to be treated in the next section.

Managing current assets

Managing accounts receivable. Trade accounts receivable are a product of credit sales. If a company were to make all sales for cash it would have no accounts receivable and no need to finance its sales by the use of current debt. Most firms, particularly in manufacturing, sell on credit and it is towards all firms with accounts receivable balances that this section is directed.

Net cash value. In the previous chapter a method for checking upon the credit policy of a firm was described in terms of the average age of the receivables balance. The average collection period (or age) is an important indicator of the liquidity of receivables. The longer an invoice goes unpaid the less likely it is ever to be paid. Doubtful accounts turn into bad debts when they are left uncollected. Hence, to assess the liquidity of a given balance of receivables it is necessary to investigate the relation between the age of an account and the likelihood of its being collected. An inspection of past accounts will reveal the proportions to use. For illustrative purposes suppose the collectable percentages are as follows:

Age of account	*Collectable percentages*
1 –30	99
31 –60	98
61 –90	95
91 –120	70
121 –	50

Applying these percentages to the receivables balance recorded at a particular time period will produce the net cash value of those receivables.

For example, in Tables 6:3 and 6:4 credit sales of £130 000 and £146 000 are classified by age groups. To calculate the net cash value of these balances the amount in each age category is multiplied by the appropriate percentage. The result is presented in Table 7:2 where columns *A* and *B* refer respectively to the data of Tables 6:3 and 6:4.

Age category (days)	*Month of sale* *A*	*B*	*Balances* *A*	*B*	*Collectable percentage*	*Net cash value* *A*	*B*
1– 30	June	September	£23 000	£19 000	99	£22 800	£18 800
31– 60	May	August	48 000	33 000	98	47 000	32 400
61– 90	April	July	33 000	47 000	95	31 400	44 600
91–120	March	June	19 000	29 000	70	13 300	20 300
121–	Earlier	Earlier	7 000	18 000	50	3 500	9 000
			£130 000	£146 000		£118 000	£125 100

TABLE 7:2 NET CASH VALUE OF RECEIVABLES

From July to October this firm increased its accounts receivable balance by £16 000. However, as was noted in Chapter 6, the average age of these receivables also increased. The effect of this growth is evident in the comparison of the net cash balances. At 1 July the net cash value was £118 000 on a book value of £130 000 (91 per cent of book value). By 1 October the net cash value has dropped to 86 per cent of the book value. Clearly both the liquidity and real value of these credit sales is decreasing, for an additional £16 000 in receivable balances has yielded only a £7000 increase in net cash value.

Cost of credit sales

Consider the balances presented in Table 7:2 and suppose that management has decided to do something about its deteriorating receivables position. What are the possible actions it can take and what credit policy ought to be adopted? Solutions vary from leaving things as they are to the opposite extreme of withdrawing credit facilities and insisting that all future sales be contracted for cash. Every solution will generate its own pattern of cash receipts and, depending upon its stringency, will entail certain costs. Thus, an increase in cash flow can be measured against the cost of generation. The net value to the company, given by a variety of alternatives will aid management in taking a decision to adopt a particular credit policy.

Suppose, for example, that the projected credit sales for the final quarter are as follows: October, £83 000; November, £89 000; and December, £68 000, for a total of £240 000. According to the calculations in Table 6:2, the average age of the receivables that result from these sales is expected to be fifty-five days. The average age of the receivables balance at 1 October is forty-nine days and as we have already seen in Table 7:2 the net cash value of this balance is 86 per cent of its stated value. Under current policies the receivables balance is expected to grow both in value and in average age during the fourth quarter. The net cash value can be expected to fall even further unless action is taken to alter the firm's credit policy. Since previous commitments cannot be readily changed, consider some possible alterations that can be put into effect during the final quarter.

Suppose a policy of net cash thirty days is proposed, accepted and enforced on all new credit sales. This would mean that cash receipts were due within thirty days of the time that the invoice was received by the customer. If the inflow of cash under this credit policy is compared to that experienced in the third quarter (see Table 6:4) it is seen that receivable balances will go down while cash inflows go up. This comparison is presented in Table 7:2 where all receipts from previous receivables are ignored. Given this projection of events, under Policy *A* the firm will receive £96 900 in cash by the end of December while Policy *B* will yield cash receipts of £204 800. This is a substantial difference in cash flows. Though no allowance for doubtful accounts has been made in either set of figures, the actual effect of implementing Policy *B* would closely approximate the results given here.

It is most unlikely that a new more stringent credit policy can be effected without cost. Management will wish to determine the probable cost of persuading customers to pay their bills within a new time limit. Obviously such cost must not exceed the benefits to be derived from the new policy. The limit to the cost is determined by calculating the discount which the firm could afford to offer as an incentive and be no worse off than under the old credit policy. In other words, the interest rate or discount that will equalise the present value of these two streams of income must be calculated.

Net sales	*October* *£83 000*	*November* *£89 000*	*December* *£68 000*
Receipts from sales in:			
Oct *A*; *B*	10 800; 40 000	18 800; 43 000	26 800;
Nov *A*; *B*		11 600; 43 000	20 100; 46 000
Dec *A*; *B*			8 800; 32 800
Total receipts *A*; *B*	£10 800; 40 000	£30 400; 86 000	£55 700; 78 800

TABLE 7:3 RECEIVABLE BALANCES AND CASH FLOWS COMPARED
Policy *A* = current credit practice
Policy *B* = net cash thirty days policy

The present value of a sum payable in the future is equal to the quantity of money that would have to be invested today at a given compound interest rate in order to generate that future sum by the specified time. If £500 is the future sum and it is to be paid three periods from now, the present value of that £500 is computed as follows: Suppose the interest rate is 5 per cent. Then £1 invested today and compounded three times will be worth £1.16 at the end of the third period. Accordingly, £500 to be paid at the end of the third period is worth £500/1.16 = £430 today.

To determine the present value of the stream of cash receipts given in the example (Table 7:3) trial and error is used to discover which interest rate will give a present value of Policy *B* equal to that of Policy *A*. If the cost of money to the firm is taken at 12 per cent per annum then the present value of the cash receipts under Policy *A* is given by:

Policy A

	Receipts: *End of month*	*Interest rate* *per period*	*Present value* *1 October*
Oct	10 800	1%	10 700
Nov	30 400	1%	29 800
Dec	55 700	1%	54 100
			£94 600

Policy *B* has a different sequence of cash receipts. By using present value tables (such as are provided at the end of this book), it can be determined that at an interest rate of 45 per cent a month the present value of Policy *B*'s receipts equals £94 100. This is approximately equivalent to the present value generated under Policy *A*. The calculations are shown below:

Policy B

	Receipts: End of month	*Interest rate per period*	*Present value 1 October*
Oct	40 000	45%	27 500
Nov	86 000	45%	40 800
Dec	78 800	45%	25 800
			£94 100

This firm could offer an incentive cash discount up to 45 per cent along with the terms net cash thirty days and be no worse off than under existing credit conditions. Clearly, it is not necessary to offer such a large discount. But it may well prove effective to offer a 2 or 3 per cent discount against payments received within ten days, to stimulate and reward those who pay promptly. The value of cash today far exceeds that of cash receipts obtained some months later. A bird in the hand is worth two in the bush.

Financing accounts receivable

Encashing receivables, like obtaining an overdraft or trade credit, is an important part of short-term working capital management. The basic objective in financing accounts receivable is to generate the maximum cash inflow at the lowest possible cost. One possible strategy was noted above: to offer a discount for prompt payment and a maximum credit period of thirty days. Although there is a large range of alternative financing policies, we shall restrict our attention to the three most important types of approach. The first is to sell, each month, all receivables to a commercial factor for cash. The second is to borrow against the receivables balance. The third is to develop a credit and collection department of such capability that other firms' receivables can be purchased and processed with the company's own assets, to yield additional earnings.

Factoring accounts receivable. The factoring of accounts receivable is accomplished by offering the entire collection of receivables to a commercial factor. If a satisfactory price is negotiated and the sale is made, the factor takes on the responsibility for collecting all accounts due. As a consequence he also accepts the risk that some accounts will prove to be uncollectable. The purchase price is determined on the basis of the net cash value of the receivables balance. If the firm in Table 7:1 was trying to factor its receivables as of 1 July or 1 October the price would be based on the net cash values of £118 000 or £125 000 respectively. Though practices can differ, the purchase price is usually stated in terms of an advance payment of, say, 90 per cent of the net cash value. The balance, less service and financing charges which may amount to 2 to 3 per cent, is paid to the firm on the average due date of the accounts.

For example, suppose a company has a receivables balance with a net cash value of £100 000. The average age of these receivables is thirty days. The factor offers £90 000 cash now, and the balance less service and finance charges in thirty days. The amount of this balance depends upon the quality of the receivables. If the credit worthiness of these accounts is high, the factor's charge is low. It is higher in cases where the risk of bad debts is high. Suppose in this instance, that the total charge is 2 per cent, then the balance of £8000 will be paid at the end of the thirty days.

To collect £90 000 at the beginning and £8000 at the end of the month, this company has to be willing to pay £2000. If accounts are sold at this rate each month of the year, the annual charges would amount to £24 000 or 24 per cent of the average receivables balance. This may appear to be a high charge to pay. However, the firm has no direct collection charges of its own. The factoring cost has to be compared with this saving. The evaluation criterion is the firm's cost of its own credit and collection department for the year. Moreover, cash today is worth more than cash at the end of the month. In any assessment of the cost of factoring the fact that the firm's own credit department will not produce 90 per cent of the cash value of all receivables on the first day of every month must be costed and allowed. An annual charge of 24 per cent of the average receivables values may well become quite an attractive proposition when the alternative costs are taken into account.

Borrowing on accounts receivable. An alternative method of raising money on accounts receivable is to pledge them as collateral for a loan. Many firms do not like the thought of having a factor collect from their customers. None the less, they cannot afford to tie up cash in receivables. A loan based on these receivables can be readily negotiated with commercial or merchant banks and may well provide a more acceptable financing vehicle.

With a loan of this type, the company retains the obligation to collect the receivables as well as the risk of doubtful accounts becoming bad debts. The usual practice is for the finance house to lend the firm a proportion, say 70 or 80 per cent, of the net value of the receivables. Interest can be charged either on a daily basis or on the actual cash advanced. A service charge may also be included. Usually, the company will pay off the loan as receivables are collected and as a result, the net cost to the firm will be less than that charged by the factor on an outright sale. It must be noted, however, that the factor carries out credit accounting, ledger keeping and collecting as part of his services. The company is responsible for all these activities if it merely borrows money on its receivables.

Buying accounts receivable. Many companies are in a position where they manage and finance their own credit sales. Such firms have credit departments and managers whose task is to service their customers' accounts and collect the receipts when due. One alternative to selling or borrowing on receivables is to go into the business of collecting receivables in a serious way. If the firm already has a credit department, why not put it to work in a more efficient and effective manner? A satisfactory credit department will find little difficulty in providing a collection service for receivables from other firms with similar customers. The question to answer has two parts and can be stated as follows: is it cheaper to sell receivables outright to a factor or to process them? Whatever set of reasons persuade a firm not to sell its receivables, economies of scale suggest it will be cheaper, per account collected, to behave as a factor and buy other firms' receivables. Accounts receivable can be purchased just as they can be sold and there is no reason why a particular business enterprise cannot act as a factor. Obviously, a minimum volume of receivables must be processed to achieve a desirable efficiency. This volume effects control. Once a credit department has been established its productivity and the rate of return can be assessed and managed just like any other productive process. As an example, suppose a company has credit sales of approximately £100 000 a month. To manage the servicing, accounting, and collection of these accounts it maintains a staff whose cost and overheads are £18 000 a year. An estimate is made of the cost, in extra staff and overheads which would be incurred if receivables turnover was doubled. Suppose it is calculated that an additional £6000 a year would provide a sufficient capacity to process £100 000 extra receivables a month. Next, an assessment of the factoring market is made. There are a number of firms who have customers of sufficient credit standing and who have a history of selling their receivables. It is discovered that such firms can supply the £100 000 receivables required each month. The company decides to offer the same terms as other factors. It will offer an immediate payment of cash of 90 per cent of the net cash value of purchased receivables. It will make a charge of 2 per cent to cover interest and handling, and will pay the balance a number of days after the contract is signed, equal to the average age of the receivables bought.

Suppose this company advertises its new factoring policy and receives, in reply a number of offers to sell blocks of accounts receivable. The alternatives are examined and one lot is selected for close inspection. The portfolio of receivables is listed in Table 7:3. They are identified by a customer account number, the terms under which they were invoiced, and the number of days yet to elapse before payment from the customer is due. The terms of sale were net cash sixty days to all customers. As can be seen in Table 7:4 the average due date is calculated by multiplying the net cash value of each account by the number of days remaining until payment to give the weighted cash value of the account. The sum of these weighted cash values is then divided by the total net cash value to give the average due date. Cheque clearance time is then added to this figure to yield, in this instance, an average due date of twenty-seven days. This means that the 8 per cent balance due will be paid twenty-seven days after the contract is signed and the initial payment of 90 per cent is made.

To evaluate this investment suppose all accounts are received on the date due. Then the initial cash investment will be 90 per cent of £107 000 which is £96 300. Receipts will arrive as shown in Table 7:4. A rough average value of invested funds determines that the rate of return over these forty-three days is approximately 4 per cent. A 4 per cent return in forty-three days is equal to an annual rate of return of roughly 37 per cent. Moreover, it is clear that £100 000 of receivables of this type can be purchased for an average investment of roughly £53 000.

Account number	*Net cash value (1)*	*Days until Payment due (2)*	*Weighted cash value: (1) × (2)*
1	£18 000	5	£90 000
2	28 000	17	476 000
3	32 000	28	896 000
4	17 000	36	612 000
5	12 000	43	516 000
	£107 000		£2 590 000

TABLE 7:4 AVERAGE AGE OF RECEIVABLES TO BE PURCHASED

Weighted average number of days to maturity

$$= \frac{\text{weighted cash value}}{\text{net cash value}}$$

$$= \frac{2\,590\,000}{107\,000} = 24 \text{ days}$$

If it takes, on average, three days to process and collect cheques then Average Due date of these receivables is twenty-seven days.

Suppose the company was to proceed as planned and incurred additional staff salaries and overheads of £6000 a year. Since it would have to make some £97 000 available for immediate investment, it could probably afford to invest more than £53 000 on average. The average value of funds invested can be raised by purchasing a new set of accounts receivable every month or as frequently as is indicated by the repayment schedules. An increase in the volume of accounts receivable handled will increase the net rate of return. A net return on capital and costs in the order of 35–40 per cent a year could be expected. Care would have to be taken to assess the risk and proportion of doubtful accounts in each lot handled. As payment is made on the net cash value of the offered receivables, this assessment would be an important part of the credit manager's job.

A decision to invest in other firms' receivables is based upon two main factors. An analysis of the company's present credit management facilities is made. Are they sufficiently effective or can they be improved to warrant an investment in additional staff and facilities? If the answer is negative, the company ought to consider factoring its own receivables. It can make better use of the invested funds in other departments of the firm. If the answer is in the affirmative, then a decision must be made as to the cost of improving the credit department, the size of the investment to be made in purchasing receivables and the expected return from the projected endeavour. It has been shown above that the rate of return on efficient credit management can be sufficiently impressive to warrant detailed scrutiny.

Days from contract signing	*Payments*	*Receipts*	*Balance of invested funds*	*Days invested*
0	£96 300		£96 300	5
5		£18 000	78 300	12
17		28 000	50 300	10
27	8 560		58 860	1
28		32 000	26 860	8
36		17 000	9 860	7
43		12 000	(2 140)	

TABLE 7:5 VALUE OF RECEIVABLES INVESTMENT

Average funds invested over the 43 days

$$= \frac{\text{sum of balances} \times \text{number of days}}{\text{total number of days}}$$

$$= £52\ 800$$

$$\text{Rate of return on average funds invested} = \frac{2\ 140}{52\ 800} = 4\%$$

Managing stocks

Stocks of raw materials, goods in progress and finished goods pose a number of management problems. On the one hand there are the questions of warehousing and storage. Decisions on what levels of stock to keep are determined by economic order and production batch size considerations. These, in turn, help to specify the minimum and maximum stock levels required. On the other hand there is the question of how to finance these stocks and how to control the investment of funds in this type of asset. Only the latter set of questions will be discussed in this section.

In the previous chapter it was pointed out that the average age of stocks on hand can be computed. The stock balances at the beginning of the period are divided by the purchases expected during the period and multiplied by the number of days in the accounting period. This calculation can be made for each category of stock as well as for the total balance. For example, within the raw material stocks used in a particular company's manufacturing process there are a variety of items such as sheet steel, copper bars, and metal rods which are purchased in substantial quantities. Raw materials, as far as this firm is concerned, also include items which are the finished products of other companies, such as die castings, gear assemblies, and many types of fittings. The manufacturing process takes some time to complete and in so doing produces a number of stages of goods in progress. Raw materials have been partially assembled into finished goods and stocks of goods in progress are normally held at a fairly high level representing a substantial amount of invested funds. Finished goods stocks are not large and every effort is made to keep them within reasonable bounds.

In Table 6:1 an example was provided of how raw materials on hand can be classified with respect to the length of time they have been in stock. The analysis can be performed on specific items as well as on the balance as a whole. Suppose the age classification of the die casting stocks are as given in Table 7:6. It can be readily seen that over 60 per cent of these die castings have been on hand for over forty-five days. Suppose a check on the composition of these aged stocks shows that some castings are used early in the productive process while others are not employed until much later. Moreover, some of the castings are speciality items which may remain in stock for many months at a time. In short, the company really uses two classes of die castings: those which are processed within thirty days and those which may take many months to clear.

Efficient management of raw materials requires that these stocks are turned over rapidly. The longer a given item remains in stock the more difficult it becomes to collect the full cost through the sale price. In many instances, however, there are some items such as special die castings, sub-assemblies, etc, which cannot be moved through the productive process with the desired speed. The financing of stocks can be readily geared to the ageing process, and it is this criterion around which the following discussion revolves.

Classification (days)	*Amount*	*Percentage each is of total*
0–15	£17 000	16.0
16–30	13 000	12.2
31–45	9 000	8.5
46–60	29 000	27.4
61–	38 000	35.9
	£106 000	100.0

TABLE 7:6 AGE CLASSIFICATION OF DIE CASTINGS

Types of stock finance. Stocks can be used to raise funds in a number of ways. The simplest procedure is to use these assets as collateral for a secured loan from a commercial or merchant bank. To do so the value of each item or class of items must be noted and approved. As in the case of accounts receivable, the loan will be based upon an agreed percentage of the net cash value of the stocks. As stocks are consumed in the productive process, the net cash value declines and unless the balance is maintained by new purchases the size of the loan has to be reduced by a proportionate amount. As a result, taking a secured loan on rapidly moving raw materials is a complicated process and may not be worth the effort. An analysis of the age classifications reveals those stocks which remain unused for the greatest periods of time. These are the items to use as collateral if loan financing is desired. If the average age of certain materials, say die castings or other speciality items is eighty days, this length of time is sufficient to make a collateral loan worthy of investigation.

Raw materials which are purchased in bulk and which take some time to be delivered to the firm can be financed *en route* by means of a trade bill and/or warehouse receipt. In either case, the financing instrument is in effect a secured loan on the value of the itemised goods. Warehouse receipts are issued by the warehousing company and can be used by the firm: to reclaim the goods when required; to borrow funds by pledging the receipt as collateral; or to sell the goods in question by presenting the receipt for sale on the commodity market. The trade bill is based upon the bills of lading which represents the goods in transit from the supplier. These bills become negotiable if endorsed by a commercial house (see Chapter 4) and can be sold outright or used as collateral for a loan. In both of these cases the firm is delaying the investment of its own funds until such time as the goods are actually delivered to their factory for processing.

An additional method of financing certain types of raw materials is available if these materials are traded on the world or local commodity markets. Items such as steel, copper, aluminium, and other metals can be bought and sold on the commodity market. Many of these commodities suffer wide price changes over time, due to shortages and excesses in demand and supply. A company which consumes extensive amounts of such items would do well to consider the problem of trying to reduce the cost of its stocks by taking an active position in the commodity markets. Commodities can be bought for present or future delivery and can be sold short or long. Purchases are usually made by buying receipts which have been put up for sale by other firms. These receipts may specify the delivery date or may represent warehoused stocks which can be collected at any time.

An investment programme of this type is similar to that described in Chapter 5 when dealing with the management of short-term money flows. With commodities the interest and handling charges as well as the expected shifts in prices have to be considered. If prices are expected to rise over the short term, immediate buying at current prices for current and future delivery will assure the company of adequate supplies and provide excess stocks for sale at a profit, if the price rise occurs. When prices are falling only the firm's imminent raw material requirements need be purchased from week to week and short sales (selling stocks that are not owned for delivery at a later date when prices are expected to be lower) can be considered as an investment opportunity. An efficiently managed commodity portfolio can produce handsome returns. If a company is already engaged in purchasing materials, an additional investment in staff and facilities can effect the competence and capacity to engage in this activity. The expected rate of return on the total investment can be readily computed for a given volume of transactions. Since the firm requires a certain level of raw materials for its manufacturing process, a cost and value analysis of the type described in the section on receivables is indicated. The worth of investing in multiples of current stock requirements can be computed. Clearly, the return on investment will be a function of the volume of transactions. Firms with large material requirements are in a better position than smaller companies to take advantage of commodity market investments. None the less, the commodity market is available to all companies whatever their size and as a source of funds to finance stocks it should not be overlooked or ignored.

Managing current liabilities

For most firms the bulk of their current liability balances consist of overdraft, short-term loans, and accounts payable. The management of overdrafts and short-term loans is a part of the management of short-term funds which has been discussed in Chapter 5. The only management problems remaining to be treated are those of accounts payable and sundry accruals such as PAYE and taxes.

Managing accounts payable. The management of accounts payable is essentially a simple operation. As noted in Chapter 6 it is both informative and useful to maintain control over the average age of the outstanding trade credit. The decision whether to settle accounts payable at once or later depends upon the discounts, if any, that are offered for prompt and early cash payment. If discounts are available from suppliers, then advantage should be taken of the offer. Such reductions in cost can always be compared to the value of keeping this amount of credit unpaid. In most cases it is a sound financial rule to accept cash discounts whenever possible.

Some suppliers do not offer cash discounts. In this event, they should be approached with a view to striking a bargain. The promise of prompt settlement will often produce an agreed discount even if this is not part of the firm's normal sales policies. If all efforts to achieve discounts for immediate cash payment fail, there is no incentive to settle the account and every reason to delay payment until the last possible moment.

The management of accounts payable can be broken down into two parts: (*a*) for all accounts on which cash discounts are available, make sure that settlement occurs before the cash due date; (*b*) for all accounts with no discount make sure that payment is not made until the agreed due date, but no later. Financial management is responsible for maintaining the credit standing of their firm as well as generating the necessary credit financing. To be known as a late payer does not enhance the firm's reputation. To be known as a firm that is aware of the value of money, and insists on bargaining for its most effective use engenders respect and in all likelihood will lead to even higher credit rating.

The remaining current liabilities offer little scope for active financial management. PAYE withholdings are taken out of wages and salaries every time employees are paid. These withholdings do not have to be paid to the appropriate authority until certain calendar dates have been reached. Firms have free use of these funds for an average thirty to forty days. If total wage and salary payments are rising, so will the amount of credit that this free source of funds represents. Since the size of the withholdings is not under the company's control, management only has responsibility to use these funds while it can and to make sure they are paid to the tax authorities when due.

Similar comments pertain to the payment of the company's tax obligations. Though tax assessments must be paid, there is no justification for paying them in advance. Tax reserve certificates are offered for sale to tempt firms, by a small discount, to settle their obligations in advance. To buy a tax reserve certificate is to make an investment with zero liquidity, for these certificates can only be used in dealings with the Inland Revenue. All other short- or long-term investments have a degree of liquidity and many exist which also provide higher rates of return. Thus, before purchasing tax reserve certificates compare their rate of return to other available short-term investments. The money market can always supply an investment with a high degree of liquidity and a due date coincident with tax outlays.

EIGHT

MANAGING FIXED ASSETS

Fixed assets may be described as those assets which cannot, as a rule, be sold and encashed without expending a great deal of time and effort. As a result, fixed assets have low liquidity. To the shareholder they represent the firm's ultimate source of wealth, while at the same time creating the greatest source of risk to his invested funds.

If a low degree of liquidity is taken as the major characteristic of fixed assets it is immediately apparent that there is no sharp line dividing current assets, such as some types of stock, from fixed assets. This is not accidental, as there is no satisfactory measure by which these types of assets can be readily classified. The division which is used is a matter of accounting convenience. There is no abrupt change in liquidity in the transition from special raw material stocks to long-term investments or land. To illustrate this notion, suppose that the liquidity of each asset was plotted against either the time required to sell it, or the discount at which it would have to be sold. The result would be a more or less continuous curve going from the most liquid asset, cash, at one end, to the least liquid, intangible asset, such as goodwill, at the other. Differences in liquidity are a matter of degree and the accounting division between current and fixed assets is based more upon a notion of time. Some assets are turned over and consumed in short-run operations—current assets; others are part of the long-run operations—fixed assets.

The distinction between short- and long-run operations has important implications for financial management. Though short and long run become indistinguishable at the limit, the techniques of management differ and involve shifts in emphasis. Short-run decisions are taken under the condition that all long-run factors are constant. These decisions cannot ignore long-run considerations altogether, but there is little that can be done about them. Hence, the emphasis is on decision making within an existing long-run framework. The management of long-run operations, on the other hand, is a process of creating the structure within which profitable short-run decisions can be made. Here, full allowance must always be made for the effects of any changes on short-run operations. Hence, the management of long-term operations is necessarily concerned with the entire financial activity of the firm.

The management of short-run decisions have been discussed in the chapters on the management of cash, short-term investments and working capital. Consequently, this chapter is concerned primarily with the consideration of long-run factors. This should not be taken to suggest that we believe that each section of financial management is an isolated entity. It is not. All sectors depend upon one another and financial management involves the successful administration of each of these facets of the business enterprise. The reader is therefore requested to bear in mind the pertinent details of the previous chapters when examining the contents of this chapter. Long-term decisions determine to a large extent the future direction of a firm's financial activity.

Fixed assets

Fixed assets were loosely defined, at the beginning of this chapter, as having low liquidity and high risk of capital loss. In general, all assets with a service life in excess of twelve months are subject to the long-run management decisions. Hence, all investments which are not consumed, turned over, or liquified within a year can be considered as fixed assets. These assets can be divided into two main groups. The first consists of those assets which are employed in a firm's daily operations, such as land, buildings, and machinery. The second category contains those investments which are purchased in order to utilise effectively all surplus cash which is generated by short-term operations. They include such securities as local authority bonds, mortgages, and industrial debentures, having redemption dates of more than twelve months. Minority interests in other firms, though frequently purchased for other reasons, must be considered a part of such long-term investments. This aspect of financial management will be treated in detail in Part 4, particularly in Chapter 13. At the present moment, comment will be restricted to the principal factors affecting the long-term investment of funds in the securities and minority holdings of other companies.

Long-term investments

Management's task is to utilise a firm's resources as efficiently and effectively as possible. Every company has skills, experience, expertise and funds which are employed in the generation of profit from short-term operations. The management of temporary cash excesses and requirements is a vital component of current operations, since idle funds are a waste of available resources. In a similar manner long-term investments which do not relate to the company's operations reduce available working capital as well as weaken the firm's financial strength. For example, a long-term loan to another firm is in part a statement that the borrowing company can earn a greater return on those funds than can the lender. If a firm has been skilful enough to earn "surplus" funds it ought to be capable of employing such funds within its own commercial endeavour. A policy of growth requires substantial finance whether it is accomplished by internal expansion or acquisition. To lend to others, except as part of a short-term money flow plan, is to deprive the firm of the use of such funds for a substantial period of time.

A second type of long-term investment is the purchase of a minority interest in another company. It may well be argued, in specific cases, that such an investment will satisfy a number of political and strategic objectives. From the financial point of view a minority interest is the same as investing in non-liquid equities. Once acquired, minority holdings are hard to sell even if these equities are actively traded on the stock exchange. Equity portfolios are managed as part of the short-term money operation and to invest long term is to prevent the financial manager from taking advantage of the firm's available resources. Minority holdings are often taken as a vehicle for influencing the companies involved. Actively pursued, this can prove to be an effective technique for gaining partial control of the environment. However, many companies do not manage with any skill the votes these holdings represent. In such instances, those firms have effectively handed over part of their funds for others to manage. Since one of the primary objectives of financial management is to seek and generate external funds for internal use, we can only repeat the adage: working capital should be under management's dircct control, not invested in the affairs of outsiders.

A third class of long-term investments occurs when a firm decides to create a pool of funds to finance future capital purchases. The need for reserves such as sinking funds, where not directed by statute, suggests a lack of ability on management's part to create adequate long-term financial plans. The objective of financial planning is to ensure that the right volume of working capital is on hand to satisfy all demands for funds. An adequate plan will generate working capital as required and there will be no need to tie up large amounts of money in such long-term investments as sinking or reserve funds.

The perceived desirability of sinking and other reserve funds is closely connected with emotional responses to money. Financial management is the science of accepting risk in order to generate profit. Without risk profits disappear, and the feelings of security derived from holding money in cash or in reserve funds is both false and expensive. Though it may appear difficult to create a working, long-range financial plan, such a plan will prove to be considerably less expensive in terms of the expenditure of time and effort than any other more haphazard alternative. To recognise in advance that a new building or machine is to be acquired is to permit short-run operations to be geared to produce the necessary funds. Such an approach is significantly more efficient than one which tries to save specific amounts of money from time to time in the hope that a sufficient reserve will eventually be created. Furthermore, it frequently occurs that the reserve, if created, is never large enough to justify the expenditure under consideration. There are many reasons why this happens, one of which is that cash reserves are always tempting to use. It is relatively easy to justify a new car for the managing director. Also it is hard for management to resist the demands of various departments for extra funds when the cash is readily available. Indeed, such demands are almost inevitable, since a firm that is weak in financial planning is not likely to be strong in cash budgeting.

Another, and equally important, reason for the inadequacy of reserves is to be found in the behaviour of the purchasing power of money. Prices tend to rise not fall, and as prices rise the purchasing power of a given sum depreciates. For example, the purchasing power of the pound sterling had fallen in 1968 to one-sixth of its value in 1938. Moreover, over the past thirty years interest rates have also risen. Although short-term rates have fluctuated up and down, the long-term trend has been upward. Whereas 2 per cent was considered a high rate of interest for much of the nineteenth century, 6 per cent has been considered favourably during the 1960s. This behaviour of interest rates is reflected in the prices of fixed interest stocks. Long dated and irredeemable government issues (gilt edged longs) have shown a steady decline in capital value.

To illustrate this point, consider the behaviour of the 3½ per cent war loan, a most widely held long-term gilt edged security. If £100 had been invested at issue date, perhaps to open a sinking fund, this sum would have been worth £47.50 if sold on the market on 10 June 1968. This represents a loss on capital of 52¾ per cent. Clearly, this security would have produced income during those years and this income has to be included to arrive at the true value in June 1968. If a generous view is taken, it can be assumed that the income would be reinvested in long-term securities of similar stature so that the fund should grow by compounding. If this income had been reinvested at the prevailing interest rates, the total cash value at 10 June 1968 would be approximately £130. Such appreciation in value represents an absurdly low rate of return, for the purchasing power of £100 had fallen to £40 during the same interval of time. Thus, the combination of rising interest rates and prices prohibit the possibility of using savings as a means to create pools of reserve liquidity.

To emphasise the point, consider the behaviour of £100 invested in equities over the same period as the war loan. On average, the present value of such a fund would be several times greater. It would show a large capital gain rather than a loss, and it would represent a store of potential wealth of considerably greater value than the original investment. The financial press has published records of growth companies where equity values have appreciated by 3000 per cent during the time that the war loan has decreased in value by 50 per cent. Even allowing for the fall in purchasing power, these equities represent nearly a tenfold increase in potential wealth. If investment in such equities has protected the value of the investor's money, it follows that an even greater appreciation in value has taken place within the firm itself. Once again the lesson to financial managers is clear. Surplus funds should be employed to advantage within the firm or management must expect to be attacked for inefficiency or bought out by other firms. Such is the core of mergers and takeovers which are discussed in Part 4.

Operational assets

There are two types of fixed assets pertinent to a company's operations. *Tangible assets* are those with definite physical shape such as land, buildings, goods and chattels. *Intangible assets* are equally necessary to the firm but like patents, trademarks, long-term advertising, research and development, market research, and goodwill they are hard to assess, weigh and value. As a result, tangible assets are generally regarded more highly than intangible ones, even though some intangible assets represent the largest proportion of appreciating value in a company's asset structure.

Most *tangible assets* depreciate in value, some more rapidly than others. Though land and buildings have generally appreciated during the last few decades, this has not always been the case. During the early 1900s land and buildings including residential property decreased in value and it is only recently that industrial property, particularly offices, have shown stability of value. The Inland Revenue is not being charitable when it permits capital allowances on assets, such as 2 per cent per annum on buildings. All assets that are used in a firm's operations decrease in value as they are worn out or consumed. Vehicles, for example, have very short service lives, and items like machine tools not only wear out but suffer from the more serious phenomenon of obsolescence.

Intangible assets, on the other hand, can be managed so that they appreciate. Goodwill, sometimes the greatest single factor in the growth of a company's equity value, is an excellent example. Without due care and attention its value can depreciate rapidly. Further examples are provided by investments in long-term advertising, market research, and product research and development. If managed intelligently they will make a significant contribution to a firm's long-term growth. Badly managed, such investments are a waste of funds as the effects of failure are worse than not investing at all.

Fixed assets and the capital structure

The prime duty of financial management, as has been stated many times already, is to ensure that the company's total earnings grow as quickly as possible. Large earnings imply a rapid turnover of funds. A rapid turnover of funds can be generated by a high rate of turnover of assets. Accordingly, if assets are to be turned over frequently, a company cannot afford to hold more than the bare minimum of its funds in assets with long service lives. If earnings growth is a major objective, investment in tangible fixed assets ought to be avoided whenever possible. Such assets are a drain on funds and tie up capital for long periods. Such funds are relatively inactive particularly when compared to those invested in current assets. As a result, it is management's job to make sure that no more than a minimum of funds are invested in this way.

It will be noted immediately that a policy of not investing in tangible fixed assets is contrary to current practice and is at variance with the normal emotional attitudes towards assets. To pursue such a policy, a manager must become sufficiently convinced of its value to effect the reorientation of attitudes required to carry it out.

To illustrate what we mean by emotional attitudes towards assets, consider the order in which assets are placed in company balance sheets in the United Kingdom, an example of which is given in Table 8:1.

Fixed assets have low liquidity and are entered first on the asset list. Current assets which have higher liquidity come at the bottom end of the list. Within each "package" of assets, various categories are further itemised in what looks like an ascending order of liquidity. This ordering of assets is part of current accounting practice. Though current practice may have taken centuries to evolve and can be presented as a scale of assets measured by liquidity, company behaviour with respect to both cash and land and buildings is at variance with the liquidity notion. For cash and property are treated almost identically. They are considered to be desirable to have and to hold and that the greater

Net worth		*Fixed assets*	
Ordinary shares		Buildings and property	
Retained earnings		Machinery	
		Goodwill and patents	
Long-term liabilities		*Current assets*	
Debentures		Stock	
Mortgages		Accounts receivable	
		Cash	
Current liabilities			
Bank overdraft			
Accounts payable			
Sundry creditors			

TABLE 8:1 OUTLINE OF BALANCE SHEET STRUCTURE

the volume held the wealthier is the company. Such attitudes and behaviour lead us to suggest that assets are ordered on balance sheets in relation to general feelings with respect to money and wealth.

In man's early history the major tangible holding of wealth was land. As civilisation progressed the possession of land tended to become concentrated into the hands of a few and those without were forced to seek substitutes. Though gold and precious stones have always attracted attention, the major substitute for land became money (cash). This evolutionary process from land to money has created, we suggest, a deeply rooted set of emotions which govern behaviour towards certain assets. It is important to recognise the effects and implications of such attitudes since they can well form a barrier to efficient financial management. In Part 1 it has already been shown that the desire to possess wealth in terms of cash and liquid assets leads to a waste of a firm's resources. A similar policy with respect to fixed assets will also produce gross inefficiencies.

The layout of assets in a balance sheet can be explained in terms of a desire to hold real assets. Over many centuries, savings in the form of money and property have come to be regarded as highly desirable. Consumption, on the other hand, is a process which uses up savings and must, as a consequence, be kept to a minimum. Current assets are equated with consumption as they are used in the manufacturing process, while fixed assets are akin to savings.

Hence, the balance sheet proceeds by listing the major items of savings first (fixed assets) and leaves the consumable items (current assets) until the end. As a further illustration of this point, it should be noted that the American attitudes towards consumption and saving are well known to differ from those held in the United Kingdom. Accordingly, it is not surprising that in American balance sheets the ordering is reversed: current assets, the more consumable and desirable come first, with fixed assets following in order of the difficulty in which they can be consumed.

The ordering of categories of assets (UK) should now become quite clear. Land and buildings are accorded the highest position since their possession creates the greatest satisfaction. Subsequent classes of assets provide ever decreasing pleasure. This notion explains why intangibles like goodwill, patents, and research and development either appear at the end of the list or are charged off annually as expenses and are never placed on the balance sheet at all. The arrangement of current assets also follows this general principle, except now the ordering is in terms of most to least consumable. Stocks are bought to be processed through the manufacturing operation. In general, all stocks will be consumed eventually, and as a result stocks come first in the list of current assets. Cash, on the other hand, can be conserved and not consumed until necessary. It is placed at the bottom of the list as the most desirable of all current assets. In effect, the ordering is circular with the first and last items being the most prized. Successive inward steps lead to progressively less desirable holdings as is evidenced by the central position of intangibles, the hardest to value and appraise.

Managing tangible fixed assets

The emotional responses to fixed assets is chiefly responsible for the large investment in such assets that characterises British companies. Though these assets are frequently required their acquisition must be based upon financial considerations. Since shareholders have the same attitude towards assets and wealth, rational judgement in such circumstances requires skill, tact, and financial understanding. Nevertheless, these decisions must be made if the company is to prosper and grow.

Efficiency in asset management requires that all assets be considered in terms of their earning power in relation to their cost. Several techniques exist, such as the discounting of expected cash flows and capital budgeting, which enable the manager to choose among the available alternatives. But before these techniques are employed a major financial policy decision must be made and accepted. It is necessary to understand the fact that fixed assets are not desirable commodities in themselves. A case can be made for holding assets which appreciate in value. If these assets generate earnings through use and appreciate in value, the discounted value of these flows may well exceed that produced by any available alternative. Funds invested in fixed assets, however, are turned over infrequently. When comparisons among alternatives are being made it must be remembered that current assets are turned over relatively rapidly. Consequently, funds invested in working capital have a greater chance of generating higher total profits. A profit on turnover of 2 per cent multiplies itself to an annual rate of roughly 27 per cent if this 2 per cent is earned each month.

Fixed assets rarely generate either funds or profits by themselves. Indeed, left alone fixed assets usually produce capital losses through depreciation. There are relatively few fixed assets which appreciate in value and most of those are not a part of normal business activity. In general, to generate a return, fixed assets require an attendant application and turnover of gross working capital. Clearly, the greater the proportion of gross working capital to fixed assets, the lower the rate of turnover required on the working capital to earn a given level of profit. Viewed more positively, for a particular level of working capital turnover, the lower the proportion of fixed assets, the greater will be the flow of funds and the resulting profit. Return on capital employed is directly proportional to the relative volume of gross working capital and inversely related to the volume of fixed assets.

Example of tangible fixed asset management. To illustrate the points made above consider the following example of asset management where the asset structures of the Liquidity and Efficiency Companies are compared. The principal criterion used is the rate of return on total capital employed. To simplify the analysis we have supposed that the rate of turnover, profit, and the time interval all remain unchanged throughout the example. It should be clear, however, that in a real situation, where rates of turnover, profits, and time periods all vary, the technique of discounted cash flow is to be used and not a simple notion of rate of return.

Liquidity Company				
Net worth	£3500	Fixed assets		£2500
		Current assets:		
Current liabilities	500	Liquid assets	1000	
		Other assets	500	
				1500
Total	£4000		Total	£4000

Efficiency Company				
Net worth	£1800	Fixed assets		£1300
		Current assets:		
Current liabilities	1200	Liquid assets	1200	
		Other assets	500	
				1700
Total	£3000		Total	£3000

TABLE 8:2 BALANCE SHEETS (ALL FIGURES IN £'000s)

The balance sheets for the Liquidity and Efficiency Companies were presented in Table 2:1 and are reproduced for convenience in Table 8:2. As can readily be seen the proportion of fixed to current assets differs substantially between these two companies. If costs and prices per unit are similar for both firms then it can be assumed that the rate of profit per unit sold is also the same. Though these assumptions doubtless do an injustice to the real facts, they permit a comparative schedule of rates of return to be drawn up. This is presented in Table 8:3. In this table we have taken the libery of using two symbols, x and y, to denote two items which remain constant throughout, whatever their actual value happens to be. The symbol x stands for the rate of turnover on gross working capital. To simplify things we have assumed that both companies achieve the same rate $=x$. The symbol y is the rate of profit measured as a percentage of sales. That is to say, both companies are supposed to be earning y per cent profit on sales.

By using these two symbols, the reader will find that the differences between these two firms stand out more readily than if actual numbers were used.

It can be seen from Table 8:3 that the Liquidity Company earns only two-thirds the return on capital employed earned by the Efficiency Company. In order to equalise this rate of return the Liquidity Company would have to turn over its gross working capital 0.66/1 or 1.5 times faster than the Efficiency Company. To increase working capital turnover, under present conditions, the Liquidity Company would have to spend more on staff and other expenses which would reduce its profit on sales. Since the comparison was based on this profit margin remaining constant and equal between these two companies, it is clear that the problem is more serious than this example portrays. The cost of raising working capital turnover is large when such a large proportion (62.5 per cent) of all assets are fixed. It follows that the possession of fixed assets is a liability to the firm, a liability which should be avoided whenever possible.

	Liquidity Company	*Efficiency Company*
$\frac{\text{Fixed assets}}{\text{Total assets}}\%$	62.5%	43.3%
$\frac{\text{Gross working capital}}{\text{Total assets}}\%$	37.5%	56.7%
Return on capital employed %	37.5xy%	56.7xy%
[x = rate of turnover on gross working capital; y = rate of profit on sales]		
Relative return on capital employed $= \frac{\text{liquidity}}{\text{efficiency}} = \frac{37.5}{56.7} = 0.66$		

TABLE 8:3 COMPARATIVE ANALYSIS

It is clear in this example that the Liquidity Company has an excessive amount of fixed assets when compared to the Efficiency Company. To restore the balance, that is for fixed assets to be 43.3 per cent of total assets, the Liquidity Company would need to sell £770 000 of its fixed assets and invest these funds in its current assets. If it did, fixed assets would stand at £1 730 000 which is 43.3 per cent of the total assets of £4 000 000. Such a generation of funds is both eminently desirable and profitable. Many ailing firms have undergone this type of surgery to the benefit of their earnings. In times of credit or cash shortages fixed assets are an important source of funds and financial managers should take such opportunities as become available to rationalise the structure of their company's fixed assets.

It is not our intention to suggest that a company can survive without the substance of fixed assets. We are stating, however, that it is frequently unnecessary to own such chattels. Held in excess amounts, fixed assets are as wasteful of resources as locking pound notes away in a vault.

Volume decision

Fixed assets pose two distinct problems: (*a*) how many to have, and (*b*) how many to own. The financial literature is full of ratios which purport to act as guides to the first of these decisions. (The second will be treated in the next section.) Some of these ratios such as fixed assets/total capital, fixed assets/total sales, and fixed assets/gross working capital, are more useful than others as they relate the volume of fixed assets to turnover in selected items. Even these ratios can only serve as rough guides to be used in comparison with other companies. For the manager who wishes to do better than industry averages we can but recommend that the best volume of fixed asets is the least possible which can be tolerated. Clearly, any such volume of fixed assets must be checked against alternative uses of such funds. The physical asset structure is the framework within which short-term operations are carried out. To achieve maximum efficiency the asset balance must be such that gross working capital is as large as can be handled under the requirement that it be turned over as frequently as possible. This balance, though difficult to attain, is what financial managers should be striving to achieve.

Ownership decision

There are a number of financial arrangements by which assets can be used without owning them. Of these, leasing, hire purchasing, mortgaging, and selling and leasing back are the most frequently used. They are discussed in turn below.

Lease or buy. There are two main costs connected with the ownership of assets. The first is a combination of wear and tear (depreciation) and the loss in value due to obsolescence. The second is the opportunity cost, the lost profit which could have been generated from working capital represented by these funds tied up in asset ownership. To adjudge the lease and buy decision it is not sufficient just to subtract the first type of cost from the cost of the lease and compare rates of return on capital employed. Return on capital is indirectly related to the volume and turnover of working capital. By leasing an asset a firm can invest the excess funds in working capital and hence increase the rate of return.

To illustrate these remarks consider the case of the Efficiency Company where the balance sheet is given in Table 8:2. Suppose the £1 300 000 of fixed assets which appear on the current balance had been leased instead of purchased. Under this condition the asset balance would shift and a comparison is provided in Table 8:4 where it is supposed that the £1 300 000 of funds released

		Owned		*Leased*
Fixed assets		£1300		
Current assets:				
Stock	500		1100	
Liquid	1200	1700	1900	3000
		£3000		£3000

TABLE 8:4 LEASE OR BUY ASSET BALANCES FOR EFFICIENCY COMPANY

from fixed assets are invested, £600 000 in additions to stock and £700 000 in additions to liquid assets (accounts receivable, short-term investments and cash). If it is assumed that the rate of turnover of working capital can be maintained under the lease condition, then the rates of return on capital in the two cases can be compared. Once again we will use the symbol x to stand for the rate of turnover of working capital and y to represent the per cent of profit on sales.

In Table 8:3 the rate of return on capital for the Efficiency Company is given by 56.7 xy per cent, where the number 56.7 is the proportion of gross working capital to total assets. Once all fixed assets are leased as in Table 8:4, this proportion is equal to 100 per cent. Accordingly, if all fixed assets are leased, the rate of return on capital employed is 100xy per cent. The increase from 56.7 xy per cent to 100 xy per cent represents a 77 per cent increase in the rate of return on capital employed. The opportunity cost of not leasing fixed assets is given by the profit the firm would have earned if it had invested those funds in working capital. For the Efficiency Company the opportunity cost is therefore specified by the calculation on rate of return and is in this case an increase of 77 per cent in the rate of return on capital employed.

If the lease were taken out under normal conditions a firm could expect that the net lease cost, after allowance for depreciation etc, would not exceed 10 per cent on a discounted cash flow basis. This figure is taken gross of tax. Although there are often tax advantages to be gained from leasing, they will be ignored for the present.

An increase of 77 per cent in rate of return on capital employed has been purchased at a net cost of 10 per cent of the funds released by the lease. To break even on the lease or buy decision it is only necessary for the actual increase in return to be equal to the net increase in cost. For the Efficiency Company the break even analysis is given by:

$$3000 \times \frac{43.3\ xy}{100} = \frac{1}{10} \times 1300$$

$$xy = \frac{1}{10}$$

where the figures on the left are total assets times the expected increase in return ($100 - 56.7 = 43.3$), and the figures on the right represent the net increase in cost (10 per cent of the assets leased). The result, $xy = 1/10 = 10$ per cent, is the break even point, which is a statement that profit margin on sales times the rate of turnover on working capital must be equal to 10 per cent.

To indicate what this figure of $xy = 10$ per cent might mean, suppose that working capital is turned over ten times a year.

Then the profit margin on sales need be only 1 per cent to achieve the break even point. A profit on sales of 1 per cent is very low, and most companies will have a profit level considerably above this. Alternatively, suppose working capital is turned over only twice a year, which is a very low rate of turnover. In this case, profit on sales must equal 5 per cent before the break even point is reached.

It can readily be seen that it requires little in the way of business management to earn more than the cost of a lease. Moreover, it could well be argued that any firm which could not do better than these minimum requirements should question its right to be in business. It ought not to be surprising that a lease compares so favourably to the ownership of depreciating assets. The firm which lends the money on the lease does not have the manufacturing capacity or productive skill of an active commercial enterprise. The lender is content to receive a fair return on his money and to leave the larger share of earnings to the organisation which is prepared to work the funds and take the risks.

Hire purchase. The criteria which apply to leasing also apply with equal force to the decision to buy tangible assets on hire purchase terms. In general the net cost of hire purchase terms exceeds that of leases. Even so the net cost may still be below the rate of return that can be generated on the funds released.

Hire purchasing is a specialised financing opportunity and only applies to a limited range of goods and chattels. In addition the items that can be obtained under a hire purchase arrangement are seldom available under a lease. None the less, it is the financial manager's job to seek such means as are available of financing the firm's assets. Since hire purchase is the most expensive of all credit facilities, reaching a discounted rate of 20 per cent on occasion, leases are preferable whenever possible. Moreover, a hire purchase agreement implies eventual ownership of the asset which increases the liability of such contracts.

Mortgages. Mortgages are available only for a limited range of assets. The rate of interest is also subject to change which makes a calculation of the true cost a somewhat hazardous undertaking. They are obtainable on assets which appreciate in value but, like hire purchase arrangements, mortgages imply eventual ownership.

Since instalment payments include some contribution to principal, these payments will exceed those of a lease. In addition, a mortgage usually requires a capital deposit, the down payment, which can be as high as 20 or 30 per cent. The combination of down payment, fluctuating interest rates, high instalments, and eventual ownership may well prove to be more expensive than a break even analysis permits. The objective is to increase earnings, and a policy of not owning assets should only be pursued up to the point where the cost is less than that of outright purchase.

Sale and lease back. Assets which have been purchased by mortgage, hire purchase, or other means frequently have a substantial residual value. This is particularly true of appreciating assets such as land, office buildings, and other property. Firms with these assets on the books would do well to consider the possibilities of remortgaging or selling and leasing back from an insurance company or other financial institution. Clearly the sale and lease back process releases funds which can be invested in working capital. Hence, the cost of such an operation can be calculated. The advantage of a sale and lease back lies in the fact that funds are released without any change taking place in the physical assets. The factory, office or other asset may be well suited to the firm's immediate requirements. In effect, sale and lease back permits a company to have the best of both worlds, at the price of an increase in running costs to be offset by an increase in total earnings. As with all leases, an opportunity is provided to plan logistics and any relocation at leisure and in advance. For the term of the lease can easily be geared to any removal or expansion plans. By incorporating leases into the long range financial plan, the company is in a better position to keep abreast of technological developments, to contain the ever present hazard of obsolescence, and to keep up with the shifts and growth in its customer's consumption and demographic habits.

Effects of taxation

All the preceding sections were concerned with decisions taken before tax. Clearly, the net effect of a lease or buy decision, for example, depends upon the allowance that can be charged to tax.

Leasehold and other rent payments are allowable along with numerous other business expenses, so that if the company tax rate is 42½ per cent, the firm will only have to bear 57½ per cent of the agreed rent payments. Ownership, precludes such tax adjustments except for those made under the heading of depreciation, and laid down by statute.

Depreciation. There are several methods of depreciating assets which are currently used by companies in preparing their accounts. The simplest is the straight line method. Under this approach equal increments are deducted each year from the original value. These increments are calculated by taking the number of years in the useful service life of the asset and dividing this number into the original value. A second and, according to many, more realistic measure, is the declining balance method. Here a fixed percentage is deducted each year from the balance of the previous year. Such an approach preserves salvage values. There are other more complex methods all of which are applied to the original value and must take into account any additions or sales that take place during a given accounting year.

The objective of these techniques is to represent the speed at which the value of the asset is being consumed. Frequently it is argued that a prudent manager will set aside funds in proportion to the amounts charged under depreciation to build a reserve for future purchases. Such sinking funds or reserves are to be avoided wherever possible, for the reasons presented in the earlier parts of this chapter. Depreciation is a cost, but one that ought to be more than offset by the additional earnings this asset has helped produce. Fixed assets are in part consumed in the productive process where the cost of such consumption is recovered through the selling price.

Depreciation is a source of funds only in respect of the capital allowances permitted on specific types of assets. Since capital allowances are laid down in statutes and rigorously applied, there is no point in charging more for depreciation than the allowances permit. These statutory allowances represent a source of working capital funds. Though exceptions occur on the sale of assets when balancing calculations are made, the general rule should be to charge depreciation according to the appropriate capital allowance.

It might be argued that larger allowances for depreciation

reduce, with respect to the shareholder, the stated net profit for the year. A reduced net profit can be accompanied by a decreased or at least not an increased dividend. In brief, an overcharging of depreciation can cover up the true earnings rate and hence permit the firm to keep more of its profit for internal use. This is a poor justification for excess depreciation charges, and dividend policies will be discussed in detail in Part 4. It may be concluded that complicated procedures for calculating depreciation are best forgotten. The amount to charge for each asset is laid down in enforceable statutes and these are the precise allowances to use. Whatever figure a company uses, tax relief can only be obtained on that which is recorded as due.

Lease and buy. Given the capital allowances ascribed to specific assets, the lease or buy decision can be calculated on an after tax basis. In this event, the advantage is even more heavily weighted in favour of a lease. For the whole of the cost of the lease is chargeable against earnings and is not subject to statutory limits. In the long run, it may turn out that capital allowances and lease charges even out. Hence, the timing of these payments must be taken into consideration before the final decision is made.

Investment grants. Government grants are made available to firms to encourage investment in new equipment and in building new plants in certain areas. These grants are an obvious source of funds to finance fixed asset purchases. However, once purchased the funds are tied up and the company must do all it can to release these funds for working capital. One way of so doing would be to sell and lease back the new factory that has just been completed. Unfortunately, leases and hire purchase arrangements cannot be used on assets already owned. The alternative to a lease and sale back is to mortgage all assets acquired under investment grants. In either event, the extra funds provided by the grants will be redirected from their idle position in fixed assets, to a more useful role as part of working capital.

Managing intangible fixed assets

Intangible fixed assets are the main class of appreciating assets that are available to most business concerns. Investments in intangibles are judged by the same criteria as are used on tangibles. The difficulties are those of assessment of worth and value. Though it is necessary to be able to estimate the value of long-term advertising, market research and research and development, the decision process is neither easy to specify nor standardise.

This allocation of value is sufficiently difficult that many companies refuse to regard such intangibles as assets at all. Instead of creating assets, they merely charge off the investments as expenses within the year they occur. This approach is supported by the tax laws which permit such items to be charged as expenses against earnings. As a result, an intangible asset structure can be built by charging all investment as expense. With the government paying roughly half of the funds, here is an excellent source of potential wealth that is frequently overlooked.

Once acquired and stated at a recognised value, intangible assets can be sold and leased back. An investment in research and development, built up over the years on allowable expenses, can always be realised and returned to working capital. The sale and lease back of intangible fixed assets is subject to the same rules and criteria as tangibles. The objective is to increase earnings. Hence, intangibles should be sold and leased back wherever the additions to earnings via increased working capital more than cover the cost of the lease.

Part Three

MANAGING THE CAPITAL STRUCTURE

9 Capital Structure 147

10 Managing the Capital Structure 168

NINE

CAPITAL STRUCTURE

The capital structure of a company depicts its long-term financial position. It is the foundation upon which the firm's short-term financial activities are carried out. The company balance sheet shows the structure to consist of all share capital, capital, and revenue reserves and capital debts. The value of this structure is equal to the gross capital assets of the company, represented by the sum of net working capital and fixed assets. Hence it is the source of funds which are used to finance long-run operations.

The financial manager views the capital structure not only as an array of long-term financing but also as a system of risks and costs associated with each individual source. Capital debt financing, for example, exposes the company to special risks not associated with the issue of shares or the retention of earnings. Some types of long-term funds leave the financial manager free to behave within a very wide brief. Others entail specific restrictions on the internal management of the firm. Again there are types of long-term finance which are relatively inexpensive to raise but may influence future financing because they impose extra risks on the company's solvency. At all times there is also a capital market factor to consider. The financial manager must always take into consideration the effects of current decisions on the future market reputation of the firm's securities. All these factors must be assessed so that management may carry out long-term financing to the net benefit of the company's earnings. Such is the essence of the management of the company's capital structure to the advantage of the ordinary shareholder's long-term interests.

The issue of capital shares and debt is the principal method of raising long-term funds from the capital markets. Each type of security possesses particular characteristics and appeals to different investors. Since the company objective is to maintain an efficient capital structure, it will want to market those securities which involve the least costs and risks and provide the greatest tax advantages. The management of capital structure is discussed in detail in Chapter 10. It presupposes a detailed knowledge of the components of the structure. The first part of this chapter is devoted to a description of the various components. The second part discusses a number of measures which management can use to assess their value.

Ordinary shares—accounting classifications

Financial accounts record the share capital in two ways, the number that has been authorised for sale and the quantity that has been sold. The accounts will also indicate the amount of shares issued but not fully paid.

Authorised ordinary shares. The memorandum of a company limited by shares states the maximum amount of nominal capital, the shares into which it is divided and the value of each share. It is this statement which constitutes the authorised capital of the company. A decision is taken when the company is first formed which sets this maximum number of shares and total nominal capital. Once this amount is fixed it becomes part of the constitution of the company. The authorised share capital is the maximum that can be issued. There are no legal restrictions on the size of authorised capital, but a change can only be effected by a resolution of the shareholders. Such a resolution is itself only possible if the Articles of Association allow such action. The Company Acts specify the regulations which govern alteration of authorised share capital. In the absence of a suitable enabling clause in the Articles, they themselves must first be altered by special resolution of the shareholders. In the case of an unlimited company, the statement of authorised capital appears in the Articles.

Since ordinary shares have a par or assigned value, the authorised capital is stated both in total value (nominal) and the number of shares with a given par value. The term "par value" was derived in the early nineteenth century when a value was placed upon shares to represent the price at which they were expected to be sold. Par value was the price at which both market and face (book) value were on a par with one another. Today the par value may or may not be the issuing price. It is rarely the subsequent stock-market price. However, it is well for financial managers to bear in mind that investors have shown a marked preference in recent years for shares to carry a low rather than a high par value. This preference is reflected in the turnover of shares with market prices under £1.00. Although par value and market price may not be equal, a high par value ensures a correspondingly high market price given by the price/earning ratio. When considering a new financing operation it is worth remembering that low par values permit more shares to be issued for a given total value. Since volume of outstanding shares and stockmarket activity are not unrelated, low par values offer advantages. Even the higher jobbing commissions associated with low priced shares does not detract from this market preference.

Issued shares. Issued shares are those for which the company has received subscriptions of cash, property, or services. They form part or the whole of the authorised pool of shares but cannot exceed it. The company's record of issued shares will be accompanied by a statement which shows the dates of sale and the sums received per share as well as in total. This total sum also appears on the balance sheet in one of two forms. If the shares were issued at par, the balance sheet figure will equal the total sum received. If the shares were sold at a premium over par value, this premium will be separately listed as capital reserve or surplus. In both cases the value of the issued shares will be given on the balance sheet as the number of shares times their par value.

Contractual obligations. There is no one standard type of ordinary share. Every ordinary share represents a unit of ownership which is registered in the name of its proprietor. Ordinary shareholders have legal participant rights as members of the company, and these rights are stated in the issue prospectus.

Ordinary shareholders are residual claimants to the assets of their company. They are the beneficiaries of any net balance of profits and other monies which may accrue. The right to share in net profit should not be confused with the right to receive dividends. The ordinary shareholder, unlike the holders of preference and fixed interest stock, is entitled to receive dividends only after they have been declared and recorded as a current liability. There are means, other than dividend payments, which a company may use to ensure its shareholders receive satisfactory returns on their investments. Participation in the net balance of profits may take the form of scrip issue. Equally, the shareholders interests may be best served by the company management reinvesting profits effectively so that share prices rise. In neither case does the shareholder receive a direct cash dividend. The result may well be a receipt of payments that are of greater value. This topic will be discussed in detail in later chapters.

Ordinary shares usually carry the right to vote at company meetings. Non-voting ordinary shares are also issued, often in the form of scrip. Since such shares do not carry voting rights they can be used to avoid diluting or affecting the control of the firm. Though most ordinary shares fit a normal pattern and the majority carry voting rights, other types, such as deferred or founder's shares, also exist. Founder's shares often have nominal value and entitle the holder to surplus profits after the ordinary shareholders have received a specified amount.

The ordinary shareholder bears the greatest financial risk in respect of the companies operations. As the ultimate owners, they are entitled to share *pro rata* in the assets that would be distributed after a voluntary or forced liquidation. However, their share is residual since all other creditors have prior claims. This acceptance of risk ensures the ordinary shareholders right to expect a satisfactory return for supplying funds for the company's operations. As a source of funds, ordinary shares represent a long-term commitment. In all but the direst circumstances they are irredeemable. Under normal conditions, financial management need never consider their redemption and can treat such funds as permanent investments in the firm.

Preference shares

Preference shares, as the name suggests, have certain prior claims to ordinary shares. They are entitled to dividends when profits are made. They have first claim of all the shareholders on the residual capital value resulting from liquidation.

Preference shares generally carry a fixed rate of dividend which may or may not be a cumulative right. If the dividend rights are cumulative then the obligation is carried forward from year to year until discharged. If a company is unable to pay its preference dividends and this failure cancels the obligation for that year, then the preference share is non-cumulative. Since dividends must be paid on preference shares before they can be paid on ordinary shares, the distinction between cumulative and non-cumulative is important to financial management. In the former case, accumulated arrears of preference dividends must be paid before ordinary shareholders can participate. In the latter case, preference share obligations become void at the end of the financial year so that an improvement in earnings can be distributed as circumstances dictate. However, it should be noted that, in both cases, the passing of a preference dividend is a serious matter being viewed with apprehension by the financial community and investing public alike. The effect on share prices and the subsequent market reputation of the companies securities can help to inhibit recovery of earnings. To avoid this effect, financial managers often consider it prudent to pay preference dividends out of reserves even when earnings do not permit a disbursement. In certain circumstances, failure to make such a distribution might cause such an alarm that technical insolvency might follow. Sometimes, preference shareholders are given the right to a second share of net profits. In this case the shares are called participating preference shares. Whatever the dividend entitlements of the preference shares issued by a company, they are always noted on the balance sheet.

Preference shares can be issued either with a redemption date or as a permanent investment in the firm. A redeemable preference share is more likely to be used when interest rates are high and the dividend required by the investor is higher than the company wishes to pay in perpetuity. By including a redeemable feature the company will have the opportunity of buying the shares back if interest rates fall and other funds can be raised at a lower price.

A further class of preference shares can be created by adding a conversion privilege. Convertible preference shares give the holder the right to exchange preference for ordinary shares at some future date. The quantities, timing, and rates of exchange are specified in the prospectus when the securities are issued and this schedule is also printed on the share certificates. At the time of issue there will usually be a gap between the current market value of the ordinary share and the price this share must attain before conversion takes place. Care must be taken to ensure that this differential is not too great or the conversion privilege will not be taken seriously by the investor. If sound judgement is exercised, the convertible provision can be a sufficient inducement to permit relatively low dividend rates to be carried by the preference shares.

When a company issues convertible preference shares, the financial manager must make due allowance for the eventual dilution of ownership and control implicit in the offer of the conversion option. In addition he must recognise the effects on his company's performance measures which are based on outstanding ordinary shares. Although the conversion schedule only specifies minimum time periods and rates of exchange, it is expected that the option will be exercised. Ownership and control can be maintained when preference shares are exchanged for ordinary shares by suitable growth of earnings. Financial managers can readily calculate the extra earnings required to counterbalance the expected dilution. The conversion timetable published in the schedule should be based on the result of this calculation. During the period prior to an exercise of the option the company has full use of the preference share funds unfettered except for the liability to pay agreed dividends. Once converted, the only effect on the capital structure is an increase in the number of issued ordinary shares. If earnings have risen, at least proportionately, in the interval, the market price should not react unfavourably.

Preference shares, like ordinary shares, are not issued in any one standard form. The issue prospectus defines the voting rights. It states the dividend rate and whether such dividend is cumulative, and participation or conversion privileges and schedules are noted. If all relevant factors are assessed correctly, the preference share will sell at par. Market conditions are liable to fluctuations which are beyond the control of any one individual and even beyond regular successful prediction. Since it takes time to mount a financing operation via a share offer, market conditions may have changed between assessment and publication of the offer. If conditions have changed so that a higher than par value is realised, a capital reserve is created. The net difference between par value and subscription price is added to capital reserves in the same manner as a surplus from an issue of ordinary shares. If issue price is beneath par value, the shares will have been sold at a discount, but this discount is not capitalised.

Reserves

Capital reserve. The capital reserve balance originates mainly from the sale of shares, whether ordinary or preference, at a price above par value. Though this is the more frequent source of capital reserves, these balances are supplemented whenever assets with substantial hidden appreciation are revalued. Fixed assets are depreciated on a company's books from the moment they are acquired. Accordingly, the accounts seriously under-value certain assets. Property and land holdings are cases in point. From time to time, whether due to tax or other considerations, companies reappraise the market value of their assets. In all cases where the new values are greater than the old, the net balance is added to the capital reserves. Since revaluations usually take place only when there is appreciation to capitalise, they can be viewed as a source of capital reserves.

Revenue reserves. Revenue reserves, frequently called retained earnings, represent the undistributed profits of the firm. Since earnings which are not paid out in dividends can be used by the firm with no external interference, revenue reserves are its major internal source of long-term funds. Though dividend policies vary from company to company, revenue reserves are usually treated as the pool into which the residue of the year's earnings are placed. Instead, retained earnings should be recognised for what they are—a source of funds over which no outsider has control. Once viewed in this manner a firm can take such action as is necessary to ensure that the supply of these funds grows from year to year and as rapidly as possible.

Capital debt

Capital debt is a source of long-term funds. A company generates these funds by promising to pay interest and capital repayments on the outstanding balance of the loan. As a result there is a risk to solvency incurred by raising money in this way. The risk is a consequence of the legal obligation to pay interest in agreed amounts by stated dates, and to return the principal sum to the investor when the debt matures. Any failure to perform these actions can have serious effects on the shareholder's interest. A business enterprise cannot operate without taking risks. The objective of debt management is not to eliminate risk but rather to choose those debt forms which hold the risks to a manageable level. A special risk involves the attitude of shareholders and bankers to the level of capital debt used by a firm. The firm's financial advisers should always be consulted on the question of type and volume of capital debt the firm should use. A particular type of debt may apparently be financially desirable. It may also be disastrous to the firm's market image.

Debentures

A debenture (bond) is a legal document by which a company acknowledges a loan. The debenture will record a statement of the interest rate payable, the terms for repayment of the principal and any other charges that are agreed. In most cases, debentures are not secured by a specific charge against a company's assets. They are either completely unsecured ("naked" bonds) or most usually secured against a floating charge. A floating charge implies that the debenture holder has a general claim against all the assets of the firm. Such a charge does not become specific except in the case of default when the claim crystallises on to specific assets. Such a flexible arrangement allows the financial manager to pursue an unfettered asset policy. Unsecured debentures contain less risk than secured bonds, for the former gives the trustee the right to delay action against a defaulter until such time as a revised repayment schedule can be worked out. On the other hand, to default on a secured bond gives the trustee the foreclosure on the specified assets. This implies a possible forced sale or a special assessment on the earnings of those assets. In either event, the trustee assumes control of part of the company's affairs and in serious cases can cause a permanent loss in the shareholder's capital. A debenture has a prior charge against the assets of the firm. The volume of debentures which a firm may issue is governed by its assets. This can be a severe restriction in the case of a company pursuing a minimum fixed asset policy. In this latter case the firm should use unsecured long-term loans, the volume of which is determined by earnings.

Debentures are generally referred to as loan capital and are issued as unsecured loan stock (fixed interest stock.) Unsecured loan stock is normally issued in units of £100. These debentures carry a stated interest rate which is payable by the company on a specified date. They may be issued to named persons and registered by the company, or they may be made payable to bearer. Bearer bonds are more readily negotiated. All fixed interest stock quoted on a stock exchange and purchased for cash, via a broker, will be payable to bearer.

As in the case of preference shares, debentures may be issued in perpetuity or they may have a specified maturity or redemption date. Redeemable debentures give the company the option to call in the bonds at a stated price, or schedule of prices, on or before maturity date. This feature tends to reduce the element of risk by allowing a firm to use its funds to repay part of the debt whenever management recommends it. Excess earnings in a good year can be used to reduce outstanding debt if the company so decides.

Debentures may be issued with a provision for conversion into ordinary shares under specified conditions. Convertible debentures can pose less risk to the firm's solvency than redeemable bonds. A reduction in risk occurs as and when the debenture holders exercise their right to convert. The conversion procedure, which is described in the indenture at the time of issue states the rate at which debentures can be converted into ordinary shares, the various time periods and price levels at which conversion may take place as well as a number of other items which refer to the remaining terms of the agreement. Though the final decision to convert rests with the debenture holder financial managers may well be able to influence this decision. Such influence is gained by drawing up, and publishing at issue, a table of conversion prices which are only slightly above the prevailing ordinary share price. As the ordinary share price rises, the debenture holders will be tempted to convert. A second, but more risky approach, is to add a redemption date to the convertible provision. In this event, if conversion has not taken place by a certain date, the company is obliged to redeem them. The risk is posed since the firm's ordinary share price may fall below the conversion price. Debenture holders will not convert under these circumstances and the company may be faced with the task of redeeming more bonds than it can afford.

Loans

Long-term loans can be arranged in direct negotiation with financial institutions. In most cases such loans will be secured by a charge against specific assets or by a floating charge. The latter form is to be preferred as the risk is spread among a collection of assets. The contract may permit the company to alter the composition of these assets to meet changing business and market conditions. Secured loans have a larger element of risk than do publicly issued debentures. For if the debt is held by a single institution or a few large investors little time is needed to call and hold creditors' meetings to formulate a course of action. On the other hand, a long and well established relation with a financial institution assures the company in difficulty that arbitrary foreclosure is unlikely to occur and that some reasonable compromise can probably be agreed. Unlike debentures, the volume of loans which a company can carry is not determined by its assets. A willing lender is more likely to be interested in a firm's ability to meet a schedule of repayments, a function of earnings.

Bills of sale and mortgages

A bill of sale is a mortgage loan taken out against specified assets. When the asset specified in the instrument is either land or property, the debt is called a mortgage. Loans raised against the security of all other goods and chattels are recorded as bills of sale. A bill of sale is viewed as a last resort action and is regarded with the utmost suspicion by all outside parties interested in the solvency of the company. This is a regrettable and irrational attitude but one which the financial manager must recognise. It may well be prudent for a financial manager contemplating such a financing operation to keep his creditors informed. Bills of sale are perfectly respectable sources of funds, particularly for a manager pursuing an efficient fixed asset policy. The attitude of the firms creditors to bills of sale is particularly irrational in view of the fact that the assets against which such instruments are secured are those which offer the greatest threat to the firms solvency when wholly owned and which also offer the lowest return in the event of liquidation. A bill of sale should be recognised as a higher cost mortgage where the lender accepts high risk for a satisfactory return on his investment.

Mortgages, whether bills of sale or not, are registered with the Registrar of Companies. They are similar in many respects to a secured debenture.

A major difference between a debenture and a mortgage is that with the latter the company undertakes to make both interest and principal payments on a regular basis. A second source of risk is that interest rates on mortgages are subject to fluctuations and normally cannot, as in the case of a debenture, be fixed for the life of the issue. Mortgages also imply eventual ownership of the assets in question, and are usually issued for shorter periods than debentures. Moreover, mortgage holders have the first call upon a firm's assets and earnings in the event of a default. In such a situation the charged assets can be sold by the creditors to the detriment of the company and its shareholders.

Assessing the capital structure

Capital structures take many forms, and any company may well have some special features of its own. Accordingly, to assess the merit of a particular structure some general tools are required which the financial manager can apply to a variety of actual situations. A factor of interest in all balance sheets is the volume and proportion of capital debt to other asset and capital balances. Another item of importance is the cost to the firm of its existing capital structure. The efficient financial manager will want to know what changes can be effected to lower that cost by taking advantage of certain tax regulations. The management of the capital structure is discussed in detail in the next chapter. The remainder of this chapter is devoted to techniques for measuring the volume of debt and the cost of the total structure.

Capital gearing and leverage ratios

One concept of capital gearing measures the relation between the volume of fixed interest bearing instruments, preference shares and debentures, and the volume of ordinary shares. A firm which has a high proportion of shareholders to fixed interest funds has a low gearing. A highly geared company will have a large proportion of its capital in the form of fixed interest bearing securities.

The concept of gearing is hard to specify in a meaningful way. It seeks to draw a dividing line between funds raised by the sale of ordinary shares and, say, preference shares. If the preference shares are non-redeemable, and non-convertible, then they are as permanent an investment in the firm as any ordinary share. Similar comments apply to funds raised by the issue of non-redeemable, non-convertible debentures. This particular notion of gearing arises since both preference shares and fixed interest stock usually attract fixed interest payments in contrast to ordinary shares. However, the payment of interest is related to a company's earnings not its capital structure.

Consider, for example, the capital structures of the two companies depicted in Table 9:1.

	Firm A	*Firm B*
Ordinary shares	£1 600 000	£800 000
Preference shares (6%)	100 000	700 000
Debentures (6%)	300 000	500 000
	£2 000 000	£2 000 000

TABLE 9:1 CAPITAL STRUCTURE OF FIRMS A AND B

Capital gearing can be defined as the ratio of fixed interest securities to ordinary shareholders' funds:

$$\text{capital gearing} = \frac{\text{fixed interest securities}}{\text{ordinary shareholders' funds}}$$

For Firms *A* and *B* their gearing ratios are given by 400 000/1 600 000=25 per cent and 1 200 000/800 000=150 per cent respectively. It can well be argued that preference shares are as much a part of long-term equity as ordinary shares. Hence the gearing ratio is best expressed by dividing long-term debt by the sum of preference and ordinary shares:

$$\text{gearing ratio} = \frac{\text{long-term debt}}{\text{preference and ordinary shareholders' funds}}$$

In this case Firms *A* and *B* will have gearing ratios of 300 000/1 700 000 = 17.6 per cent and 500 000/1 500 000 = 33.3 per cent respectively. Clearly, the attitude to preference shares makes a striking difference.

Another approach to the notion of leverage implied by gearing is given by the ratio of long-term debt to total capital employed.

$$\text{leverage} = \frac{\text{long-term debt}}{\text{total capital employed}}$$

This measure considers all long-term funds to be identical with respect to a company's operating position. All capital is invested in the firm's operations and it is considered meaningless to point to any one aspect and say that it was financed by preference share funds as distinct from some other source of money. All funds are fungible, and the relevant question to ask is what proportion of the total capital employed is represented by long-term debt. For Firms *A* and *B* the debt to total capital employed ratios are given by 300 000/2 000 000 = 15 per cent and 500 000/2 000 000 = 25 per cent respectively.

Gearing or leverage is also measured by taking the ratio of long-term debt to total assets. This ratio is supposed to reflect the number of times such debt is covered by the assets owned by the firm. A proportion of debt to assets of up to 50 per cent is considered satisfactory. However, the previous chapter stressed the importance to financial management of not owning more than the barest minimum of fixed assets. If such an asset policy is pursued, ratios of debt to assets become quite meaningless.

The principal difficulty with all these ratios is that their meaning and usefulness depend upon: (*a*) all firms issuing uniform types of preference shares and debentures, (*b*) all firms treating fixed assets as desirable investment in themselves, and (*c*) a set of standards against which an individual company's ratios can be judged. Since there are no standard types of debentures or preference shares, and firms differ with respect to their ownership of assets, there cannot be a single set of standards for these ratios. For example, an issue of convertible debentures which is designed to lead to total conversion to ordinary shares is not the same type of debt as is represented by an unsecured non-redeemable debenture issue. In a similar manner, preference shares with a conversion privilege differ from those without this feature, whether redeemable or not.

The one feature all debt securities have in common is their fixed interest rates. Hence, one ratio that does measure the total volume of debt which a firm can handle is the times interest earned:

$$\text{times interest earned} = \frac{\text{profit before tax}}{\text{fixed interest charges}}$$

Once again, this measure is valuable only if a standard can be employed to evaluate actual cases. The lower the value of this ratio the more serious is the company's financial predicament. The essence of leverage is that it provides extra capital upon which additional earnings can be made. If these additional earnings are not generated then the fixed interest charges, which have prior claim, consume the bulk of the year's profits. Consequently, a times interest earned of four or five times is a minimum level to maintain. Measured against a company's expected profits before tax, this level will indicate the maximum fixed interest debt that the firm can manage and afford. For example, if Firm *B* has earnings of £200 000 before tax and fixed interest charges of £30 000 (6 per cent on 500 000 of debentures), then its times interest earned is 6.7 times. This measure does not take preference share dividends into account as they are distributed after taxes have been paid. If a firm has issued preference shares with cumulative dividend rights, due care must be taken to ensure that under normal conditions these dividends can be paid with ease.

Cost of capital

In order to finance a proposed investment a company may raise the required funds in a number of ways. It can borrow from banks, expand its current liabilities, sell short-term securities, sell some marketable assets, raise loans on existing assets, issue additional securities such as debentures, preference or ordinary shares, or use funds generated from operations. Each of these sources has a cost which is usually taken to be the interest rate charged. When retained earnings are employed this notion of an interest charge is sometimes used to suggest that there is no cost attached to these funds. If it could always be shown that the funds raised by any one operation were used to finance a particular investment and that all earnings from this investment could be traced and recorded, then there would be some merit to this approach. In general, however, investments are interconnected and earnings from one set of machinery depend upon the existence of, and earnings from, the remaining plant and machinery. In short, funds are fungible, and it is more reasonable to view a firm as having a set of desirable investment opportunities on one side and a variety of sources of funds on the other. If the financial resources of a firm are to be considered as a whole, then a single procedure is required for evaluating the cost of capital funds. The criterion by which investments are judged is whether their discounted projected earnings are greater than the cost of their finance. Hence, the cost of capital funds is the base line or cut off point against which all investments are to be evaluated.

The cost of capital to a firm may be described as the weighted average of the cost of each type of capital. The weight is determined by taking the ratio of the value of each class of securities to the total value of all securities issued by the firm. Since we are concerned with the capital structure, these securities include all ordinary and preference shares and all long-term interest bearing debt.

Cost of ordinary shares. The cost of ordinary shares is directly related to the rate of return required by the ordinary shareholder. For the shareholder to invest his funds in a company he must be persuaded that the discounted value of his future returns, from his subscription, is not less than the present quoted market price. Shareholders can receive returns on their investments in the form of cash dividends, scrip dividends, share price rises, or some combination of these possibilities. The cost of ordinary shares is the discount rate that equates these future returns to the current market price.

As a simple illustration, suppose that a firm pays cash dividends, as a policy, and expects to apply a proportion of any future earnings growth to increased dividends. The cost of ordinary shares to this firm can be specified:

$$\text{cost of ordinary shares} = \frac{\text{dividend}}{\text{market price}} + \text{growth rate of dividend}$$

Suppose the ordinary shares have a market price of £2.00 (40s), that the firm is currently paying a cash dividend of £0.14 (2s 9d) per share and that it expects an earnings growth which will allow dividends to be increased by 2 per cent per year. The cost of ordinary shares to this firm can now be calculated.

$$\begin{aligned} \text{cost of ordinary shares} &= \frac{0.14}{2.00}\ \frac{(2\text{s } 9\text{d})}{(40\text{s})} + .02 \\ &= .07 + .02 \\ &= .09 \text{ or } 9 \text{ per cent} \end{aligned}$$

Dividends do not have to be paid solely in cash. Suppose, for example, that this firm only paid £0.04 (9d) a share in cash and also issued free scrip to the proportion of one fully paid share for every twenty held by the shareholder. The net payment received by the shareholder would be the same as in the first illustration. However, the net value of such a payment would depend upon three things: whether the Inland Revenue regarded the scrip as an option dividend; what the shareholder did with the scrip; and the behaviour of market price. If the Revenue regarded the scrip as an option dividend, the recipient would be taxed as though a cash dividend had been received. Regular and widespread selling of such scrip by holders, some of whose tax rates would not warrant such a sale, would persuade the market that this was to be expected future behaviour. Consequently, the market jobbers would always mark down their purchase price for the company shares in expectation of the sale of scrip issues. This mark down in market price would occur regardless of the future earnings considerations. A general policy of widespread early selling is twice detrimental to the shareholders net income. If the scrip issue is not regarded as an option dividend and is held for such a time that more than a year has elapsed since the original purchase of the shareholding, then proceeds from a subsequent sale would be treated as a capital gain and taxed at the capital gains rate, the present maximum liability being 30 per cent. In this case the market would judge the increased share issue solely in terms of expected earnings. Indeed the price could be expected to rise due to the leverage effect of retained earnings. In this case the shareholder would benefit twice and his net income would be increased accordingly. From the long-run point of view, it is very much in the shareholders' interest to accept scrip in place of dividends and financial management must communicate this fact to their members. This topic is discussed in detail in Chapter 10.

It is also very much in the interest of the company not to pay cash dividends. By issuing scrip instead of cash a company effects an immediate reduction in its cash outflows. On the other hand, to flood the market with additional shares will only drive the market price down. Hence, for scrip issues to be a success they must be accompanied by a proportional increase in the firm's earnings. If earnings are increasing at, say 5 per cent per year an increase in issued shares of anything up to 5 per cent per year will not reduce the earnings per share. Since working capital can be increased by the amount not paid out in cash dividends, it is more than possible for a firm to increase its rate of earnings growth in this manner.

An extreme position would be for a company to pay out neither cash nor scrip and to concentrate its energies on producing ever greater earnings per share. If successfully managed, a continued increase in earnings would be matched by a steady increase in the market price. Shareholders would be paid their dividends through the increase in the share price. Such a policy might not please all shareholders, as it would require them to sell shares from time to time to generate any cash they required. It would also cause difficulties for the Institutions and Trust Funds who are governed by the Trustee Acts of 1925 and 1961 which prevent the conversion of capital into income. None the less, it is a possible form of dividend policy, about which more will be said in the next chapter.

Cost of preference shares. The cost of preference shares is readily computed from the fixed cash rate. A 6 per cent preference share will cost the firm in cash dividends disbursed each year, 6 per cent of the book value of those shares:

$$\text{cost of preference shares} = \text{cash dividend rate}$$

Since cash dividends on preference and ordinary shares are paid out of earnings after tax, the cost of these two types of capital is an after tax cost.

Cost of capital and revenue reserves. The cost of keeping funds in capital and revenue reserves is much less easy to determine. They represent capitalised asset appreciation, the premium paid over par value for issued shares and undistributed earnings. If these funds had been distributed as cash dividends, shareholders could have reinvested this money and earned whatever rate of return they are personally able to achieve. As a result, there is an opportunity cost to keeping these funds within the firm. It is at least equal to the rate of return the shareholder could earn if these reserves were disbursed.

A second approach maintains that if these reserves did not exist, the company would have to acquire a similar amount of additional long-term capital. Capital and revenue reserves do not have fixed interest charges. To be comparable, the additional capital would have to be raised by the issue of ordinary shares. Accordingly, the cost of capital and revenue reserves is equal to the cost of ordinary shares.

Whatever view is taken (revenue reserve policies are described in detail in the next chapter) it is clear that capital and revenue reserves cannot be considered to be free or costless funds.

In our opinion the simplest and most realistic method is to consider both capital and revenue reserves to be the property of the ordinary shareholder. Consequently, the cost of keeping these reserves inside the firm is equal to the cost of the ordinary shares:

$$\text{cost of capital and revenue reserves} = \text{cost of ordinary shares}$$

Cost of debt. The cost of long-term debt is the effective interest charge on the outstanding balance of the borrowed funds. Since interest on debt is an allowable business expense, the after tax cost is reduced by this allowance. For example, a debenture issue of £1 000 000 with a 6 per cent interest charge will cause the company to spend £60 000 a year in interest payments. If this company is paying tax on its earnings at 42½ per cent, the after tax cost is 57½ per cent of the £60 000 or £34 500. Hence the effective cost of these debentures is given by:

$$\text{effective cost of 6 per cent debentures} = \frac{60\,000}{1\,000\,000} \times \frac{57\tfrac{1}{2}}{100}$$
$$= 3.45 \text{ per cent}$$

It should be noted that as a result of the difference in timing of disbursements of interest warrants to debenture holders and the payments of tax, the company has the use of some free funds.

Interest warrants are computed net of tax at the standard rate. The tax withheld by the company (approximately 41 per cent at the present rate) is such a source of free funds until the company is required to pay the tax collector. This aspect of financing by debentures might be considered to marginally affect the cost of capital. Over time the effect is averaged out by corporation tax payments. However, the funds made available by tax withholdings should not be kept idle pending payment. They should be put to work as noted in Part 1 of this book.

Weighted average cost of capital. The weighted average cost of capital is calculated by multiplying the relative proportion of each type of capital by its cost and then adding the resulting weighted costs together. To illustrate this procedure consider the capital structure of the Liquidity and Efficiency Companies. In Table 2:1 the net worths of these two companies are listed as £3 500 000 and £1 800 000 respectively. The capital structures which these total figures represent are displayed in Table 9:2 in terms of the book values of the itemised securities.

	Liquidity Company	*Efficiency Company*
Ordinary shares	£1 700 000	£600 000
Preference shares (6%)	800 000	—
Reserves	1 000 000	500 000
Debentures (6%)	—	700 000
	£3 500 000	£1 800 000

TABLE 9:2 CAPITAL STRUCTURES

The weighted average cost of capital, calculated on an after tax basis, is presented in Table 9:3. It is supposed that the costs of ordinary shares and reserves are the same for both firms. A cost of 9 per cent, derived in the earlier examples, is chosen for illustrative purposes. The preference shares carry a 6 per cent dividend and the debentures have a 6 per cent interest charge which is equivalent to an effective after tax rate of 3.45 per cent.

The difference in the cost of capital for these two companies is striking. The Liquidity Company which has no long-term indebtedness pays for this privilege in terms of a higher cost of

Source of capital *Liquidity Company*		(*a*) *Proportion of total capital*	(*b*) *Cost*	(*c*) *Weighted cost*
Ordinary shares	£1 700 000	48.5%	9%	4.37%
Preference shares (6%)	800 000	22.8%	6%	1.37%
Reserves	1 000 000	28.7%	9%	2.58%
Debentures	—	—	—	—
	£3 500 000	100.0%		8.32%
Weighted average cost of capital for Liquidity Company= 8.32%				
Efficiency Company				
Ordinary shares	600 000	33.3%	9%	3.00%
Preference shares	—	—	—	—
Reserves	500 000	27.8%	9%	2.50%
Debentures (6%)	700 000	38.9%	3.45%	1.34%
	£1 800 000	100.0%		6.84%
Weighted average cost of capital for Efficiency Company= 6.84%				

TABLE 9:3 WEIGHTED AVERAGE COST OF CAPITAL

financing its operations. Though it might be argued that the Efficiency Company was highly geared, the outstanding debt only represents 38.9 per cent of its total net worth. What is more important to note is the fact that the Liquidity Company has 22.8 per cent of its total capital tied up in preference shares. Suppose, for the moment, that it could redeem these shares at book value. To raise the necessary funds it issues a 6 per cent convertible debenture. After these transactions have been completed the cost of capital will be reduced. The reduction is given by the difference between the after tax charges on preference shares and debentures (6 − 3.45 = 2.55%) multiplied by the relative proportion of this capital (22.8%), this net reduction is 22.8% × 2.55% = 0.58%. Consequently, the weighted average cost of capital would now be 7.74 per cent, more than half a per cent lower than before.

Half a per cent may seem a small amount and one not worth bothering about. This view appears to be reinforced as there is no question that additional debt increases the risk of insolvency.

Companies, however, are in business to make profits. To make profits risks must be incurred. To illustrate the effect of additional debt on earnings consider once again the switch from preference shares to debentures noted above. In Table 9:3 the Liquidity Company is shown to have £800 000 of 6 per cent preference shares outstanding. As a result, the company will incur an annual obligation to pay a cash dividend of £48 000. This £48 000 will come from after tax earnings. Under the new arrangement where there are no preference shares and £800 000 of 6 per cent debentures, the interest payment liability will stand at £48 000. Since interest payments are allowable expenses, 42½ per cent of £48 000 is deducted from total earnings before taxes are assessed. The after tax cost of these interest payments is 57½ per cent of £48 000 which equals £27 600. Therefore, the net contribution to after tax earnings, of a switch to debentures, is £20 400.

Debt may appear to increase risk, but it also reduces the cost of capital and as a consequence increases earnings. If these extra earnings are reinvested in working capital they can be made to grow in a never ending cycle. Long-term debt is a source of earnings growth. The methods by which manipulations of the capital structure can be managed, in order to increase the value of retained earnings and to ensure future earnings growth, is the subject of the next chapter.

TEN

MANAGING THE CAPITAL STRUCTURE

Companies are in business to make profits. Investors are ready to lend their funds in exchange for an adequate rate of return. These two factors are instrumental in bringing the partners together. The key to the relationship is earnings. The needs of both parties will be satisfied if earnings grow at a consistent rate. The company looks for a growth of total earnings. The investor looks for growth of earning per ordinary share. These outlooks are consistent with each other. There are many ways to achieve earnings growth, from cutting costs to increasing sales, and financial managers can make their own substantial contribution, through the efficient management of the capital structure.

In the earlier part of this book we have concentrated on the management of the various facets of working capital. On many occasions it was pointed out how an increase in working capital could be turned into earnings growth. The increases in working capital were generated by squeezing excess cash out of the system and by selling off or leasing fixed assets. A major source of working capital remains to be explored. This source resides in the capital structure.

Before proceeding to examine the management of the capital structure in detail, it will simplify matters if a statement of objectives can be agreed. It is our opinion that the principal objective for a company is to increase its earnings per share. Though it might be argued that the real goal is to increase the market price of its shares, a company has only a limited control of the market forces which determine share prices. Earnings per share, dividends, and the price to earnings ratio are the three main factors which determine price. Of these a company can directly control the first two. Effective management of these two factors is the only way to influence the third. If earnings are not and cannot be expected to grow, price to earnings ratios are unlikely to grow. A steady rate of growth in earnings will lead the market to expect future growth and price earnings ratios are raised in anticipation. In this situation the market price will increase very quickly and it is part of management's job to see that such increases do not get out of hand.

The management of earnings growth is the surest way by which a company can manage its share price. Since the value of a firm at any point in time is, in part, determined by the price the market is willing to place on its shares, the management of earnings is of prime importance. Financial policies which increase earnings should be pursued with the utmost vigour both in the long- and short-term. Long-term policies are concerned with the manipulation of the capital structure, the topic to which this chapter is devoted.

Level of capital debt

Capital debt is usually measured as a percentage or proportion of shareholders' equity. As long as this proportion stays below some agreed level, the lender is not apprehensive and is unlikely to ask for special guarantees to be attached to the loan. Though this notion of gearing is more widely used then the ratio of debt to total capital employed (see Chapter 9), both are concerned with proportions that are derived from balance sheet figures. As such they represent the lender's point of view, not the firm's or the financial manager's. The investor is willing to lend as long as the prospect of his being repaid is not impaired. His prospect includes the possibility of a forced liquidation and if the gearing or debt to net worth ratios are too high he cannot be sure that all his money will be repaid. This is not to say that a lender could not be found to take high risks. All lenders accept risk in some measure and their expected return on an investment takes the degree of risk into consideration. With a high risk a lender will anticipate a proportion of bad debts and will raise his required rate of return accordingly. A firm presenting a high risk situation will certainly be able to raise debt capital at a price. It is for management to decide whether the firm can afford the price.

A company pays its debts whether current or long-term out of earnings. Under all conditions it wishes to avoid a forced liquidation and, as a result, a firm looks to its ability to pay interest and principal repayments out of earnings. One measure that financial managers use is the times interest earned. As long as earnings exceed interest costs by a good margin a company can be confident that its solvency is maintained.

It cannot be repeated too often that earnings are the basis for debt management. Without earnings the firm cannot meet interest charges let alone repayments of principal. With positive earnings, debt is manageable, and with earnings that grow in proportion to increases in capital employed, an ever increasing debt is readily contained. Since earnings are the funds from which debts are paid, the volume of debt must be measured against those earnings. As in the case of current liabilities there is a measure which relates the total liquidity of a firm to its earnings and total debt position. The total liquidity measure is given by:

$$\text{total liquidity} = \frac{\text{current liabilities} - \text{liquid assets} + \text{long-term debt}}{\text{earnings}}$$

The result is the number of years it will take to pay off the total debt position out of earnings. As such, this calculation provides an upper limit on the volume of debt to carry. It is the task of financial management to decide the number of years to set as the target. If all debt were in the form of non-redeemable, unsecured debentures, then a figure of twenty or thirty years might be considered a safe guide. If these debentures were redeemable and the option could be exercised within the next eight years then the manager would use the formula to estimate whether earnings would prove sufficient if maintained at the current level.

To illustrate how to use this debt measurement technique, consider the debt position of the Efficiency Company. The capital structure is noted in Tables 2:1 and 9:2 and recapitulated below in Table 10:1. The current gearing ratio for this company (gearing = fixed interest/ordinary shareholders funds) is 700 000/1 100 000 = 63.5 per cent. The debt to total capital employed ratio (long-term debt/net worth) is 700 000/1 800 000 = 39 per cent. Both of these figures indicate a moderate degree of indebtedness, but neither tells whether this degree is excessive. The only way to judge the volume of debt is by knowing the level of earnings. Earnings before taxes for the year in question were £540 000, which is a rate of return on capital employed of 30 per cent. Though this might seem to be out of line with other companies' experience, the Efficiency Company has earned approximately 30 per cent on capital for some years. We shall take this rate of earnings as the basis for calculations.

Net worth:			*Fixed assets*		£1 300 000
Ordinary shares	£600 000		*Current assets:*		
Reserves	500 000		Stock	500	
Debentures (6%)	700 000	1 800 000	Liquid	1200	1 700 000
Current liabilities		1 200 000			
	Total	£3 000 000		Total	£3 000 000

TABLE 10:1 EFFICIENCY COMPANY BALANCE SHEET

The total liquidity for the Efficiency Company will be given by:

$$\text{total liquidity} = \frac{\text{current liabilities} - \text{liquid assets} + \text{long-term debt}}{\text{earnings}}$$

$$= \frac{1\,200\,000 - 1\,200\,000 + 700\,000}{540\,000}$$

$$= 1.3 \text{ years}$$

The Efficiency Company management could pay off all outstanding debt out of earnings by the end of $1\frac{1}{3}$ years.

Despite what the gearing and other ratios might indicate, the Efficiency Company can afford a great deal more debt. The amount of this additional debt depends upon the number of years management is willing to take for repayment. This is a decision that must be taken within the long-term financial plan, taking due note of the character of the firm's present and future debt. For illustrative purposes, suppose management has planned a considerabel expansion and decides to use a ten-year repayment schedule as the upper bound on the liquidity of the firm's indebtedness. The volume of extra debt which such a schedule will permit is calculated from the total liquidity formula previously noted. It is the quantity of new debt, which, when added to the original indebtedness, will equate total liquidity to the new time schedule (ten years).

Solving for the new debt in the equation gives the value of the additional debt that the firm can seek and take on. In the case of the Efficiency Company the additional volume is £4 700 000. Since

$$\frac{\text{current liabilities} - \text{liquid assets} + \text{long-term debt} + \text{new debt}}{540\ 000} = 10$$

$$\therefore \text{new debt} = 5\ 400\ 000 - 700\ 000 = 4\ 700\ 000$$

This calculation indicates that even if earnings only remained at their current level over the next ten years, the company could afford an additional £4 700 000 in long-term debt. Clearly, if it did raise extra funds, earnings would rise. A rise in earnings would reduce the debt repayment time which would imply that still more debt could be managed.

Suppose the additional £4 700 000 is raised by the management. The gearing ratio would now be 700 000+ 4 700 000/1 100 000= 490 per cent and the debt to total capital employed ratio would be 700 000+ 4 700 000/1 800 000+ 4 700 000=83 per cent. Both ratios are extremely high, which is further evidence of their misleading nature. We have just seen that the company can certainly afford such a level of debt.

So far we have been concerned with debt in general. One specific point merits further attention. There has been no mention of the type of debt best suited to a company's needs. Though expert financial advice should be sought before commencing financing arrangements, there is one type of debenture which should be considered with the greatest care. The debenture in question is one with a privilege of conversion to ordinary shares. If the conversion schedule is correctly assessed, convertible debentures have two great advantages. In the first place, the debt is self liquidating as earnings grow. The ordinary share price will reflect the earnings growth and as conversion prices are met, debentures will be exchanged for ordinary shares. It might be argued that the conversion of debentures will in turn lower the price of ordinary shares due to the increase in the number outstanding. Though this can well happen during the immediate conversion period only poor financial management will permit this effect to continue. Share prices respond to earnings and if a company is unable to increase its earnings share prices will indeed falter and perhaps fall. The experience both in America and England is that companies which regularly issue convertible debentures have histories of rising share prices. The reason for this behaviour is connected with the second advantage associated with convertible debentures.

The second great advantage of convertible debentures concerns the change of capital structure that takes place as the option is exercised. Since the debentures have not been redeemed the company has not had to repay any of the principal. The only cost has been the annual interest charge, 42½ per cent of which is an allowable expense. If the company continues to make a consistent rate of return on capital employed, the funds raised on the debentures will have increased earnings by a proportionate amount. That the debt is being converted into ordinary shares does not affect the volume of capital employed. It only reduces the proportion of debt in the structure. As the volume of debt decreases, the company can afford to purchase more. Debt has been exchanged for shareholders equity which reduces the leverage ratio as well as providing the liquidity with which to finance more debt. Consequently, convertible debentures can become a part of a never ending financing cycle. A cycle that can be readily managed to yield a constant return on capital which in turn will generate increasing share prices.

Preference shares and break even analysis

Preference shares, unless convertible, are a relatively expensive source of capital when compared to the cost of long-term debt. Dividends on preference shares are disbursed from after tax earnings. Thus, for example, a preference share would have to carry a dividend as low as 3.45 per cent before it would be as inexpensive as a 6 per cent debenture to a company liable for corporation tax at the rate of 42½ per cent.

Not all preference shares on company books carry such a small dividend. Equally, it is true that not all debentures have a 6 per cent interest rate. The break even point for a preference share can be calculated once the long-term interest rate and the company's tax rate are known. The break even point can be stated as:

$$\text{break even point} = (1 - \text{tax rate}) \times \text{long-term interest rate}$$

For the company tax rate of $42\frac{1}{2}$ per cent and a long-term interest rate of 8 per cent, the break even point for a preference share is $57\frac{1}{2} \times 8 = 4.6$ per cent. This means that if the manager had a choice between raising new funds by either a debenture or a preference share issue, unless the latter dividend rate was 4.6 per cent or less it would be cheaper to issue 8 per cent debentures.

This analysis is straightforward when considering alternative means for raising new funds. The decision procedure is quite clear. *Do not issue preference shares unless the dividend rate is less than or equal to the break even point determined by an alternative debenture issue.* Clearly other considerations can override these cost considerations. As a general rule, however, it is worth noting the cost and avoiding the issue of preference shares whenever the break even point is not reached. In practice it would prove impossible to issue non-redeemable, non-convertible preference shares with a dividend rate very much lower than prevailing interest rates. The underwriters would perceive that no investors would subscribe to the share at or near par. Anticipating that they would be left with the total issue, they would refuse to provide a guarantee except at a self defeating discount. The company's advisers would acquaint the management of the situation and prevent such an issue. Preference shares, presently recorded on company books, with very low coupon rates will sell in the market at a large discount to par such that the gross yield to the investor reflects the prevailing interest rates. Any new issue of preference shares must also reflect such rates in the absence of other incentives to investors.

Many companies have preference shares outstanding on their books. The question posed by these shares is whether to replace them or not. If the preference shares can be redeemed, a break even calculation should be made to discover the advantage, if any, to be gained by raising the necessary funds through a debenture issue. It could well be the case that the preference shares were issued at a time when long-term interest rates were relatively low so that the cost of the outstanding shares is well below the break even point. In such a case, no alterations are required. Such preference shares are costing the firm less to maintain than a new debenture issue. On the other hand, it could occur that the preference shares on the books have a dividend rate which places them above the break even point. The firm ought now to consider redeeming these shares with funds raised by debentures.

The redemption of preference shares can be negotiated for cash, a combination of cash and a new debenture, or a straight exchange of preference share for new debenture. Consider the last case. Some shareholders might feel that a debenture was not equivalent to a preference share and resist the exchange. Others would rightly view the exchange as offering a better rate of return and a more secure investment. On such a straight exchange of securities it would be sound management to offer the preference shareholder a convertible debenture issue. In the event, his investment can eventually be converted into ordinary shares which provide an incentive to accept the exchange. An exchange of preference share for debenture of similar value incurs no income or capital gains tax liability. Securities can be swapped so that the net cost to the firm is reduced while the potential gain to the preference shareholder is increased.

To redeem preference shares for cash or cash and debentures is expensive for both company and shareholder. The firm loses working capital to the cash payment. The shareholder incurs a tax liability for any receipt, pro rata in excess of his original investment. Since redemptions usually are negotiated at a premium over par, there is little that can be said in favour of this approach. Even when the preference shareholder demands a premium to sweeten the exchange, all efforts should be made to pay this premium in securities, whether in scrip or convertible debentures, to avoid the cash drain and the tax liabilities. Clearly, the cost of the cash drain and the tax can be computed to determine two premium offers, one made up of securities alone the other a combination of cash and securities. The shareholder can then choose the package he prefers and if the offers have been well presented the balance ought to be in favour of the all securities exchange.

As can be seen the general advice to take when considering the issues of preference shares is "don't." On occasion it will make financial sense to ignore this advice. At this point, the merits of convertible preference shares ought to be considered. Any issue of preference shares must cause a substantial drain on after tax earnings. This cash outflow is made at the expense of ordinary shareholders' dividends and the company's retained earnings position. As such it is to be avoided whenever possible and certainly when the cost of the preference share dividend is above the break even point.

Retained earnings policies

Retained earnings (revenue reserves) are a company's major source of internal funds. In the previous chapter it was suggested that these funds are not free and that their cost can be considered to be equivalent to that of the firm's ordinary shares. Though this notion of cost can serve as an approximation, the real cost decision on internal financing turns on the relative cost of retaining earnings as compared to the cost of distributing the funds to shareholders. The financial manager should question whether it is cheaper, and hence more profitable to the shareholder, to reinvest earnings in the firm or to distribute them as cash dividends. The cost decision consists of two parts, the cost of retaining earnings and the cost of distributing them. *The decision rule is to retain earnings when the cost of retention is less than the cost of disbursement.* Such a rule is easy to state, but until each component is defined it is difficult to employ.

The cost of retained earnings is an opportunity cost. This opportunity cost is determined by specifying the earnings that shareholders forego by leaving the funds in the business. One obvious benefit that accrues to the shareholder is the absence of a tax payment on the dividend income. If earnings are paid out as dividends each shareholder must pay tax at his personal rate on this income. Another benefit is the addition to earnings that the firm can generate by reinvesting. Since increasing earnings will, in time, be reflected in the share price the shareholder receives this appreciation instead of a cash dividend. If the shareholder wishes to convert the appreciation into cash, only moderate care need be exercised to ensure that only long-term capital gains tax is paid. Some shareholders will have personal tax rate below the capital gains rate. These persons can encash their shares at any time. The majority of shareholders, however, will have to delay such sales until all gains can be classified as capital appreciation to be taxed at the present maximum of 30 per cent.

A further item to consider is the cost to the firm of replacing the funds paid out in cash dividends. If a company is to maintain its capital structure over the short as well as the long run, then funds paid out in dividends must be replaced by other financing. The cheapest form of funds for this purpose is a loan, hence the loan cost must be included in the calculation.

These various costs can be combined into a formula which specifies the cost of retaining earnings:

$$\text{cost of retaining earnings} = \{D - C(1 - ct)\} \times (1 - st) \times R(1 - st)$$

where D = gross amount of cash dividends
C = cost of loan to replace dividends paid out
ct = company tax rate
st = shareholder tax rate
R = rate of return shareholder can earn by investing dividends

To illustrate the use of this formula, suppose that the Efficiency Company proposes to pay out a little more than a third of its after tax earnings in cash dividends. Earnings before tax and after interest payments are £498 000 and if the tax rate is 42½ per cent, after tax earnings will be approximately £286 000. Let us suppose that the shareholders decide to declare a gross dividend payment of £100 000. At current market rates, a loan can be arranged for £100 000 at 7½ per cent. It will cost the firm £7500 to replace the £100 000 it proposes to pay out. The company tax rate is 42½ per cent and an estimate has to be made of the average income tax rate paid by the company's shareholders on dividend and investment income. Though the standard rate could be taken as the minimum average tax, the Efficiency Company made an extensive survey of its shareholders and discovered that the average rate they paid on investment income was 50 per cent. The Efficiency Company in the same survey discovered that, on average, their shareholders expected to earn 9 per cent gross on their investments. Substituting these figures into the formula produces the cost of retaining £100 000 of earnings:

$$\begin{aligned}\text{cost of retaining earnings} &= \{£100\,000 - 7\,500(1 - .425)\} \times (1 - .50) \times .09(1 - .50)\\ &= \{100\,000 - 7500(.575)\ \{ \times (.50)(.09)(.50)\\ &= 95\,687 \times (.50)(.09)(.50)\\ &= £2153\end{aligned}$$

If £100 000 is not distributed as a cash dividend, the shareholders will be deprived of £2153 of additional net income. Against the cost of retention must be balanced the loss in the firm's earnings, incurred by shareholders as a consequence of any distribution. If earnings are distributed the firm will have less funds to invest. Hence the cost of distributing earnings is equal to the profits the firm would have earned for the shareholder if these funds had been reinvested in the business. To compute this cost the normal after tax rate of return on capital is multiplied by the amount of earnings to be distributed as dividends. For example, the Efficiency Company earns, on average, a 30 per cent return on capital before interest and taxes. Their after tax earnings for the last year are £286 350, a 16 per cent return on total capital of £1 800 000. Suppose this rate of return is in keeping with previous and expected future performances. Then the cost of distributing £100 000 of earnings will be given by:

$$\begin{aligned} \text{cost of distributing earnings} &= £100\,000 \times .16 \\ &= £16\,000 \end{aligned}$$

Given both the cost of retaining earnings and the cost of distributing them, it is now possible to compare the two in the following ratio:

$$\text{relative cost of retaining earnings} = \frac{\text{cost of retaining earnings}}{\text{cost of distributing earnings}}$$

The relative cost of retaining earnings is a statement of the comparative costs of retention and distribution. If the cost of distributing earnings exceeds that of retaining them, then it is clear that the firm should retain and not pay dividends. This situation occurs when the value of the ratio is less than one. The decision rule can now be stated: *do not distribute earnings if the relative cost of retention is less than one.*

To illustrate the behaviour of this rule consider the calculations given above for the Efficiency Company. The cost of retaining £100 000 of earnings is £2153, while the cost of distributing this amount is £16 000. Accordingly, the relative cost of retaining these earnings is £2153/£16 000 = 0.13. The Efficiency Company ought not to distribute these earnings. Both the shareholders' and the company's financial interests will be better served if these earnings are reinvested internally.

For many companies the relative cost of retaining earnings will be less than one. In other words, many companies which currently distribute a substantial proportion of their earnings are disbursing to the detriment of themselves and their shareholders. This is a strong statement to make, since cash dividends are viewed with such apparent pleasure by the investing public. Cash dividends, however, are only worth receiving by the investor as long as the tax paid on this income is less than or equal to the long-term capital gains rate. As has been shown above, cash dividends are only worth paying out if the investor can earn an after tax return which exceeds the earnings rate of the company.

A retained earnings policy implies that many firms should retain and reinvest their earnings. A token payment in cash might be made if management considers this to be sound public relations. In general, if the relative cost of retaining earnings is less than one, earnings should be retained.

To retain earnings means that no cash dividends are paid. There are not very many companies who currently follow this policy of retaining all after tax earnings. Though management can determine whether it is profitable to retain, most firms are in the habit of paying cash dividends. It is our suggestion that financial management review and reassess their retained earnings policy. Dividend policies will be discussed in a later section of this chapter. For the moment we shall concentrate our attention upon possible decisions with respect to retained earnings.

Managing earnings

The key to the management of earnings is the relative cost of retention. It is necessary for financial management to calculate this relative cost. If the answer is a value less than one then it is clear that the greater the proportion of earnings retained the greater the return to shareholder and company alike. Not every firm will view a policy of retaining all earnings with equanimity. For those who insist on distributing some cash, a policy should be selected where the emphasis is on retention. A policy of retaining 80 per cent of all earnings would be an example of such a rule. An alternative would be a decision to retain a fixed amount each year irrespective of the size of the total pool of earnings. A difficulty arises in a poor year when total earnings might not reach the target figure. Again in a good year the target might represent only 50 per cent of earnings. A fixed percentage of the earnings is a more flexible rule, since it will produce a straightforward decision under all circumstances.

It is entirely possible that the calculation of the relative cost of retaining earnings can yield a value greater than one. In this case, the company ought to distribute all of its earnings. A value greater than one occurs when the shareholders can earn a higher net of tax return on the distributed earnings than can be generated from a reinvestment of funds within the company's activities. Though companies consistently in this position will be reluctant to part with their earnings, their managers ought to recognise the fact that the return on investment they produce is not on a par with the level provided by the market as a whole. Under these circumstances a policy of maximum distribution of earnings, including proceeds from the sale of all assets, ought to be adopted.

Dividend policies

Dividends are usually paid out in one of two forms: cash or shares. From the financial manager's point of view cash dividends are the most important as they represent a direct depletion of working capital. Cash dividends are paid out of earnings. Accordingly, the retained earnings balance (revenue reserves) is not as large as it could have been. In addition, the cash that is paid out is taken from working capital which in turn reduces the company's earning power. Share dividends (scrip issues) on the other hand, are a net contribution to the firm inasmuch as the value of issued shares is increased and working capital balances are undistributed. Of the two dividend forms, shares are much to be preferred.

It might well be argued that a distribution of shares does not represent cash to the shareholder. Shareholders enjoy receiving cash income and many rely on this source to finance their own activities. Large, corporate investors are particularly attached to receiving cash or franked income, a substantial proportion of their annual income being derived in this way. This attitude is, in part, determined by the preferential tax rates accorded certain institutions and in part by the requirements of the Trustee Acts. However, it is no part of the task of financial management to gear their activities to a particular section of the investing community. The choice of investment is vested in the lender who can match his special requirements to the best situation offered by the entire market. In any case, it requires very little evaluation to show that rates of growth of earnings increase when a retention policy is pursued. The cumulative advantages far outweigh any minor short-term advantages which franked income provides even for special investors. Investors who do require a cash dividend income have available the whole range of capital debt instruments issued by the firm. Their special requirements should not restrain the ordinary share.

A second argument raised in defence of dividend payments concerns the behaviour of share prices. It is frequently maintained that share prices reflect dividend policies and that a fall in cash dividends will be accompanied by a drop in share price. Since shareholders do not react favourably to a persistent fall in share prices dividends must be at least maintained and whenever possible increased. This approach to the disbursement of cash dividends is only profitable if income and company taxes are a minor irritant and not a factor of major economic importance. Where companies pay corporation tax and shareholders pay tax and surtax on earnings at the prevailing United Kingdom rates, cash dividends are a luxury neither can afford.

In the previous section a formula was presented which permits the relative cost of retained earnings to be calculated. By turning this ratio upside down, the relative cost of distributing cash dividends is obtained:

$$\text{relative cost of distributing cash dividends} = \frac{\text{cost of distributing earnings}}{\text{cost of retaining earnings}}$$

If the figures previously used to compute the cost of retention for the Efficiency Company are taken, this ratio yields a value of £16 000/2153 = 7.4. Since the ratio was turned upside down, the rule to follow with respect to paying out dividends is: *cash dividends ought not to be distributed as long as this ratio is greater than one.*

The Efficiency Company with a value of 7.4 ought not to distribute any cash dividends.

Suppose for the moment that a company had been accustomed to paying out some 30 per cent of its earnings in cash dividends. It had not calculated the cost and believed it was following a sensible dividend policy. Suppose further that managers were suddenly made aware of the cost of these dividends to their shareholders and the firm. Persuaded by the logic of the argument they computed the cost and discovered to their horror that it would benefit all parties if they stopped paying cash dividends immediately. Having established a record for steady dividend payments what is the company to do? They were aware that a sudden unexplained cut in cash dividends would be accompanied by a dramatic fall in share price. It would also damage their reputation with the financial institutions of the City.

A solution to this dilemma can be achieved by both announcing, with suitable notice, the reasons for the change in dividend policy and publishing the calculations that made the decision inescapable. It might also be useful to change the dividend policy in line with a capital reorganisation. These announcements would emphasise the fact that all earnings were now being reinvested in the firm and the extra profits generated by this process would be reflected in a proportionate increase in share price. Share prices are known to depend more heavily on earnings than cash dividends. Moreover, it should be pointed out to shareholders that as the share price rose they could take cash dividends by selling off a proportion of their holdings. If sales were made at appropriate times, this income would only be taxed at the capital gains rate which, for many shareholders, is less than their marginal tax rate on unearned income. As a sweetener, a reorganisation of the capital structure might accompany the dividend proposals. Suitably managed, such an offer would appeal, would reassure the market and might even be used to increase capital funds.

A company management may view a no dividend policy to be too drastic for their shareholders to accept. An alternative policy can make an annual scrip issue in lieu of cash dividends. The scrip issue is made by distributing shares out of the authorised but, as yet, unissued pool of ordinary shares. A scrip issue of this sort could be made at the old dividend rate, say 5 per cent. For every hundred shares issued, five new shares would be distributed. Shareholders who held odd amounts could be offered a cash balance. The value of such an issue would, of course, depend upon market price. In general the scrip rate should be calculated to generate a gross cash potential equal to the old dividend total. It would be left to the individual shareholder to decide whether to realise the cash potential by selling the scrip in the market. Such decisions would no doubt revolve round relative tax rates. It would be the task of management to pursue earnings policies which at least maintained the market price of the company shares.

The advantage of a scrip issue lies in the fact that the shareholder receives a dividend which he can decide when to encash. If personal tax rates are low, the scrip can be sold at any time. If personal tax rates are above the capital gains tax rate, any sales should be delayed until the original holding of shares on which the scrip is received has been held for twelve months. The only disadvantage to the company is that it must now increase its earnings by the same proportion as it issued scrip. Share price stability is a least essential, so that earnings per share must not go down. With the number of shares issued being increased by scrip issues earnings must rise by an equal amount. Earnings growth depends upon a growth in working capital. Since scrip issues permit all earnings to be reinvested in working capital, a reasonable return on these invested earnings will produce the necessary extra earnings per share.

To illustrate the productive cycle of reinvested funds, consider again the capital structure of the Efficiency Company as noted in Table 10:1. The value of ordinary shares is given at £600 000. If they were issued with a par value of 5s then there are 2 400 000 shares in the hands of shareholders. A 2½ per cent scrip issue would entail making a dividend share issue of:

$$\frac{2.5}{100} \times 2\,400\,000 = 60\,000$$

Since these shares would come from the authorised pool they would also have a par value of £0.25 (5s). The market value of these shares would depend upon the price/earnings value being placed upon them by investors. Earnings for this last year, before dividend are £286 000 which yields an earnings per share figure of 286 000/2 400 000 = £0.12. Suppose the market accorded the Efficiency Company a price earnings ratio of fifteen times. The current market price would be in the order of £1.80 a share. A dividend issue of 60 000 shares would have a market value of approximately £108 000.

Originally the Efficiency Company was considering a cash dividend of slightly more than a third of its earnings or £100 000.

By issuing a scrip dividend of $2\frac{1}{2}$ per cent, instead of cash, it can offer its shareholders a dividend value of £108 000. The cost to the share price can be measured in terms of the extra earnings the firm must generate to keep earnings per share at least as high as £0.12. The new issue contained 60 000 shares. The extra funds available for reinvestment are £100 000. To maintain the earnings rate at £0.12 a share the firm must earn at least $0.12 \times 60\,000 =$ £7200 on this additional £100 000. Since it currently manages to earn a net 16 per cent on capital employed it could confidently expect to earn at least twice the required amount in the coming year.

One further point is worth mentioning. The higher the price/earnings multiple accorded by investors, the cheaper it is for a firm to issue scrip dividends, and the more profitable to the shareholder. If the Efficiency Company had a price/earnings of thirty instead of fifteen times, it would only have to issue 30 000 shares or a $1\frac{1}{4}$ per cent scrip dividend to give its shareholders a dividend value of £100 000. On a 30 000 share issue it would have to earn £3600 a year to maintain earnings per share. Since the firm earns roughly 16 per cent on capital there would be a net addition to after tax earnings of $16\,000 - 3600 =$ £12 400 which is over £0.01 a share. The following year another scrip issue could be made with a similar multiplication of earnings from the reinvested funds.

Rights issues

A further method of paying scrip dividends is the rights issue. At the same time, a rights issue raises additional funds for the company since a subscription is received from the shareholder. In so far as the subscription is less than subsequent market price, the discount represents a potential source of cash to the shareholder. The discount is equivalent to the free scrip issue. By retaining earnings and raising new funds, through a rights issue based on those earnings, the company can rapidly expand working capital. To be successful, the size and price of the rights issue must be correctly assessed. If the issue is to be strictly geared to retained earnings then size and price might be calculated as follows.

It is assumed for the sake of illustration that the market and the company shareholders expect a gross yield on investments of 5 per cent regardless of the method of payment. In carrying out calculations the financial manager must also be aware that share prices have to be maintained by keeping the earnings per share at least constant. The formulas which the manager might use are:

A: number of rights shares to issue =

$$\frac{\text{retained earnings} \times \text{earnings rate on capital}}{\text{earning per share}}$$

B: price of rights share =

$$\text{market price} \times \frac{\left[\begin{array}{l}\text{number of rights shares} - \\ (\text{number of ordinary shares} \times \text{scrip rate})\end{array}\right]}{\text{number of rights shares}}$$

—where scrip rate = the scrip proportion that will just equate the total potential cash from the scrip offer to the desired cash dividend.

In the previous illustration of free scrip dividends, it was noted that the Efficiency Company was considering a cash dividend of £100 000. The net earnings rate on capital is 16 per cent and the earnings per share with a price/earnings ratio of fifteen is £0.12. The market price is £1.80 a share. The scrip rate was calculated to be 2½ per cent.

The number of rights shares which the Efficiency Company could issue on the basis of additional retained earnings is given by:

$$\text{number of rights} = \frac{100\,000 \times 0.16}{0.12}\text{shares}$$
$$= 133\,000 \text{ shares}$$

The price at which the Efficiency Company rights shares could be offered is given by:

$$\text{price} = \frac{£133\,000 - \left[\frac{2.5}{100} \times 2\,400\,000\right]}{133\,000} \times 1.80$$
$$= \frac{£133\,000 - 60\,000}{133\,000} \times 1.80$$
$$= £0.98$$

The offer to the Efficiency Company shareholder would then take the form of a rights issue of one rights share for every eighteen ordinary shares held, at a price of £0.98.

It might well be argued that the shareholder would expect an additional sweetener in order to subscribe to the rights, a price of £0.90 might be suggested. However, it should be pointed out that a sweetener already exists in two forms. A tax benefit is available as shown in the previous section. In addition, the rapid increase in both retained earnings and additional funds will ensure even more rapid growth in the future and, consequently, increasing share prices.

Taken to its logical conclusion, there is no financial reason why very large rights issues should not be hung on dividend payments. The only limit to this operation is management's ability to generate earnings from capital, and this is the whole object of business enterprise. For those effective financial managers who wish to use large rights issues, formula *A* should be modified as follows:

$$C\text{: number of rights to issue} = \frac{\left[\begin{array}{l}\text{(retained earnings + gross proceeds of rights issue)} \times \\ \text{earning rate on capital}\end{array}\right]}{\text{earnings per share}}$$

The number then depends both on retained earnings and the amount of funds management requires. Management must make the decision as to the quantity of additional funds it can handle. After assessing this amount of funds management must then add the cost of issuing and an amount to cover any additional discount that the shareholder may require as an incentive to take up the offer. The total is the gross proceeds.

The discount which the shareholder may require can be found by a trial and error process which equates formulas *C* and *B* simultaneously. The standard to use in this process is: does the price look acceptable? Obviously such a price cannot exceed the value indicated for a rights issue based on retained earnings alone. It is the task of management and their institutional advisers to correctly assess the situation. This is not a difficult task and is carried out for all other share issues.

Price/earnings multiples

Price/earnings ratios are a product of high rates of taxation. Prior to modern tax legislation companies were able to keep or distribute almost all the profits that they made. Shareholders, in turn, could keep the bulk of distributed profits and as a result were much in favour of large dividends. High personal tax levels prevent the shareholder from enjoying the benefit of cash dividends. Company taxes reduce the total amount of earnings available for distribution. Accordingly, share prices have become an important vehicle for trasnferring wealth from the company to the shareholder. Until quite recently these transfers (capital gains) were not taxed at all. The advent of tax on capital gains has put further emphasis on the ability of firms to generate wealth for their shareholders by means of share price rises. For the capital gains tax levy is lower than the standard tax rate on personal income. Hence, it is obviously preferable to receive income in the form of capital gains.

To provide share price increases for its shareholders has become a major objective of the modern firm. Share prices, however, are a product of investment interest in the particular share and the enthusiasm of the market in general. Since investors pay high tax rates on dividend income, companies which pursue a policy of maximum earnings growth are in high demand. Growth in earnings will be reflected in a high price which in turn permits capital gains to be taken and enjoyed. A growth in the rate of earnings growth will lead to a rise in the price/earnings multiple as investors bid up the share price to take part in that earnings growth. Clearly, it is a demanding task to maintain a given rate of growth of earnings per share let alone an increasing rate of growth. None the less, this should be the principal objective, for only when price/earnings ratios are maintained and increased can the shareholder receive the maximum return on his investment.

A high price to earnings multiple also reduces the cost of ordinary share capital to a firm. Suppose a company has generated a consistent pattern of earnings growth over the years and is currently enjoying a price/earnings multiple of thirty times. This company pays no cash dividends but has always paid a scrip dividend of at least 2 per cent. The usual way to calculate the cost of ordinary share capital, as given in the previous chapter is to divide the dividend by the market price and add a value representing the expected growth rate in dividends. This company however, is providing earnings growth, not dividends and is doing so without disbursing cash. Hence, it is the market by placing a premium on earnings growth that generates the price growth which in turn provides the investor with his return. In effect, the company achieves a high rate of return to its shareholders without paying out a penny in cash. The higher the price/earnings multiple, the greater will be the return to the shareholder every time earnings are increased. On the other hand, a fall in earnings which precipitates a drop in the price/earnings multiple can bring share prices down with great speed. Management's task, however, is to increase earnings. If it fails in this endeavour it is as well for the signals to be unmistakably clear. Few measures indicate failure or success with so great a speed and clarity as major movements in the market price of ordinary shares.

The pursuit of earnings growth is vital to the financial health of modern companies. Though some managers may deplore the effort required to achieve this objective, the fault, if any, lies in the tax structure, not in the demands of investors. Investors require a return and as capital gains are taxed at less than most personal tax rates, it is obvious that capital gains are preferred to cash income. That it is also cheaper for a company to pay its shareholders in capital gains is an additional consequence of tax legislation. Without earnings growth there are neither extra funds for reinvestment nor gains to be enjoyed by shareholders. The generation of earnings, the growth of earnings, and the retention of earnings must be the major objectives of financial management.

Part Four

MANAGING THE CORPORATE STRUCTURE

11	Corporate Structure	191
12	Managing the Corporate Structure	208
13	Mergers and Takeovers	226

ELEVEN

CORPORATE STRUCTURE

All business activity takes place within a political and legal environment. This environment has many aspects which are of importance to financial managers. If the firm is engaged in exporting or dealing with world markets and business conditions, the total business environment will have innumerable aspects to note. Whatever the frame of reference, local or global, the effective manager will be prepared to take advantage of all opportunities legal and financial that the environment offers. Though the constraints and alternatives of international business are beyond the scope of this book, the major relevant factors on the British scene are repeated under different guises elsewhere. No one disputes the need for governmental and administrative controls even though particular aspects may generate more difficulties than others.

Efficient business management is attained by using a variety of internal financial and administrative control mechanisms. Control within a given business environment is achieved by taking advantage of the given structure and by attempting to influence the nature of the constraints as they undergo change. Since governments take time to act most financial decisions must be taken within an existing context. Managers may differ in their opinions of the economic and social merits of the prevailing system, but it is there and decisions must be taken within its framework.

To manage within a system it is necessary to be aware of its constraints and limitations as well as the processes by which it behaves. One aspect of note is the legal environment. In Britain company law as distinct from common law is primarily laid down in statutes. Clearly, financial managers need not know the vast array of detail which constitute the successive Acts of Parliament dealing with company affairs any more than they need to be aware of the volumes of precedents which govern common law. The knowledge of law in detail is a task for a firm's accounting and legal advisers. Nevertheless, effective management does entail a minimum knowledge of the major factors which affect a company's financial position. It is the purpose of this chapter to describe and identify those aspects, and it is the object of Chapter 12 to present the financial opportunities this system provides.

Partnerships, close, and public companies

Legal environment. The legal community recognises two distinct types of business enterprise: those that have and those that do not have limited liability. The privilege of limited liability is is granted by the completion of certain formalities. A company operating under this condition is an entity in its own right. Its behaviour is controlled by company law. Such companies are subject to the Act of 1948 which consolidated, incorporated and amended all previous acts, and the Act of 1967. The owners, no matter how described, are protected by those laws. For example, the owners' responsibility for any debts incurred by the firm is limited to their agreed monetary obligations. If the owners hold fully paid up shares and have given no other specific guarantees, their liability is discharged by the purchase of the shares. Creditors are in turn limited to seeking payment from the company itself, payments which can come from the generation of earnings or the sale of assets.

The second type of business enterprise does not operate under limited liability. Their owners are jointly and severally liable for the debts of the enterprise up to the full extent of their personal wealth. This group of firms consists mainly of single owner businesses and partnerships. Although partnerships are subject to the Act of 1890 and single owner firms to some statutes, enterprises with unlimited liability are controlled primarily by common law.

Limited and unlimited liability firms represent two very different types of corporate structure. Under certain conditions each offers its owners special advantages. The more important advantages of limited liability are listed below:

1 A limited company is a legal entity in its own right. On the other hand, all rights, obligations and duties accrue to individuals in a partnership.

2 Under limited liability owners have no personal liability to the company. Each owner stands to lose only the nominal value subscribed for his shares. If such shares are fully paid, any liability is discharged by the forfeiture of part or all of his subscription. If the shares are not fully paid, liability extends to the amount of subscription remaining on call. Partners, however, are jointly and severally liable for all debts incurred by the firm. Each partner is an agent of all the partners and is liable for the firm's debts.

3 Property ownership is vested in a limited liability company and is distinct from any assets owned by the firm's members. Creditors can claim only against the company's property. In a partnership, all partners have a joint interest in property held. Accordingly, on the death of any one partner the value of all such property is realised for tax purposes, although in practice the problem is circumvented by suitable agreements. In addition, creditors have a claim against the personal property of partners as well as the property of the partnership itself.

4 Companies may sue and be sued only in their own right and name. Partners may sue and be sued as individuals.

5 A company is endowed with perpetual succession. The death of an owner has no legal effect on its life and activity. On the other hand, the death of a partner terminates the partnership. If trading is to continue the partnership has to be reconstituted.

6 The shares in a company are fully transferable. All rights and obligations are vested in the shares and they can be transferred from owner to owner. A partner may assign his ownership only to the extent of the receipt of dividends and profits. He cannot assign the right to participate in management except under agreement with all the other partners.

7 There is no upper limit to the number of owners (shareholders) a public company may have, though there must be at least seven. A private company is more restricted in that the minumum number is two and the maximum is fifty owners, in addition to such past and present employees who are or were also shareholders. Partnerships are restricted to no more than twenty members (ten in the case of a bank), though this limit can be circumvented by

associate partnerships. This generation of large partnerships will be discussed in detail later in this chapter since it affects the technique of financing such operations.

In contrast to the advantages of limited liability outlined above there are a number of legal factors which favour partnerships.

1 Under the *Ultra Vires Rule* a company has certain restrictions placed upon its business operations. A company is not permitted to engage in any activity which is outside the provisions of the objects clause in its Memorandum of Association. The Memorandum of Association is created when the company is first formed. This restriction exists to protect the interest of shareholders by ensuring that they have full knowledge of how their invested capital is being employed. In addition this rule protects the company's creditors who are assured that their funds will not be used for illegal or unspecified ventures. Not even the unanimous consent of all shareholders can validate an activity which contravenes the objects clause. A limited facility does exist by which the objects clause can be altered but this process usually requires the consent of court. This restriction has serious implications for financial management which will be discussed in Chapter 12.

A partnership, on the other hand, can carry out any type of business activity as long as the partners are mutually agreed.

2 A company must publish accounts and file copies with the registrar. These accounts must be checked and approved by a recognised external auditor.

3 Companies must hold shareholder meetings and the notice required as well as the proceedings of such meetings are specified by statute.

The last two requirements involve a company in considerable expense and inconvenience. Since partnerships are not bound by these rules they need not incur these expenses.

Economic considerations

Taxation. The legal framework is supplemented by a number of important economic factors, one of which is taxation. Though taxation creates a host of financial problems there are no clear advantages either to individuals or to companies under all conditions. Taxation is a complex problem favouring companies in some instances and individuals in others. Moreover, the incidence of tax is a political decision, and is subject to frequent change. Alterations in the tax structure can invalidate previous arrangements, and new taxes will usually require a reassessment of the company's tax status. The relative merits of companies and partnerships with respect to income tax will be discussed later. In general it cannot be stressed too heavily that financial managers have a duty to make sure that their firms operate in a manner which attracts the least possible tax. No one is required to pay more tax than the necessary minimum, and the avoidance of tax liabilities is a perfectly legal endeavour.

One clear way in which a company is at a disadvantage to a partnership is in the matter of registration fees and capital duty. The formation of a company is expensive while a partnership can be legally constituted at nominal cost. Similarly it is both difficult and expensive to wind up a company, whereas a partnership can be dissolved by mutual agreement.

Borrowing. In general terms, companies have an advantage in generating finance for their operations. First of all, it is easier for a company to borrow long-term funds, particularly on the basis of floating charge. Since a floating charge is not attached to any specific asset, financial management has great flexibility. Partnerships borrow mainly on mortgage which restricts flexibility. A mortgage attaches to an asset and the asset cannot be sold without the lender's permission. A second point to note is that companies have considerable freedom to raise capital on the open market. The facilitity to invite subscriptions from the general public either by way of a share or debenture issue exists in a restricted form in the case of private companies, but is denied entirely to partnerships.

Partnerships are not restricted in their legal ability to raise funds, but borrowing takes place by private arrangement which usually involves specific charges against assets. Though it is possible for partnerships to borrow on promissory notes and against a floating charge, it is the attitude of the lender which governs the ability to borrow. The credit standing of a partnership is determined by more personal and subjective criteria than those which are applied to a limited company.

A public company is judged as to its credit-worthiness on the financial criteria noted in Part 2. The reputation of the firm's management is of some importance, but management's capabilities are reflected in a company's published financial statements. A highly regarded management will influence demand at the time of a new share or debenture issue. Investors may well over subscribe the initial issue and subsequently drive up the market price. Nevertheless, the size and selling price of the new issue will be determined solely on the company's earnings and other financial grounds.

In contrast, lenders judge partnerships at least as much on the personal reputation of the partners as on any available financial information. Borrowing limits are not necessarily set in line with financial criteria. The business acumen, integrity and wealth of one or more of the working partners is just as likely to be the final arbiter. This can lead to serious financial shortages, particularly on the death of a partner with great personal wealth. On the other hand, since all partners are equally liable, lenders can be encouraged to accept the risk. Once the funds are received a partnership has greater freedom to trade than a company.

Dilution of equity. A second feature of the relative power to raise funds lies in the question of participation in ownership. It is often difficult for a partnership to raise substantial amounts of capital without offering a share of the business. Such a fief of the equity entitles the lender to participate as a partner. In practice the lender acts as a sleeping partner and takes no part in management. Limited partnerships are employed and registered for this purpose. In a limited partnership, the sleeping partner supplies funds and is provided a limitation of liability to the extent of his subscription. Working partners must accept unlimited liability in return for the same rights and obligations of a normal partnership.

A company, on the other hand, can raise long-term funds without diluting the equity, without affecting management, and without altering the ownership and control. Companies are controlled by holding a sufficient number of shares which carry voting rights. What proportion of votes is sufficient to maintain control will be discussed later. The point to note, at present, is that additional funds can be raised by a variety of means which do not affect control. For example, the issue of non-voting ordinary and preference shares as well as debentures all provide capital without affecting control. Whether such issues alter ownership is more a matter of management's attitude towards its investors than a legal consideration.

Cost of raising funds. Partnerships have an advantage over companies in respect to the cost of raising funds. A partnership can raise capital and borrow money at a nominal charge. Money is raised by individual partners persuading other individuals or companies to join the enterprise as a partner or merely to lend funds to the partnership. Though the investor may charge a high interest rate to cover his risk, the set up cost is quite small.

Companies incur great expense when raising long-term funds. In addition to the personal activity of management, the services of specialised bodies have to be purchased. These specialists are the operators of the new issue market. They are the middlemen who match the demand for funds, by companies, to the supply in the hands of investors. The central authority in the market is the Stock Exchange of which London is the largest and quotes 90 per cent of the securities listed in Britain. It should be noted, however, that the Stock Exchange does not supply any funds. It merely acts as a market in which shares can be bought and sold after issue. The Stock Exchange does not control the initial transactions which lead to public subscription to the shares of a company. Once issued it provides a quotation in the shares as long as its rules and procedures have been met. This market in quoted shares offers substantial advantages to investors which in turn assures business enterprises of a large pool of available funds.

The two-tiered system necessitates the services of special institutions that effect the issue of securities and arrange for a transfer market to be established. There are four major institutions concerned with the new issue market. The first is the stockbroker who brokers the operation by introducing the company to the issuing house and by giving general advice on the state of the securities market. The issuing house is responsible for advising the company on the form, size, and price of the issue as well as all rules and regulations. In addition, the issuing house is responsible for the day-to-day operations of the issue and arranges for a Stock

Exchange quotation. Most issuing houses are merchant banks, investment banks, or financial trusts. The majority are members of the Issuing Houses Association. Issuing houses who are not members of the Association usually specialise in issues for small companies. This latter group carries out most of its business by placing these shares with large institutions, though they do hold such shares themselves as investments and to provide small businesses with expansion capital. The third member of the group is the underwriter. An underwriter performs the service of selling the new issue by presenting to the company, for a fee, a guarantee that all shares will be sold at a given price. If the issue is not fully subscribed it is the underwriter who is left with the unsold shares, not the company. The issuing house will frequently act as the underwriter. The final member of the marketing operation is the Stock Exchange which provides a market quotation.

The institutions which manage the new issue market are there to advise companies on the type of security to issue. Each type of security can be subscribed in a number of ways, and advice will be given as to the best method to use. If a Stock Exchange quotation is required further information will be provided so that the issue will meet all the necessary requirements. At this point the size, price, and terms of the issue will be determined. The whole operation requires considerable planning and control. One of the objectives of the issuing house is to create a ready transfer market, and good public relations play an important part in this operation. The company's principal aim is to raise the requisite funds, and as the underwriter guarantees to provide the money, all participants must cooperate fully.

When a company requires funds it approaches its stockbroker who will arrange for an issuing house to advise the firm on all aspects of the operation. Although the public ultimately provide the funds, the issuing house guarantees the issue so that the company is assured of its capital. This guarantee is known as underwriting. The issuing house acts as the main underwriter but does not always take the risk against its own resources. Sub-underwriting is often sought and insurance companies take a large proportion of this rewarding investment opportunity. Financial managers of big firms should consider sub-underwriting as an investment for very short-term cash surpluses. Smaller firms would need to band together in a consortium to generate the necessary surplus funds. To participate in an underwriting it is merely necessary to inform an issuing house of a willingness to put a given sum of money at risk.

Clearly each institution in the issuing process charges a fee for its services. These fees take the form of commission and are based on the size and method of issue as well as on the reputation of the company. Since its own reputation is also involved, the issuing house will investigate the company seeking public subscription. This concern for reputation helps to protect the public from fraudulent and speculative issues. It also means that financial managers must have their companies' financial affairs in good order. All these factors involve expense, and a company which wishes to raise long-term funds in this way must be prepared to face these costs.

There are several methods of inviting subscriptions to a new issue. The first and major outlet is the public issue. It is achieved by a direct offer of a fixed number of shares at a stated price. The costs of the operation are met by the company out of the proceeds from the issue. These expenses comprise brokerage fees, issuing house fees, underwriting commission, Stock Exchange quotation fee, capital duty where nominal valued capital is involved, and general expenses.

A variation of the direct public offer is a sale by tender. This method differs from the public issue in only one respect: the subscription price is not fixed in advance. A minimum tender price is published and investors are invited to tender a price at which they would be willing to accept a specified number of shares. The Stock Exchange maintains a close check on this method of issue in order to prevent abuse. The Exchange will not allow a multitiered price structure. Accordingly, a single price is usually struck which will just clear the entire issue and at the same time ensure that an adequate market has been generated with a widespread shareholding. In practice, the price is set slightly above the minimum to cover the issuing turn. All other costs are identical to those incurred in a public issue. None the less, there can be a substantial advantage to be gained by using the tender method. In the direct public issue the predetermined price may not fully reflect the wealth of the company on offer. In the past decade market prices of new issues have risen rapidly after issue. This premium is a cost paid by the company to persuade investors to provide the required funds. When this premium is excessive it represents both an unnecessary loss of funds and poor management in the striking of a correct sale price. It also leads to heavy stagging of the issue and a disorderly market, both of which constitute poor public relations. It is financial management's job to ensure that a reasonable price is struck which will encourage investors without underselling the firm. The tender method, properly handled, is likely to achieve a selling price that more closely reflects future market prices.

A second method of effecting a new issue is an offer for sale whereby a company sells the whole issue to a stockbroker or an institution at an agreed total price. Under this arrangement the company may not have to pay the cost of any subsequent reissue. This depends upon the public offer price which is determined by the original purchaser. If the issue price exceeds the contract price the issuing house recovers its costs out of the profits on the turn.

A third method of issuing securities consists in placing. Shares are placed by selling them to institutions who are willing to hold them as investments. The issuing house may require the usual fees or it may be able to recover these costs in the placing price. This method is best employed by small companies which are unable to generate sufficient public interest. Indeed, the Stock Exchange has strict rules to govern placing activities and often refuses to acknowledge this method when a large public demand can be anticipated.

These issuing methods are all external financing operations which involve the general public in one guise or another. Often a firm wishes to raise money but perceives an advantage in containing the whole operation within itself. The issue of rights is a technique for satisfying this requirement. A rights issue is achieved by offering securities for a subscription, either entirely or preferentially, by existing shareholders. The offer is made in proportion to existing holdings. The offer price is made at a discount on expected market price, and represents a direct source of income to shareholders. A rights issue has the smallest initial cost of any method of raising new funds. Though an issuing house fee may be incurred, the fee is usually much smaller than that for a public issue and underwriting is rarely necessary.

A final method of issue, that of issue by introduction, is a completely specialised activity. Issue by introduction can only be used by a new company and does not raise new money. The process is one where existing unquoted shares are introduced on to the market and transfer facilities are acquired. Accordingly, though the company does not receive any funds shareholders are provided with a ready market for their shares. As a prelude to a subsequent new issue it is an invaluable device. To raise funds, at the same time as an introduction, a company can offer a rights issue to its shareholders. The money is provided by the original shareholders, but the imminence of a quotation ensures that they will be able to realise this investment as and when they choose.

Corporate structure

Unlimited liability. Firms with unlimited liability range from single proprietor businesses, to partnerships of from two to twenty people, to very large partnership associations and unlimited companies. All partnerships are subject to the same legal requirements, but size has an important effect on the dilution of ownership the effect of taxation and the power of borrowing. Size affects the level of taxation because the Inland Revenue accepts the division of profits laid down by the partnership agreement. The greater the number that share in a particular income stream, the lower will be the marginal tax rate of each partner and hence the lower the total effective tax assessment on the firm. This ability to split total earnings has particular relevance for single proprietor firm and family businesses. Though the creation of a partnership may appear to dilute the equity, individual ownership can prove to be very expensive especially when heavy surtax payments accrue. Similarly, if a small partnership is faced with increasing surtax payments, a further division of the profits may well reduce the total tax paid by a substantial amount.

Dilution of equity and ownership is always a hard decision to take, as ownership produces vast emotional rewards. Unfortunately, under the prevailing tax structure total ownership can prove to be a very expensive proposition. Moreover, every £1 paid out in tax is a drain on working capital. Increasing the number of partners reduces the total tax burden even though it also dilutes the equity. Consequently, the choice is that of parting with ownership to permit growth of total income or maintaining ownership and incurring ever increasing tax liabilities.

The unlimited company is an anomaly. The major benefit of incorporation, that of a limited liability, is foregone. There are, however, certain advantages to be gained by being an unlimited company as distinct from a partnership. Perhaps the most important is that shares can be issued and transferred. In addition the cost of establishing such a company is small, no capital duty is payable on registration, and several tax advantages apply. If the company is not close it is easy to build reserves from retained earnings as surtax is not paid on earnings. There is no restriction on membership and shareholders have most of the legal rights of incorporation except the limitation on their liability. Liability for company debts is divided in proportion to equity share. Shareholders cannot be sued and any legal action is taken against the company itself. In contrast to the limited company, it is possible for a member to return his share to the company. Equity can be disposed with considerable freedom and a company can buy and sell its own shares. The share capital defines voting and dividend rights and ensures transferability of these rights as distinct from partnerships.

The unlimited company is not frequently used as a corporate structure. It is usually unable to raise capital by public issues. It is not prevented from so doing by legal restrictions, but by the investing public who are unwilling to accept an unlimited risk. This is particularly true for companies which generate large liabilities as part of their normal trading operations. There are some specialised uses of this corporate structure. It is used by professional and semi-professional bodies, large estates and mutual benefit and loan societies.

Limited liability. Companies with limited liability are divided into three types: public companies, private companies, and overseas companies. The main features of public companies have already been noted in the first part of this chapter. Every incorporated company is a public company even when no general public subscription is involved. Specific steps must be taken to create a private company. The articles of a private company must contain provisions to limit the number of members to fifty in addition to members working in the firm. Furthermore the transfer of shares must be limited and the general public must be prohibited from subscribing to the firm's capital.

Private companies do have certain privileges that are denied public companies. The first is that the minimum number of members is two instead of the seven required of public firms. Another is that there are few restrictions on the appointment of directors or on the commencement of business. Shares can be transferred by delivery so that the raising of funds is relatively inexpensive. The restriction on the number of shareholders, however, makes it more difficult to raise capital funds.

Overseas companies are controlled by the same provisions as British companies. The registrar has to be notified of the establishment of such concerns. After certain formalities have been completed, an overseas company has the same power to own land and conduct its affairs as a company incorporated in Britain.

Taxation. The incidence of taxation depends upon whether an enterprise is liable to personal and surtax charges or to corporation tax rates. It does not matter whether the firm has limited or unlimited liability.

Partnerships are taxed as individuals. Personal and surtax rates are applied to each partner's share of the firm's net profit. If the partnership is generating handsome earnings, the high surtax charges will drain the enterprise of working capital. Surtax payments restrict growth, and if retained earnings are to be increased, a partnership must consider the problem of going public.

The advent of corporation tax has placed special tax pressures on all close companies. Indeed, the tax disadvantages of the close company are so severe that many such firms have already reformed themselves as partnerships or have taken the necessary step to dilute the equity and escape the confines of the close company regulations. Since a close company may be unlimited, private, or public it is worth noting the main factors which subject a firm to this category of tax treatment.

A close company is defined as being under the control of five or fewer participators. If the company is director controlled, the company is considered close even if there are more than five directors. A participator may be an individual or a group of individuals who are associates. For example, a number of direct line relatives, a set of trust settlements, or a close company by itself are all considered as single participators. Control is defined in terms of the possession of or entitlement to more than 50 per cent of the equity.

The disadvantages of close companies are almost exclusively a function of the tax charges. The advantages pertain to ownership and control. Unfortunately, current tax structures make total ownership a most expensive proposition whether conducted under the guise of a partnership or a close company. All companies pay corporation tax at the prevailing rate. For ordinary public and private companies corporation tax is the only tax that is applied to their earnings. Any surplus (retained earnings) can be reinvested or paid out in dividends as the company sees fit. In a partnership all earnings are taxed as income in the hands of the individual partners even when those funds are reinvested in the firm. As soon as such partners begin to pay surtax rates, the firm as a whole will be paying out an ever increasing proportion of their profits in tax. As a result, the partnership will be less and less able to finance expansion from retained earnings. In contrast, the ordinary public or private company can always retain that proportion of its earnings which is not paid out in corporation tax. At current rates corporation tax is 42½ per cent of earnings, while personal and surtax rates combined depend upon income and have no upper limit.

The tax liability for close companies is such that it can place them at a disadvantage to both partnerships and ordinary companies. In addition to paying corporation tax on all its agreed trading profits—net pretax audited profit plus depreciation less capital allowances—the close company also pays shortfall tax. The shortfall is a standard percentage of the after tax earnings which are presumed to be distributed as dividends. The directors of a close company may decide to declare only a minimum dividend in order to increase working capital. If this dividend distribution falls short of the standard amount the difference is still treated as though it had been disbursed. The shortfall is taxed by dividing it among the owners and directors and charging them tax at their highest personal tax or surtax rate. The standard amount is determined by taking 60 per cent of the agreed trading profit after corporation tax has been paid. To this sum is added not more than the whole of the company's distributable investment income. Certain small profit relief is presently granted and minor abatement allowances accrue on franked investment income. The Inland Revenue is presently making concessions to the notion of shortfall where a close company can show just evidence that such a distribution would be detrimental to the future conduct of the business.

This can, at best, be a limited concession and the eventual liability of the firm must be very high indeed.

To clarify the description consider the following example. A close company has agreed profits for the year amounting to £200 000 and franked investment income of £25 000. The company is director controlled and is wholly owned by three people whose shares total 60 per cent, 30 per cent and 10 per cent respectively. The basic tax computation is given in Table 11:1.

	Agreed profits	£200 000
Less:	Corporation tax at 42½ per cent	85 000
	Profits after corporation tax	£115 000
Add:	Franked investment income	25 000
	Total distributable income	£140 000

The required standard for this close company is given by:

(1) Distributable investment income	£25 000
(2) 60 per cent of profits after corporation tax $\frac{60 \times 115\,000}{100} = 69\,000$	69 000
Standard	£94 000

TABLE 11:1 TAX PAYMENTS FOR A CLOSE COMPANY

The directors of this close company have already received a salary of £10 000 each for their managerial services and have been charged PAYE on their monthly remittances. They are all liable to surtax on their salaries and it will be supposed that each director has to find an extra £1500 to satisfy this surtax assessment. Suppose further that these directors are anxious to reinvest in their firm as large a proportion of the after tax profits as possible and declare no dividends. If the company had not been close, retained earnings could have been increased by the total distributable income of £140 000. However, as the company is close, tax and surtax is charged on the shortfall of £94 000 in order to bring the dividend distribution from an actual zero to the theoretical standard. Hence, the three directors will be taxed as though each had received an extra income of £56 400, £28 200 and £9400 respectively. At estimated surtax rates these directors will pay a total tax bill of £84 000 on the £94 000 shortfall. Total distributable income will be reduced by this £84 000, which will leave the firm £56 000 to be added to retained earnings.

It is worth summarising the tax effects of being a close company. In this simple example, a given company has earned a total of £200 000 and has received a franked investment income of £25 000. If it were an ordinary company the total tax bill would be 42½ per cent of the £200 000 or £85 000. The franked income is not taxed so that the effective tax rate is £85 000 on an income of £225 000 or 39 per cent. Because this same enterprise is a close company the tax bill is £85 000 plus the shortfall tax of £84 000. Thus the total effective tax rate is £169 000 on an income of £225 000 or 75 per cent. In short, this company is paying an extra £84 000 or 36 per cent of its total income in tax for the privilege of remaining close.

It should be noted that this is a much simplified example of the effects of taxation on close companies. The essential features are all correct but the provisions of the 1965 Finance Act are sufficiently complex to warrant taking professional advice. Among other important factors there are restrictions on directors' remuneration which affects the tax computations. There are also concessions which auditors are best able to obtain.

Ownership and control

The normal corporate path followed by most growing firms is from early beginnings as a single proprietorship to a partnership. As growth continues the partnership is dissolved and a private company is formed. Eventually the private company goes public. It is always difficult to forego the pleasure of personal ownership. It is an even bigger step to consider the possibility of losing control. It must be noted, however, that what constitutes ownership and control in practice is very different from the individual concept of possession. Ownership and control are legally unquestionable when an individual or associated group exercise rights, by possession or entitlement, of greater than 50 per cent of the equity. In practice it is not necessary to hold such power over the equity to achieve working control. Effective control can be maintained, in all but dire emergencies, by holding the largest share of any of the members. If the larger shareholders are a part of management the threat to their control is negligible. Outside shareholders, however large, rarely challenge the sovereignty of a large managing shareholder. Indeed, large outside shareholders are most likely to be financial institutions and investment trusts. Such enterprises have an established record of uninterest in the day-to-day activities of the companies of which they are shareholders. As long as firms are not obviously guilty of neglecting their duties, shareholders can be relied upon for passive support.

Individual firms differ with respect to their corporate structure and the distribution of their shares. If a firm's shares are widely distributed a 10 per cent holding by an active manager should prove sufficient to maintain control. Clearly, the precise number of shares will vary with each situation. The point to note is that a manager can effectively control a firm with substantially less than a 51 per cent holding. It follows, therefore, that once total control is to be abandoned the objective must be to issue shares to as many individuals as possible. By ensuring a widespread division of the issued equity the percentage retained by the original owners assumes a controlling position. A second factor which affects control is share price. The greater the value of each ordinary share the more expensive it becomes for anyone else to acquire a substantial interest. Effective control can be readily maintained by pursuing a policy of growth based on retention of earnings and the division of issued shares into ever smaller individual holdings.

TWELVE

MANAGING THE CORPORATE STRUCTURE

Throughout this book it has been repeatedly emphasised that management's primary task is to generate the maximum possible level of earnings. Growing earnings, particularly when reinvested will raise share prices as well as stimulate internal growth. It is our opinion that the efficient management of earnings is the best foundation for a policy of growth. Growth, though much prized by shareholders and investors alike, is only partially supported by the legal and tax framework. The tax structure, as described in the previous chapter, discriminates against particular corporate forms. Since tax laws change but slowly, the most suitable response is to accept the system and operate within it to the best advantage. If growth and retention of earnings can be accepted as the fundamental objectives, the management of the corporate structure is a straightforward operation. It is a task of selecting the structure which is most suited to the earnings goal.

The corporate structure is usually regarded as being concerned with the question of ownership and control. In so far as this is true it is but a minor consideration. The major objective of a business enterprise is to create a stream of income both now and in the future. The value of a firm is the present value of this income stream. Some firms may not consider a high value to be of great importance but without earnings no firm can survive. In an inflationary system, stability of earnings is not good enough. Earnings must increase at a faster rate than purchasing power falls if any growth is to be achieved.

From financial management's point of view it is inefficient to maintain a corporate structure which inhibits the growth and retention of earnings. It can be argued that the pleasure derived from ownership outweighs the cost in taxation and growth. Unfortunately, this is to a large extent a spurious argument, as it is debatable as to who really has the rights of ownership and control. Under a partnership or close company arrangement it would appear that the partners or directors had full authority and control. But examine the division of profits and it is clear that the Inland Revenue receives the largest share. In a partnership all income is charged at personal tax rates and in a close company the premium is paid in shortfall tax. In both cases, ownership of voting rights leads to loss of control over the income stream. It might well be asked: what price ownership and who really has control? Since the tax structure has a higher priority on earnings than shareholders, the objective must be to reduce the effects of taxation. To reduce the level of tax, a corporate structure which entails a dilution of equity should be adopted. Such a reduction in equity holding by particular individuals can lead to an increase in their control over the income stream, an apparent paradox. In this curious world where ownership is heavily taxed, there are considerable advantages to be gained by examining the problem of ownership and control with respect to the tax structure.

The ultimate objective of earnings and profit is consumption. A person who builds an enterprise so that he may be succeeded by his descendants is storing earnings for future consumption. If ownership is retained, growth will be retarded since a large proportion of all earnings will be paid out in tax. The pleasures of ownership can be viewed as consumption of current earnings, because a company which restricts its liability to corporation tax alone spends a smaller proportion of its earnings on tax. It is financial management's task to decide whether the privilege of ownership is worth its cost. This chapter examines corporate structure in terms of such costs.

Managing debt

There are two major stimulants to growth which are directly affected by the corporate structure: the ability to raise debt, and the level of taxation. In some respects the capacity to raise debt is interlinked with the level of taxation. In the previous chapter it was pointed out that lenders perceive specific corporate structures as presenting different amounts of risk. Indeed, the size of the available pool of borrowable funds depends upon the form of the corporate structure. Similarly, the corporate form specifies the level of taxation that will be applied to earnings.

A company has a larger pool of funds to draw upon, at a given cost of servicing, than a partnership. Though more funds can be raised, the cost of raising capital is greater for a company than a partnership. It is an exercise in financial management to calculate the relative advantages for a specific structure. It is unlikely that an established public company would alter its corporate structure to take advantage of an investment opportunity. But all other types of firms might well see fit so to do. A public company can take advantage of the opportunities by creating subsidiaries with the desired corporate form.

The calculation is an exercise in present value analysis. It proceeds by taking the set up costs of a given corporate form and adding to it the cost of raising debt and the future stream of interest payments which are discounted at the relevant cost of capital. The cost of capital is determined by proceeding as indicated in Chapter 10 making due allowance for the effective tax rate that will be applied to the estimated earnings of the proposed firm. A comparison of the net present costs for a variety of corporate structures will indicate the type of structure most suited to the proposed enterprise. If a change in structure is being examined, any cost saving would have to be balanced against the cost of any corporate upheaval.

The availability of debt must be carefully considered when setting up or assessing the structure of a particular firm. If the structure prohibits the raising of sufficient debt, then the cost of this corporate form is overwhelmingly large. Either the investment opportunity has to be rejected or the corporate structure changed. The cost of this alteration must be weighed against the net present value of the investment as well as the future opportunities it may entail.

Another factor to consider is the level of debt which a company can afford. The volume of debt in relation to capital structure was discussed in Chapter 10. Volume of debt is also related to corporate structure since availability and what the firm can afford are closely connected. Lenders can always be persuaded to provide funds at some price. Management must determine whether the firm can afford the price. Taxation is clearly involved in this calculation and this problem is discussed in detail in the next section.

A final aspect of debt management arises from constraints generated by the provisions of the objects clause of the memorandum and to a lesser extent by the Articles of Association. As noted in Chapter 11, all activities which contravene the objects clause are illegal. Objects clauses frequently specify the type and limits of debt financing. In other cases, limits on debt are specified only by implication. These provisions can cause a number of problems. A desirable investment may require unacceptable debt financing. In this event the investment has to be rejected or a new company has to be formed to take advantage of the investment.

The objects clause can effect a wide array of a firm's financial decisions. In Parts 1 and 2 a number of techniques for cash and current asset management were discussed. In addition a range of investment opportunities which are available from the financial community were presented. The entire financial system can be prohibited to a firm whose objects clause is sufficiently restrictive. For a firm in this position, a subsidiary company, or partnership with the required investment rights, may well be indicated. A number of public companies handle their surplus cash investment activities in this manner.

Managing taxation

The management of taxation is directly related to the problem of ownership and control. Clearly, a major objective is to manage a firm so that its earnings attract the lowest possible tax charge. Since the tax structure discriminates against particular corporate structures, the management of taxation is determined by management's attitude towards ownership and control. Since the retention of earnings is of crucial importance, debt financing ought to be closely examined. Debt provides a way to offset the excessive tax charges which accrue to partnerships and close companies.

The owners take the final decision as to the corporate structure most suited to their requirements. Financial managers, however, must point out the costs of each alternative. Once a decision is taken it is the manager's task then to reduce the effect of taxation within the bounds set by the given structure.

The decision on corporate structure must be taken in full

recognition of the costs of taxation on projected earnings. In a going concern the decision might be that of changing the existing structure or that of setting up a subsidiary with a more suitable tax liability. In each case it is necessary to estimate the effects of tax on future earnings. To simplify matters, the alternatives can be considered to be a partnership, a close company, or an ordinary public company. Each alternative has certain advantages under different conditions. The capital structure, turnover, projected earnings, and number of participators all have a direct bearing on the choice of company structure. These issues are now discussed in terms of small and large firms.

Small firms

Until the advent of corporation tax, many small businesses found legal and tax advantages by having the structure of a limited liability company rather than a partnership. Since corporation tax and the restrictions on close companies were introduced, the tax charges on these firms have been large enough to persuade a number to reform themselves as partnerships. Though some partnerships are at a severe disadvantage, the formation of a close company is not usually an answer. Close companies incur higher tax charges than non-close or public companies. To reform a close company into a non-close private or public company involves cost and the dilution of equity. However, the savings on tax are earned annually, while the set up cost is only incurred once. Tax charges are applied every year and it is easy to calculate how long it will take for the savings on taxes to pay for the cost of setting up the new structure. Unfortunately, it may well occur that the choice is not between being a close or non-close company. If the firm is small and investors are not willing to provide the necessary capital the decision on corporate structure revolves around the relative tax advantages of a partnership and a close company.

The choice between a partnership and a close company depends heavily on the size of earnings and the number of participators in the business. If the chargeable profits are large the total tax and surtax liability of a partnership may exceed the total tax on a close company where such tax consists of corporation and shortfall liabilities and the owner/directors' personal assessments. If such is the case, the close company ensures a smaller tax charge even though this tax charge is far in excess of that paid by a non-close company.

To illustrate the break even point between partnerships and close companies we shall present a number of examples. In these examples the tax calculations are based upon the tax liabilities of average individuals. Clearly, a specific individual's tax assessment will depend upon his personal allowances. Marital status, number of children, insurance and pension payments all affect the actual charge. Though such detail is beyond the scope of this volume, specific individual liabilities will only affect the major calculations at the margin. If the decision to accept or reject a given corporate structure depends on a particular individual's tax allowances, no change is worth while. It is both cheaper and easier to manage allowances than it is to alter a corporate structure.

The examples begin by going back to the year 1965 and considering a small, private company with annual trading profits of roughly £20 000. The finance Act of 1965 has just been announced and the financial manager has been asked to calculate the probable tax charge for the coming year. This firm has been classified as a close company as the equity is equally divided between its two directors. The Finance Act has introduced a corporation tax, a restriction on deductible income to £7000 for these two owner/directors whose profits are insufficient to warrant a 15 per cent allowance, and a shortfall tax. The directors are concerned for their firm as they realise that retained earnings are essential to the financial health of their enterprise. To date they have only taken the barest living expenses as salaries of £1000 each so as to plough back as large an amount of each year's profits as possible. In the absence of shortfall concessions they wish to know the best corporate structure to use in the future.

The financial manager calculates the new tax charges and presents these to the directors. The figures are given in Table 12:1. He points out that he has listed director's remuneration at the allowable level of £7000 since this reduces the tax charge. Since the directors can reinvest their salaries in working capital by means of directors loans, a listed salary of £3500 does not mean that more than the usual £1000 need be spent on living expenses.

Having arrived at the tax charge for the close company of £10 200 the financial manager decided to estimate the tax cost under the supposition that the close company was reformed as a partnership. His estimate of the partnership's tax charges are given in Table 12:2. The saving, by using a partnership

Estimated earnings		£20 000
Allowance for directors' remuneration:		
15% × £20 000 = £3000		
Therefore minimum allowance used:		
2 directors @ £3500 gives allowance		7 000
Earnings chargeable to corporation tax		£13 000
Corporation tax of 42½% on £13 000		£5 525
Required standard for distribution:		
60% × (13 000 − 5525) = £4465		
Income tax on shortfall of £4465 @ 41.2% (8/3)		£1 840
Personal taxation on directors' salaries (£3500)		1 975
Surtax on standard shortfall		860
Total tax charge		£10 200
Funds available for reinvestment	= earnings − tax	
	= £9800	
Directors' living expenses	2000	
Total possible retained earnings	= £7800	

TABLE 12:1 TAX AND RETAINED EARNINGS FOR CLOSE COMPANY WITH EARNINGS OF £20 000

Estimated earnings		£20 000
Partners' earnings are £10 000 each		
Personal taxation on partners' earnings estimated per tax schedule		£8 400
Funds available for reinvestment	= earnings − tax	
	= £11 600	
Partners' living expenses	2 000	
Total possible retained earnings	= £9 600	

TABLE 12:2 TAX AND RETAINED EARNINGS FOR PARTNERSHIP WITH EARNINGS OF £20 000

form, is £1800 or 9 per cent of total earnings. Looked at another way the extra £1800 is an increase of 23 per cent on the retained earnings that the close company could achieve. Since the owners are determined to reinvest all available funds, it is clear that an alteration in corporate structure can lead to a substantial addition to retained earnings.

In practice the tax advantage of the partnership form will be amplified by the absence of PAYE deductions. Under the close company structure PAYE is deducted from the directors' salaries and payed to the Inland Revenue within forty days. Hence, the company's retained earnings will be reduced by the PAYE payments throughout the year. It is possible to "pay" directors fees instead of salaries. On average, however, the loss to retained earnings amounts to half the total personal tax charge and takes place six to fifteen months before the similar charge has to be paid by a partnership. Accordingly, in large partnerships, the timing of tax payments can provide significant additions to the flow of funds.

On the evidence produced so far it would appear that this firm should reconstruct itself as a partnership. Before so doing, however, the owners must face the question of a partnership's unlimited liability. If the owners are unable or unwilling to accept this risk, then it is clear that the limited liability of the close company is costing them some £2000 a year. In many cases it is possible to insure the liability risk in a partnership. Unless the annual premium exceeds £2000 a partnership is still the more advantageous corporate structure. Any decision to reform must obviously take account of other financial and non-financial criteria. The tax computation merely gives notice that an investigation is necessary. Professional advice is necessary before a final decision is taken.

Another point to consider is the question of growth. If annual earnings remain at the £20 000 level, it would appear that the close company ought to reform itself into a partnership. But what happens to the tax level and retained earnings if, through hard work, the firm's earnings rise to £40 000? To answer this question the financial manager calculates the approximate tax charges that would accrue on estimated earnings of £40 000 under the assumption that the two directors remain as joint owners or partners. The results of his calculations are shown in Tables 12:3 and 12:4.

Estimated earnings		£40 000
Allowance for directors' remuneration: 15% × £40 000 = £6000		
Therefore minimum applies: 2 Directors at £3500		7 000
Earnings chargeable to corporation tax		£33 000
Corporation tax of 42½% on £33 000		£14 025
Required standard for distribution: 60% × (33 000 − 14 025) = £11 400		
Income tax on shortfall of £11 400 @ 41.2% (8/3)		£4 700
Personal tax on directors' salaries		1 975
Surtax on standard shortfall		2 600
Total tax charge		£23 300
Funds available for reinvestment = earnings − tax	= £16 700	
Directors' living expenses	2 000	
Total possible retained earnings	£14 700	

TABLE 12:3 TAX AND RETAINED EARNINGS FOR CLOSE COMPANY WITH EARNINGS OF £40 000

Estimated earnings		£40 000
Partners' earnings are £20 000 each		
Personal taxation on partners' earnings estimated per tax schedule		£25 200
Funds available for reinvestment = earnings − tax	= £14 800	
Partners' living expenses	2 000	
Total possible retained earnings	= £12 800	

TABLE 12:4 TAX AND RETAINED EARNINGS FOR PARTNERSHIP WITH EARNINGS OF £40 000

With earnings at the £40 000 level the advantage lies with the close company structure. This advantage is based on the assumption that no dilution of equity has taken place. An increase in the number of partners or directors will lower the tax charages. There are limits to the number of participators who can claim tax allowances if the original ownership and control is not to be impaired. Blood relations offer possibilities as long as they are not minors, in which case their income is considered to belong to the parent. Unfortunately, tax savings cannot be extended indefinitely in this manner. At a fairly low level of gross earnings both partnerships and close companies begin to pay out a disproportionate amount of their earnings in tax. Consequently, growth by reinvestment of retained earnings is severely restricted under these two corporate structures. At best it depends upon a decision of HM Inspector of Taxes.

To facilitate growth a major policy decision must be taken by the owners. The objective is to raise additional long-term capital which can take the form of debt or equity financing.

The sale of equity entails a dilution of ownership, and since a public issue is frequently impossible for a small company, debt financing is the more suitable financial operation. Financing by debt will be discussed in greater detail in the section on "Managing ownership and control."

Large firms

In order to ensure a high rate of retention of earnings, owners must take advantage of the best alternatives available. So far we have discussed the tax effects of corporate structure on the earnings of a small firm as it grows from a gross earnings level of £20 000 to £40 000. From Tables 12:1 and 12:2 it is clear that at the £20 000 level the firm should be constituted as a partnership. Even when earnings grow to £40 000 a suitable division of the equity would ensure that a partnership attracts less tax. In either case, however, a more rapid growth rate could be achieved by debt financing. Whatever means are taken to reduce the tax charges, the firm will eventually be faced with the fact that further rapid growth cannot be obtained in the context of either a partnership or a close company. Though debt financing offers proprietor controlled companies excellent opportunities for growth, there is a relatively low limit to the amount of debt such an enterprise can raise. At this stage in the firm's development the structure of a public company becomes mandatory.

There are several ways by which owners can retain control and a measure of ownership under a public company structure. Whatever means is used, a public company is the only answer to the problem of generating long-term growth. Though a close company can well serve to advantage during the early stages of development it is not a suitable long-term structure. The cost of remaining close should be recalculated as earnings rise so that management is always aware of the tax drain this structure imposes. To illustrate this point, an example is now presented of a close private company that has reached the point where "going public" is indicated. The same calculations could have been performed for the case of a large partnership. A large partnership can be transformed into a public company without going through the intermediate stage of a private company. In both cases similar calculations are made.

Tables 12:5 and 12:6 present the relevant financial data of the Efficiency Company. Originally this firm was arranged as a partnership and its tax liability is illustrated in Table 12:2. This structure was retained as long as debt financing was available. As it grew in size, and additional debt became harder to find, a close company was formed. The tax liability is illustrated in Table 12:3. Further debt financing permitted the company to grow to its present level. The situation is presented in Tables 12:5 and 12:6. It should be noted that the data in Table 12:5 is the same

Net worth:		*Fixed assets*		£1300
Ordinary shares	£600			
Reserves	500			
Debentures (6%)	700			
Total	£1800	*Current assets:*		
		Stock	500	
		Liquid	1200	
				1700
Current liabilities	1200			
Total	£3000	Total		£3000

TABLE 12:5 EFFICIENCY COMPANY BALANCE SHEET
(All figures in £'000s)

Earnings before tax and interest (30% of net worth)	£540 000
Interest on debentures: (6% non-convertible, non-redeemable)	£42 000
Earnings before tax (approximately)	£500 000
Total liquidity of long and short debt (see Chapter 10)	1.3 years
Extra long debt that can be afforded on current earnings with total liquidity being no greater than 10 years (see Chapter 10)	£4 700 000

TABLE 12:6 EFFICIENCY COMPANY RÉSUMÉ OF FINANCIAL STATISTICS

as that used in Chapter 10 in the analysis of the management of capital structure.

The most important factor in the decision to go public is the before tax earnings of £500 000. The problem of the apparent loss of ownership and control encountered by going public is considered in the next section. At present we are strictly concerned with the tax cost of remaining close.

Suppose for illustrative purposes that the Efficiency Company is still jointly owned by the two directors. If they go public they will act as the joint managing directors and will each exercise direct control over 10 per cent of the voting equity. The remaining directors of the public company would have less than 10 per cent of the voting equity and no other single member would own more than 3 per cent. In order to make comparable calculations, it is assumed that the directors take similar remuneration under both corporate forms. As a close company the least tax charge accrues if the directors take the maximum allowance of 15 per cent of earnings. It is assumed that as a close or public company the directors are listed as receiving 15 per cent of £500 000 or £75 000. Clearly, retained earnings can be increased by an appropriate division of this sum. Moreover, if the two owners only controlled 51 per cent instead of 100 per cent of the close company's equity and split this 51 per cent among some associates the tax burden would be considerably reduced. The point at issue, however, is the cost of remaining close, and no matter how income is split, there will always be a substantial tax saving to be earned by going public. In this case the tax charges for the close and public

Estimated earnings		£500 000
Allowance for directors' remuneration:		
15% × £500 000		
2 directors' remuneration		75 000
Earnings chargeable to corporation tax		£425 000
Corporation tax of 42½% on £425 000		£180 625
Required standard for distribution:		
60% × (425 000 − 180 625) = £146 625		
Income tax on shortfall of £146 625 @ 41.2% (8/3)		£ 60 483
Surtax on standard shortfall		£ 73 312
Total tax charge		£314 420
Funds available for reinvestment	= earnings − tax	
	= £185 580	
Directors' living expenses	75 000	
Total possible retained earnings	£110 580	

TABLE 12:7 TAX AND RETAINED EARNINGS FOR CLOSE COMPANY WITH EARNINGS OF £500 000

Estimated earnings		£500 000
Allowance for directors' remuneration:		
15% × £500 000		
Directors' remuneration		75 000
Earnings chargeable to corporation tax		£425 000
Corporation tax of 42½% on £425 000		£180 625
Total tax charge		£180 625
Funds available for reinvestment	= earnings − tax	
	= £319 375	
Directors' living expenses	75 000	
Total possible retained earnings	£244 375	

TABLE 12:8 TAX AND RETAINED EARNINGS FOR PUBLIC COMPANY WITH EARNINGS OF £500 000

companies are presented in Tables 12:7 and 12:8 respectively.

From the results listed in Tables 12:7 and 12:8 it is clear that the cost of remaining close is approximately £134 000 a year. In other words, if the Efficiency Company went public it would immediately have an extra £134 000 of earnings available for reinvestment. This increase in retained earnings would grow if earnings rose above the £500 000. Though the £75 000 allocated to the directors in the close company could, in part, be reinvested in the firm, this manipulation is irrelevant to the decision to go public. Even if this whole sum could be retained tax free, which it certainly cannot, the cost of remaining close would still be prohibitive.

Managing ownership and control

The whole point of being a close company is to retain personal ownership of a firm. In the case of the Efficiency Company the owner/directors have worked hard and developed an enterprise that is now earning over £500 000 a year. Given the tax structure it should be perfectly clear that though they own the firm they do not control the distribution of its earnings.

As a close company the owner/directors maintain control of £110 580 plus director's income net of tax, say £20 000, or roughly £130 000 from earnings of £500 000. In short, the Inland Revenue has immediate access to, and control of, 74 per cent of the company's earnings. As a public company the directors would control £262 000 of the £500 000 annual earnings, for the Inland Revenue only have access to, and control of, 47 per cent of their earnings. The directors own 100 per cent of the equity of the close company and control of 26 per cent of the earnings. As joint managing directors with as little as 20 per cent of the equity they would control 53 per cent of a vastly increased stream of earnings (see Table 12:9). Hence, it is more than pertinent to ask, what is the meaning of ownership and control?

The decision to go public is without question the prerogative of the owners. It should be clear, however, that an ownership which permits control over 26 per cent of the earnings is in many respects an ownership of only 26 per cent of the firm. The primary objective of a business enterprise is to generate earnings. If control cannot

	Close company		Public company	
Earnings	£500 000	100%	£500 000	100%
Tax paid on company	315 000	63%	181 000	36%
Directors' personal tax	57 000	11%	57 000	11%
Earnings controlled by directors	£128 000	26%	£262 000	53%

TABLE 12:9 OWNERSHIP AND CONTROL OF EARNINGS OF EFFICIENCY COMPANY

be exercised over earnings what is the point of owning the means of producing them?

In the suggested public company structure for the Efficiency Company it was proposed that the original owners would retain a total of 20 per cent of the voting equity. Some might feel that 20 per cent was too little to maintain effective control of the firm. Whatever proportion is chosen it is highly unlikely that a proxy fight would unseat the major shareholders, particularly if the remainder of the board owns less than 10 per cent.

By going public the managing directors of the Efficiency Company would now be running a firm which had a vastly increased potential for growth. In addition, they would have sold 80 per cent of their equity for a substantial capital sum. This sum would include a premium over current value to take account of the firm's expected growth. Since the proceeds from the sale would be taxed as capital gains, the owners would retain at least 70 per cent of the total sum. A large capital sum might well pose its own investment problems. With suitable advice, such sums can be invested so that the tax charge incurred on the revenue is a matter of personal preference. Revenue can be taken as income or capital gains and if managed properly the tax paid will be far less than was originally charged on the ascribed earnings of the close company.

As a public enterprise the Efficiency Company has an enormous growth potential. To begin with its after tax earnings are more than 50 per cent greater as a similar close company. As a result, the compound effect of reinvesting these earnings will be very large indeed. If this firm pursues a dividend policy designed for growth (see Chapter 10) the market price of the firm's shares will also rise. Though 20 per cent of the new public company's equity may seem a small amount, a record of continued earnings growth will soon create a market value for that 20 per cent which is far in excess of the original total value of the close company.

A final point to consider is that of death and estate duties. Under a close company structure an owner's share is taxed at an assessed value. If this equity represents his major asset, the tax funds may have to be raised by a forced sale of the equity. Such a sale can have disastrous effects on the future management of the close company. As a public company, the equity will still be taxed, but the raising of the tax payments will not affect the firm's finances. The equity can be used to borrow the necessary funds or it can be sold on the market. In either event, the company itself will not be seriously affected.

Managing close companies

It can occur that the owners of a close company will decide to remain in this state and pay the annual cost of not diluting the equity or going public. It is still the financial manager's task to take advantage of all available opportunities. Though the public structure offers the best vehicle for retaining earnings and stimulating growth, there are certain financial operations which can help a close company to grow. Unfortunately, the best that can be done for a close company is to create growth in goodwill. The close company is not able to generate a continuing sequence of large net profits as the Inland Revenue takes an increasingly large share. The time inevitably arrives when the company can no longer justify non-distribution of earnings and severe shortfall penalties will be applied.

A close company can stimulate growth by debt financing. A large volume of debt provides the capital for growth, but cannot provide the retained earnings. Growth, as it occurs, will be reflected in the value of the firm's goodwill. Goodwill and growth are stores of potential wealth which can be realised by a public issue. Consequently, a close company which uses debt financing to ensure growth cannot create real wealth for the owner until the goodwill is realised by going public. The operation of debt financing is merely a prelude to an eventual public issue.

To illustrate these remarks consider the effect, on the earnings of the Efficiency Company constituted as a close company, of the additional debt they could afford. In Chapter 10 it was pointed out that at the current rate of pre-tax earnings, the Efficiency Company could afford an extra £4 700 000 of long-term debt (see also Table 12:6). They can afford this debt as long as management is capable of utilising the extra capital to earn their current pre-tax rate of return. The earnings generated on this additional capital will, before long, permit even more debt to be raised. For a close company, debt represents a powerful mechanism for creating growth, and as has been shown in Chapter 10, long-term debt should be as large as lenders will allow.

There are two main constraints which place a limit on the amount of debt. The first is the drain on funds due to the required interest payments. The second is the interest price that has to be paid, a price which depends upon the availability of debt to the firm. Loans can always be found if the interest rate compensates for the risk. Since interest on debt is fully chargeable against tax, and since the bulk of after tax earnings are paid out in tax, a close company can afford to service debt with all its before tax earnings. The point to note is that the close company cannot retain its earnings indefinitely. It is in the long-run interests of such a company to spend its earnings to service debt instead of on taxes. It follows that a close company can afford very high interest rates on its loans.

For example, suppose the Efficiency Company were offered £2 000 000 of long-term funds at a cost of 12 per cent. The interest payments would be £240 000 a year which, at the present rate of earnings, would merely reduce the tax charges. However, the Efficiency Company has generated a before tax return on capital of 30 per cent. If this rate of earnings is maintained, earnings will rise by £600 000 which will more than cover the £240 000 of servicing costs. Indeed, as long as the rate of return on capital employed is greater than the interest charge, the net cost to the firm is nil. Clearly there is a limit to this method of purchasing growth and to capitalise on this endeavour an eventual public issue must be contemplated. In this context, if debentures with conversion rights to a future public issue are raised, the volume of debt that can be obtained is large. The cost of servicing would be nominal as growth would eventually pay for the debt.

Managing partnerships

Debt financing is also indicated as a method of purchasing growth for a firm operating under a partnership structure. Once again the eventual object must be a public company. Debt financing offers the owners the maximum retention of ownership and control with a large capital appreciation once the goodwill is realised in a public issue.

There is no doubt that effective financial management is directed at growth and that earnings growth demands a corporate structure based on a public company. Though there are several paths a growing enterprise may follow, the selection of the specific route is a decision based on personal choice and financial advantage.

THIRTEEN

MERGERS AND TAKEOVERS

Throughout this volume the management of earnings has been taken as the primary task. Each section and chapter has focused, in its own way, on the problems of earnings generation and growth. Part 1 was concerned with the management of cash and a company's liquidity and solvency. The objective is to increase the flow of funds through a firm's operations which in turn leads to a growth in earnings. Part 2 was devoted to asset management. Working capital and fixed assets were both treated as sources as well as uses of funds and earnings. Once again an increase in the rate of turnover of funds in these assets leads to earnings growth. Part 3 and the preceding chapters of Part 4 are concerned with the long-term capital and corporate structure within which the firm's operations are conducted. It was shown that the size and rate of growth of earnings depended heavily upon the particular capital and corporate framework chosen. If earnings growth is the chief objective, financial managers must guide their firms through this entire range of decisions. The reward for effective financial management is an increase in the market value of the company, an increase which benefits all concerned.

Financial managers affect the value of their companies by their management of the earnings flow. An increase in the rate of earnings growth will lead shareholders and other investors to bid up the company's share price. If this growth in earnings can be sustained investors will begin to bid up the price to earnings ratio in their desire to participate in this earnings stream. Increases in the price to earnings ratio raise the market value of a company's issued capital. Clearly, shareholders benefit from a rise in share prices. The point to note is that a rising share price is a major advantage to the firm itself. Mergers and takeovers are based upon an exchange or purchase of shares. The higher the price/earnings of a firm's shares the more readily that firm can take over others rather than be taken over.

This chapter is devoted to the subject of mergers and takeovers. In a world of expanding trade where the multinational and international organisations are becoming increasingly common, it is essential for a firm to know how to compete in merger and takeover battles. On a national basis the issues are similar and the problems associated with mergers and takeovers are an important element of financial management.

So far this book has been devoted to the financial activities necessary to the internal generation of earnings and growth. Though mergers and takeovers are important as sources of such growth, financial managers usually regard the acquisition of a firm as an outlet for extra earnings. Companies are purchased for many reasons: to reduce competition; to acquire additional production, marketing, and transportation facilities; to obtain the services of exceptional managers; to diversify; and to purchase goodwill and other intangible assets. Many of these and other such reasons are beyond the brief of the financial manager. The decision to merge or take over is the prerogative of the chief executive. The task of the financial manager is to point out the financial advantages and disadvantages of suggested candidates for merger and takeover, and to advise on the best means of effecting the acquisition once it is selected. Of these three items the first two are concerned with the question of what to acquire, the last with the problem of how to take over. These issues are discussed in turn.

Definition of mergers and takeovers

There is a considerable difference between a merger and a takeover, and it is necessary to describe these activities before considering the mechanics of their operation. Unfortunately, there is some confusion as to what is meant by a merger and a takeover since the line dividing them is diffuse. To clarify the position we shall consider mergers to be those activities which lead two or more firms to amalgamate their operations within an entirely new capital and corporate structure. Takeovers will embrace all acquisitions of one enterprise by another where the corporate identity of the one taken over disappears and only the other remains.

In a merger a new company is created, usually with a new name, which in turn reflects the identities of the merging parties. A total reorganisation of the capital structure takes place. The shareholders of the original firms are offered an exchange for share capital in the new firm on some equitable basis. In effect an entirely new corporate entity is formed with a suitable corporate structure. This new company then takes over all the merging parties and sets up its capital structure to effect this takeover to the greatest advantage to all concerned.

The question of what constitutes an equitable exchange of capital shares is a task for the respective financial managers. Each has a duty to obtain the best possible bargain for his shareholders. The decision on what to charge per share clearly depends upon the value placed on the company itself. This problem will be discussed in the next section.

Any amalgamation which permits the corporate and capital identity of one party to survive is a takeover not a merger. In a takeover the shareholders of the surviving company are affected only in so far as the terms of the purchase cause a dilution of equity. This aspect of takeovers is discussed when the operation itself is outlined. In general, existing shareholders of the surviving company will not perceive any change in their securities. This is not the case for the shareholders of the company that is being taken over. The nature of the change will depend on the mechanics of the takeover. It may involve an exchange of securities, a complete realisation of equity for cash, or some combination of these alternatives. The advantages of the various ways of purchasing companies will be discussed in due course, both from the point of view of the company and the original shareholder.

Value of a company

In a merger or takeover the financial manager must ensure that there is an equitable exchange of his company's securities for those of another. Whether he is acting as a party to a merger or as a participant in a takeover, his job is to drive the best possible bargain for the enterprise he represents. Though bargaining requires skill in negotiation, it is enhanced by a knowledge of the real value of his firm.

There are three principal methods that are used to value a company: book value, present value of the future earnings, and stock market value. The former is at best misleading, and the latter two are closely related.

Book value. Book value is the audited written down monetary worth of the total net assets owned by a firm. The total net assets are composed of gross working capital plus fixed assets minus liabilities. Unfortunately, opinions differ as to what constitutes the real value of any given asset. These difficulties are compounded by the fact that the value of an asset in a going concern differs sharply from the value accorded that same asset in a company undergoing liquidation. In a takeover a firm's assets are valued by a variety of auditing techniques. These values are affected by depreciation and stock valuation policies as well as the opinions of the decision makers in the acquiring organisation.

In Part 2 of this book we have shown that it is sound financial management to own as few fixed assets as possible. If a company pursues an efficient fixed asset policy valuation becomes difficult if related to another firm which takes pride in the ownership of its assets. Furthermore, intangibles such as goodwill are notoriously difficult to evaluate.

Book values represent an historical record. Except when assets are revalued, they only describe what an asset is worth in terms of purchase price and depreciation charges. A firm may own vast quantities of assets and, because they are obsolete, their real value is close to zero. Alternatively, companies with large property holdings which have risen in market value may understate these values on their books. Book values say nothing about the ability of the firm to generate earnings. Since earnings are the key to financial health, book values are at best, highly misleading.

Present value of future earnings. If earnings are accepted as essential to the continued existence of an enterprise, then the value of a company depends on its ability to generate earnings. A way to evaluate earnings is to take the present value of the expected earnings stream discounted at the appropriate cost of capital. The major difficulty of this method lies in the assessment of the size of the future earnings. That this assessment requires skill cannot be denied. An effective financial manager, however, will be able to transfer his experience in assessing the future earnings of his own firm to that of the new. In addition, there already exists a guide to this process of evaluation. The guide is the market price of the company's issued securities.

Market value. Though it has been argued that it is possible to know the price of everything and the value of nothing, the market price of an article is one measure of its value. A sale requires a willing buyer as well as a seller. What is true for individual articles is also true for firms. In this respect the current market price of a company's securities sets a lower limit to the value of the firm. Market prices reflect investors' anticipations of future earnings and dividends, their confidence in the company's management, and the efficiency with which the firm's operations are conducted. The market price is an arms length value of the entire company as presently constituted. As a result, it represents the investors' estimate of the present value of the future earnings.

From management's point of view the market price is the base line from which to negotiate. The company being taken over is not likely to accept such a price unless its share prices are falling. Inertia alone will necessitate a premium. The acquiring firm regards the market value as the price to which they will endeavour to get close. It is up to the management of both firms to arrive at a satisfactory compromise. In the case of a merger each firm will be striving for as large a slice as possible of the new capital to be issued.

A major drawback to market valuations lies in the ability of investors to make accurate assessments of a company's future earnings. This is particularly true if a firm's shares are not actively traded. If share prices cannot be used as a reliable guide, other estimates will have to be made by the managers involved.

What to take over

A company is in business to make profits and to increase its earnings. In the previous two chapters we have emphasised the value of retained earnings. Money is a scarce resource and financial managers must employ their funds efficiently. Among the many investments competing for attention is that of the takeover. To be acceptable, an investment must yield a suitable rate of return consistent with its risk. A takeover does not differ from other types of investments and is to be viewed in terms of the present value of its future earnings stream. Since investors will have placed a market value on the shares of a candidate for takeover, financial managers will seek out those firms where the market price does not fully discount the potential future value. Such situations exist for many reasons, some of which are: inefficient management, inappropriate corporate and capital structures, excessive liquidity, and too many fixed assets.

A good takeover situation will have considerable hidden potential which has not yet been realised and which more effective management can use to generate additional earnings. Firms which are inefficiently run are either unaware of or unable to make use of this potential. As a result, the purchase price is lower than would be appropriate if these earnings were fully realised. The takeover of an enterprise with hidden potential is not likely to be difficult to achieve. Efficiently run firms will resist a surrender of their autonomy and identity. An undervalued company has less scope for negotiation and the firm making the acquisition can afford to be generous.

Suitable takeover situations have certain characteristics which financial managers would do well to recognise. These characteristics are listed and discussed below. Though they may not all be present in a given situation any one may be sufficiently attractive in itself. Their presence can be ascertained from the financial data published in balance sheets, profit and loss statements, or in the market reports in the financial press.

Characteristics of takeover situations

Unused cash. In Part 1 we demonstrated that a company which maintains a large balance of idle cash is wasting profitable investment opportunities. Firms of this sort frequently pursue liquidity for its own sake. Its earnings are likely to be low and the market price usually reflects this inefficiency. This is a suitable candidate for takeover by a company which is capable of proper cash management. Information on a company's liquidity is directly obtainable from the cash, near cash, and investment entries on published balance sheets, and indirectly from a determination of the values of the ratios specified in Part 1.

Accounts receivable. In Chapter 6 a method was presented for determining the average age of accounts receivable balances. By applying this technique to the published data of a firm a measure is obtained of the efficiency with which it collects its debts. A long average life indicates inefficiency, high costs of servicing debtors, and consequently lower than necessary earnings. Once again there is an opportunity to improve this company's financial activities and the slack in the market price will indicate that it is a suitable takeover situation.

Volume of debt. Several measures of gearing and leverage are discussed in Part 3 as well as a method for computing the volume of debt a company can afford. Many companies are unaware of their ability to manage such a level of debt and fail to make use of the funds they could so readily purchase. Firms which make slight use of debt are an attractive proposition for aggressive financial managers. Once again the volume of a firm's debt is to be found in published financial statements and an undergeared company will have a market price which will make a takeover a profitable investment.

Asset policies. In Chapter 8 the management of fixed assets is discussed in detail. It is pointed out that ownership of assets beyond the bare minimum is not financially sound. A company that owns large quantities of fixed assets has great earnings potential through the sale or sale and lease back of those assets. Funds released from fixed assets can be invested in working capital to generate additional earnings. Such a firm is well placed as a candidate for a takeover.

Earnings growth. It has been noted frequently throughout this book that earnings growth is the major objective of financial management. Growth is affected by many factors one of which is the industry in which a firm is engaged. Certain industries, particularly those concerned with new technologies, are recognised growth areas. Any firm that lags behind the average in such an industry is a potential takeover candidate.

In general, a low growth in earnings is an indicator of lax financial management and a takeover opportunity. This is true of all industries. A slowing down of earnings growth may be due to a falling market, or a lack of direction or a breakdown in financial management. Financial managers ought to be searching for such opportunities and should not be put off by the reputation or size of the company in question. Companies which are stagnating are vulnerable to takeover by more aggressive and efficient firms.

Price/earnings ratios. The price to earnings ratio represents investors' assessment of the future stream of earnings for a particular company. An industry's average level of price to earnings ratio depends upon a number of factors. The industry's growth potential is crucial. General economic and political factors are also important. Within an industry some firms will have price to earnings ratios that are higher than the average. These companies are expected to realise a faster than average growth. If they should fail in this endeavour their market price will drop rather sharply. A lower than average ratio indicates a low expected rate of growth and may well suggest the presence of a number of the takeover characteristics discussed above.

A low price to earnings ratio is a strong indicator of a possible takeover situation. Clearly, such a company could be caught in a declining industry and be on its way to extinction. Though such situations merit careful attention, due care must be taken not to be misled by this single factor. In general, takeovers are most profitable when the acquiring company has a higher price to earnings ratio than the firm it is purchasing. In financial terms it does not matter what the higher value may be, although a ratio in excess of the average places the buyer in the soundest position. On the other hand, a merger is indicated when the price earnings ratios of the interested parties are on a par with one another. Indeed, economies of scale alone may suggest a merger, even among companies with below average but similar ratios.

To illustrate these remarks consider the Efficiency Company which has been discussed in various sections of this book. This firm has 2 400 000 shares outstanding and earnings of £290 000 in the current period. If this company is accorded a price to earnings ratio of thirty times then the market price of the ordinary shares would be given by:

$$\text{price} = \frac{\text{earnings}}{\text{shares}} \times \text{P/E ratio} = \frac{290\,000}{2\,400\,000} \times 30$$

$$\text{price} = £3.60$$

If the price/earnings ratio were only fifteen times then the market price of these same shares would be £1.80.

Any firm wishing to purchase the Efficiency Company would have to pay at least twice as much if the price to earnings were thirty rather than fifteen. Presumably the high price to earnings ratio entails a rapid growth in earnings which might well justify such an investment. It would most certainly be an expensive investment unless the buying company had an even higher earnings multiple.

How to take over

A company seeking to acquire another can accomplish the purchase in several ways. One possibility is to offer cash for the whole of the outstanding equity. Another approach is to exchange the securities of the buying company for the equity in the firm being taken over. There are many such ways of accomplishing the transaction since each package can contain a different mixture of securities and cash. One point to note is that it is not essential to the takeover process to acquire 100 per cent of the company being bought. In Chapters 11 and 12 the meaning and cost of ownership and control were explored in some detail. In a takeover less than 100 per cent will still give the buyer control over the earnings and financial policies of the acquired firm. Minority interests may or may not prove troublesome, but it should not be forgotten that control can be achieved for less than 100 per cent of the ownership of the voting equity.

Any method of takeover purchase which involves the payment of cash is, in our opinion, inefficient. A part or whole cash purchase represents an unnecessary drain on working capital and a loss of potential earnings. Cash payments conflict with the major objective of a takeover which is to increase earnings. Moreover, a cash payment ought to be unwelcome to the original shareholders since it will most likely subject them to a capital gains charge. A purchase for securities is the soundest means to effect any takeover. It is in the best interests, both short and long term, of all concerned.

A takeover by means of a share exchange can be accomplished in two ways. The first is a straight exchange of ordinary shares at an agreed rate. This can lead to a substantial dilution of the equity in the buying company, particularly if the premium to be paid is high. Large dilutions represent a risk to the remaining shareholders. The share price is likely to fall over the short run unless the increase in earnings is sufficient to offset the dilution. If financial management has assessed the takeover properly, the risk is minimal and the additional earnings will not only service the new issue of shares but also will add a net balance to total earnings. A second method of acquiring a firm for shares is by an exchange of shares for convertible debentures. The rate and prices for conversion are settled during the negotiations. If the full price is paid in convertible debentures, the additional earnings must cover the debenture interest and contribute a net addition to total earnings. In this event, the earnings increase will raise the market share price which in turn will service the conversion to ordinary shares as it takes place.

The price to earnings factor can now be re-examined as an indicator of a takeover situation. Consider the Efficiency Company once again. With a price to earnings ratio of thirty the market price of the issued shares will be roughly £3.60. The Efficiency Company could finance a takeover by issuing a convertible debenture of, say, £1 000 000 with a suitable coupon rate and a conversion privilege at the price of, say, £4.50 a share. The debentures issue then represents a future issue of 1 000 000/4.50 =222 000 ordinary shares after full conversion has taken place.

If the Efficiency Company had a price to earnings ratio of only fifteen, the same debenture issue of £1 000 000 could be offered with a different conversion rate. Since at fifteen times earnings the market price will be roughly £1.80 a share the conversion price might well be set at £2.25 a share. The debenture issue of £1 000 000 now represents an eventual issue of 440 000 ordinary shares. Clearly a debenture issue which represents 440 000 shares is twice as expensive as one which represents only 220 000 shares. This expense can be measured both in terms of dilution and the earnings growth required if market share price is to be maintained.

It should now be clear why a high price to earnings ratio is important to the management of growth by takeovers. The Efficiency Company with a ratio of thirty can purchase a firm with a price to earnings of fifteen times for half the price it would have to pay if its own ratio was fifteen. In addition, there is an advantage to the shareholders of the firm being taken over if the buying company has a higher price to earnings multiple. Whether those shareholders are paid in convertible debentures and/or shares, the new securities will appreciate in value more rapidly than their original equity could have done in the absence of the takeover.

How to avoid takeover

There are many advantages to be gained by being involved in a takeover bid. However, the owners may well decide that no matter how generous the offer their long-run interests will be best served by remaining independent. A firm attracting a takeover bid is most likely to be suffering from one of the noted deficiencies. The defence against a takeover bid lies primarily in an increase in managerial and financial efficiency. In brief, management must reverse the trends which have placed their company in a position to be taken over.

Once management has recognised its shortcomings it will be evident that many of them are related to their financial operations. This book is directed at precisely those problems. It contains a sufficient number of techniques and illustrative examples to assist a firm threatened with takeover to work its way out of this position. Indeed, if financial control is properly achieved a company, once threatened, may soon be in a position to contemplate takeovers of its own.

To take a reasonable liberty with the words of Lord Justice Sumner we may state that:

"There should be firms who endeavour so to arrange their affairs as not to attract taxes enforced by the crown so far as they can legitimately do so within the law."

The management of taxation is but one of the important ways by which earnings can be increased without expanding sales. Many other such techniques have been presented in this volume. It is our hope that they will be recognised for what they are—methods for increasing company earnings which in turn will raise the real wealth of the entire community.

APPENDICES

1	Present Value of £1	238
2	Present Value of £1 per annum	246

APPENDIX 1

Present Value of £1 at interest rate *I* received *N* years in the future

N/I	**1%** *0.010*	**2%** *0.020*	**3%** *0.030*	**4%** *0.040*	**4.5%** *0.045*	**5%** *0.050*	**5.5%** *0.055*	**6%** *0.060*
1	0.99	0.98	0.97	0.96	0.96	0.95	0.95	0.94
2	0.98	0.96	0.94	0.92	0.92	0.90	0.90	0.89
3	0.97	0.94	0.92	0.89	0.88	0.85	0.85	0.84
4	0.96	0.92	0.89	0.85	0.84	0.81	0.81	0.79
5	0.95	0.91	0.86	0.82	0.80	0.77	0.77	0.75
6	0.94	0.89	0.84	0.79	0.77	0.73	0.73	0.70
7	0.93	0.87	0.81	0.76	0.73	0.69	0.69	0.67
8	0.92	0.85	0.79	0.73	0.70	0.65	0.65	0.63
9	0.91	0.84	0.77	0.70	0.67	0.62	0.62	0.59
10	0.91	0.82	0.74	0.68	0.64	0.59	0.59	0.56
11	0.90	0.80	0.72	0.65	0.62	0.55	0.55	0.53
12	0.89	0.79	0.70	0.62	0.59	0.53	0.53	0.50
13	0.88	0.77	0.68	0.60	0.56	0.50	0.50	0.47

N/I	**1%** *0.010*	**2%** *0.20*	**3%** *0.030*	**4%** *0.040*	**4.5%** *0.45*	**5%** *0.050*	**5.5%** *0.055*	**6%** *0.060*
14	0.87	0.76	0.66	0.58	0.54	0.47	0.47	0.44
15	0.86	0.74	0.64	0.56	0.52	0.45	0.45	0.42
16	0.85	0.73	0.62	0.53	0.49	0.42	0.42	0.39
17	0.84	0.71	0.61	0.51	0.47	0.40	0.40	0.37
18	0.84	0.70	0.59	0.49	0.45	0.38	0.38	0.35
19	0.83	0.69	0.57	0.47	0.43	0.36	0.36	0.33
20	0.82	0.67	0.55	0.46	0.41	0.34	0.34	0.31
21	0.81	0.66	0.54	0.44	0.40	0.32	0.32	0.29
22	0.80	0.65	0.52	0.42	0.38	0.31	0.31	0.28
23	0.80	0.63	0.51	0.41	0.36	0.29	0.29	0.26
24	0.79	0.62	0.49	0.39	0.35	0.28	0.28	0.25
25	0.78	0.61	0.48	0.38	0.33	0.26	0.26	0.23
26	0.77	0.60	0.46	0.36	0.32	0.25	0.25	0.22
27	0.76	0.59	0.45	0.35	0.30	0.24	0.24	0.21
28	0.76	0.57	0.44	0.33	0.29	0.22	0.22	0.20
29	0.75	0.56	0.42	0.32	0.28	0.21	0.21	0.18
30	0.74	0.55	0.41	0.31	0.27	0.20	0.20	0.17

N/I	**6.5%** *0.065*	**7%** *0.070*	**7.5%** *0.075*	**8%** *0.080*	**8.5%** *0.085*	**9%** *0.090*	**9.5%** *0.095*	**10%** *0.100*
1	0.94	0.93	0.93	0.93	0.92	0.91	0.91	0.91
2	0.88	0.87	0.87	0.86	0.85	0.83	0.83	0.83
3	0.83	0.80	0.80	0.79	0.78	0.76	0.76	0.75
4	0.78	0.75	0.75	0.74	0.72	0.70	0.70	0.68
5	0.73	0.70	0.70	0.68	0.67	0.64	0.64	0.62
6	0.69	0.65	0.65	0.63	0.61	0.58	0.58	0.56
7	0.64	0.60	0.60	0.58	0.56	0.53	0.53	0.51
8	0.60	0.56	0.56	0.54	0.52	0.48	0.48	0.47
9	0.57	0.52	0.52	0.50	0.48	0.44	0.44	0.42
10	0.53	0.49	0.49	0.46	0.44	0.40	0.40	0.39
11	0.50	0.45	0.45	0.43	0.41	0.37	0.37	0.35
12	0.47	0.42	0.42	0.40	0.38	0.34	0.34	0.32
13	0.44	0.39	0.39	0.37	0.35	0.31	0.31	0.29

N/I	**6.5%** *0.065*	**7%** *0.070*	**7.5%** *0.075*	**8%** *0.080*	**8.5%** *0.085*	**9%** *0.090*	**9.5%** *0.095*	**10%** *0.100*
14	0.41	0.36	0.36	0.34	0.32	0.28	0,28	0.26
15	0.39	0.34	0.34	0.32	0.29	0.26	0.26	0.24
16	0.37	0.31	0.31	0.29	0.27	0.23	0.23	0.22
17	0.34	0.29	0.29	0.27	0.25	0.21	0.21	0.20
18	0.32	0.27	0.27	0.25	0.23	0.20	0.20	0.18
19	0.30	0.25	0.25	0.23	0.21	0.18	0.18	0.16
20	0.28	0.24	0.24	0.21	0.20	0.16	0.16	0.15
21	0.27	0.22	0.22	0.20	0.18	0.15	0.15	0.14
22	0.25	0.20	0.20	0.18	0.17	0.14	0.14	0.12
23	0.23	0.19	0.19	0.17	0.15	0.12	0.12	0.11
24	0.22	0.18	0.18	0.16	0.14	0.11	0.11	0.10
25	0.21	0.16	0.16	0.15	0.13	0.10	0.10	0.09
26	0.19	0.15	0.15	0.14	0.12	0.09	0.09	0.08
27	0.18	0.14	0.14	0.13	0.11	0.09	0.09	0.08
28	0.17	0.13	0.13	0.12	0.10	0.08	0.08	0.07
29	0.16	0.12	0.12	0.11	0.09	0.07	0.07	0.06
30	0.15	0.11	0.11	0.10	0.09	0.07	0.07	0.06

N/I	**10.5%** *0.105*	**11%** *0.110*	**11.5%** *0.115*	**12%** *0.120*	**13%** *0.130*	**14%** *0.140*	**15%** *0.150*	**16%** *0.160*
1	0.90	0.90	0.90	0.89	0.88	0.88	0.87	0.86
2	0.82	0.80	0.80	0.80	0.78	0.77	0.76	0.74
3	0.74	0.72	0.72	0.71	0.69	0.67	0.66	0.64
4	0.67	0.65	0.65	0.64	0.61	0.59	0.57	0.55
5	0.61	0.58	0.58	0.57	0.54	0.52	0.50	0.48
6	0.55	0.52	0.52	0.51	0.48	0.46	0.43	0.41
7	0.50	0.47	0.47	0.45	0.43	0.40	0.38	0.35
8	0.45	0.42	0.42	0.40	0.38	0.35	0.33	0.31
9	0.41	0.38	0.38	0.36	0.33	0.31	0.28	0.26
10	0.37	0.34	0.34	0.32	0.29	0.27	0.25	0.23
11	0.33	0.30	0.30	0.29	0.26	0.24	0.21	0.20
12	0.30	0.27	0.27	0.26	0.23	0.21	0.19	0.17
13	0.27	0.24	0.24	0.23	0.20	0.18	0.16	0.15

N/I	**10.5%** *0.105*	**11%** *0.110*	**11.5%** *0.115*	**12%** *0.120*	**13%** *0.130*	**14%** *0.140*	**15%** *0.150*	**16%** *0.160*
14	0.25	0.22	0.22	0.20	0.18	0.16	0.14	0.13
15	0.22	0.20	0.20	0.18	0.16	0.14	0.12	0.11
16	0.20	0.18	0.18	0.16	0.14	0.12	0.11	0.09
17	0.18	0.16	0.16	0.15	0.13	0.11	0.09	0.08
18	0.17	0.14	0.14	0.13	0.11	0.09	0.08	0.07
19	0.15	0.13	0.13	0.12	0.10	0.08	0.07	0.06
20	0.14	0.11	0.11	0.10	0.09	0.07	0.06	0.05
21	0.12	0.10	0.10	0.09	0.08	0.06	0.05	*0.00*
22	0.11	0.09	0.09	0.08	0.07	0.06	*0.00*	*0.00*
23	0.10	0.08	0.08	0.07	0.06	*0.00*	*0.00*	*0.00*
24	0.09	0.07	0.07	0.07	0.05	*0.00*	*0.00*	*0.00*
25	0.08	0.07	0.07	0.06	*0.00*	*0.00*	*0.00*	*0.00*
26	0.07	0.06	0.06	0.05	*0.00*	*0.00*	*0.00*	*0.00*
27	0.07	0.05	0.05	*0.00*	*0.00*	*0.00*	*0.00*	*0.00*
28	0.06	*0.00*	*0.00*	*0.00*	*0.00*	*0.00*	*0.00*	*0.00*
29	0.06	*0.00*	*0.00*	*0.00*	*0.00*	*0.00*	*0.00*	*0.00*
30	0.05	*0.00*	*0.00*	*0.00*	*0.00*	*0.00*	*0.00*	*0.00*

N/I	**18%** *0.180*	**20%** *0.200*	**22%** *0.220*	**24%** *0.240*	**30%** *0.300*	**40%** *0.400*	**50%** *0.500*	**60%** *0.600*
1	0.85	0.83	0.82	0.81	0.77	0.71	0.67	0.63
2	0.72	0.69	0.67	0.65	0.59	0.51	0.44	0.39
3	0.61	0.58	0.55	0.52	0.46	0.36	0.30	0.24
4	0.52	0.48	0.45	0.42	0.35	0.26	0.20	0.15
5	0.44	0.40	0.37	0.34	0.27	0.19	0.13	0.10
6	0.37	0.33	0.30	0.28	0.21	0.13	0.09	0.06
7	0.31	0.28	0.25	0.22	0.16	0.09	0.06	*0.00*
8	0.27	0.23	0.20	0.18	0.12	0.07	*0.00*	*0.00*
9	0.23	0.19	0.17	0.14	0.09	*0.00*	*0.00*	*0.00*
10	0.19	0.16	0.14	0.12	0.07	*0.00*	*0.00*	*0.00*
11	0.16	0.13	0.11	0.09	0.06	*0.00*	*0.00*	*0.00*
12	0.14	0.11	0.09	0.08	*0.00*	*0.00*	*0.00*	*0.00*
13	0.12	0.09	0.08	0.06	*0.00*	*0.00*	*0.00*	*0.00*

N/I	**18%** *0.180*	**20%** *0.200*	**22%** *0.220*	**24%** *0.240*	**30%** *0.300*	**40%** *0.400*	**50%** *0.500*	**60%** *0.600*
14	0.10	0.08	0.06	*0.00*	*0.00*	*0.00*	*0.00*	*0.00*
15	0.08	0.06	0.05	*0.00*	*0.00*	*0.00*	*0.00*	*0.00*
16	0.07	0.05	*0.00*	*0.00*	*0.00*	*0.00*	*0.00*	*0.00*
17	0.06	*0.00*	*0.00*	*0.00*	*0.00*	*0.00*	*0.00*	*0.00*
18	0.05	*0.00*	*0.00*	*0.00*	*0.00*	*0.00*	*0.00*	*0.00*
19	*0.00*	*0.00*	*0.00*	*0.00*	*0.00*	*0.00*	*0.00*	*0.00*
20	*0.00*	*0.00*	*0.00*	*0.00*	*0.00*	*0.00*	*0.00*	*0.00*
21	*0.00*	*0.00*	*0.00*	*0.00*	*0.00*	*0.00*	*0.00*	*0.00*
22	*0.00*	*0.00*	*0.00*	*0.00*	*0.00*	*0.00*	*0.00*	*0.00*
23	*0.00*	*0.00*	*0.00*	*0.00*	*0.00*	*0.00*	*0.00*	*0.00*
24	*0.00*	*0.00*	*0.00*	*0.00*	*0.00*	*0.00*	*0.00*	*0.00*
25	*0.00*	*0.00*	*0.00*	*0.00*	*0.00*	*0.00*	*0.00*	*0.00*
26	*0.00*	*0.00*	*0.00*	*0.00*	*0.00*	*0.00*	*0.00*	*0.00*
27	*0.00*	*0.00*	*0.00*	*0.00*	*0.00*	*0.00*	*0.00*	*0.00*
28	*0.00*	*0.00*	*0.00*	*0.00*	*0.00*	*0.00*	*0.00*	*0.00*
29	*0.00*	*0.00*	*0.00*	*0.00*	*0.00*	*0.00*	*0.00*	*0.00*
30	*0.00*	*0.00*	*0.00*	*0.00*	*0.00*	*0.00*	*0.00*	*0.00*

APPENDIX 2

Present Value of an Annuity of £1 at interest rate *I* for *N* years.

N/I	**1%** *0.010*	**2%** *0.020*	**3%** *0.030*	**4%** *0.040*	**5%** *0.050*	**6%** *0.060*
1	0.99	0.98	0.97	0.96	0.95	0.94
2	1.97	1.94	1.91	1.89	1.86	1.83
3	2.94	2.88	2.83	2.78	2.72	2.67
4	3.90	3.81	3.72	3.63	3.55	3.47
5	4.85	4.71	4.58	4.45	4.33	4.21
6	5.80	5.60	5.42	5.24	5.08	4.92
7	6.73	6.47	6.23	6.00	5.79	5.58
8	7.65	7.33	7.02	6.73	6.46	6.21
9	8.57	8.16	7.79	7.44	7.11	6,80
10	9.47	8.98	8.53	8.11	7.72	7.36
11	10.37	9.79	9.25	8.76	8.31	7.89
12	11.26	10.58	9.95	9.39	8.86	8.38
13	12.13	11.35	10.63	9.99	9.39	8.85
14	13.00	12.11	11.30	10.56	9.90	9.29
15	13.87	12.85	11.94	11.12	10.38	9.71

N/I	**1%** *0.010*	**2%** *0.020*	**3%** *0.030*	**4%** *0.040*	**5%** *0.050*	**6%** *0.060*
16	14.72	13.58	12.56	11.65	10.84	10.11
17	15.56	14.29	13.17	12.17	11.27	10.48
18	16.40	14.99	13.75	12.66	11.69	10.83
19	17.23	15.68	14.32	13.13	12.09	11.16
20	18.05	16.35	14.88	13.59	12.46	11.47
21	18.86	17.01	15.42	14.03	12.82	11.76
22	19.66	17.66	15.94	14.45	13.16	12.04
23	20.46	18.29	16.44	14.86	13.49	12.30
24	21.24	18.91	16.94	15.25	13.80	12.55
25	22.02	19.52	17.41	15.62	14.09	12.78
26	22.80	20.12	17,88	15.98	14.38	13.00
27	23.56	20.71	18.33	16.33	14.64	13.21
28	24.32	21.28	18.76	16.66	14.90	13.41
29	25.07	21.84	19.19	16.98	15.14	13.59
30	25.81	22.40	19.60	17.29	15.37	13.76
31	26.54	22.94	20.00	17.59	15.59	13.93
32	27.27	23.47	20.39	17.87	15.80	14.08
33	27.99	23.99	20.77	18.15	16.00	14.23
34	28.70	24.50	21.13	18.41	16.19	14.37
35	29.41	25.00	21.49	18.66	16.37	14.50

N/I	**1%** *0.010*	**2%** *0.020*	**3%** *0.030*	**4%** *0.040*	**5%** *0.050*	**6%** *0.060*
36	30.11	25.49	21.83	18.91	16.55	14.62
37	30.80	25.97	22.17	19.14	16.71	14.74
38	31.48	26.44	22.49	19.37	16.87	14.85
39	32.16	26.90	22.81	19.58	17.02	14.95
40	32.83	27.36	23.11	19.79	17.16	15.05
41	33.50	27.80	23.41	19.99	17.29	15.14
42	34.16	28.23	23.70	20.19	17.42	15.22
43	34.81	28.66	23.98	20.37	17.55	15.31
44	35.46	29.08	24.25	20.55	17.66	15.38
45	36.09	29.49	24.52	20.72	17.77	15.46
46	36.73	29.89	24.78	20.88	17.88	15.52
47	37.35	30.29	25.02	21.04	17.98	15.59
48	37.97	30.67	25.27	21.20	18.08	15.65
49	38.59	31.05	25.50	21.34	18.17	15.71
50	39.20	31.42	25.73	21.48	18.26	15.76

N/I	**7%** *0.070*	**8%** *0.080*	**9%** *0.090*	**10%** *0.100*	**11%** *0.110*	**12%** *0.120*
1	0.93	0.93	0.92	0.91	0.90	0.89
2	1.81	1.78	1.76	1.74	1.71	1.69
3	2.62	2.58	2.53	2.49	2.44	2.40
4	3.39	3.31	3.24	3.17	3.10	3.04
5	4.10	3.99	3.89	3.79	3.70	3.60
6	4.77	4.62	4.49	4.36	4.23	4.11
7	5.39	5.21	5.03	4.87	4.71	4.56
8	5.97	5.75	5.53	5.33	5.15	4.97
9	6.52	6.25	6.00	5.76	5.54	5.33
10	7.02	6.71	6.42	6.14	5.89	5.65
11	7.50	7.14	6.81	6.50	6.21	5.94
12	7.94	7.54	7.16	6.81	6.49	6.19
13	8.36	7.90	7.49	7.10	6.75	6.42
14	8.75	8.24	7.79	7.37	6.98	6.63
15	9.11	8.56	8.06	7.61	7.19	6.81
16	9.45	8.85	8.31	7.82	7.38	6.97
17	9.76	9.12	8.54	8.02	7.55	7.12
18	10.06	9.37	8.76	8.20	7.70	7.25
19	10.34	9.60	8.95	8.36	7.84	7.37
20	10.59	9.82	9.13	8.51	7.96	7.47

N/I	**7%** *0.070*	**8%** *0.080*	**9%** *0.090*	**10%** *0.100*	**11%** *0.110*	**12%** *0.120*
21	10.84	10.02	9.29	8.65	8.08	7.56
22	11.06	10.20	9.44	8.77	8.18	7.64
23	11.27	10.37	9.58	8.88	8.27	7.72
24	11.47	10.53	9.71	8.98	8.35	7.78
25	11.65	10.67	9.82	9.08	8.42	7.84
26	11.83	10.81	9.93	9.16	8.49	7.90
27	11.99	10.94	10.03	9.24	8.55	*7.92*
28	12.14	11.05	10.12	9.31	8.60	*7.92*
29	12.28	11.16	10.20	9.37	*8.64*	*7.92*
30	12.41	11.26	10.27	9.43	*8.64*	*7.92*
31	12.53	11.35	10.34	9.48	*8.64*	*7.92*
32	12.65	11.43	10.41	*9.50*	*8.64*	*7.92*
33	12.75	11.51	10.46	*9.50*	*8.64*	*7.92*
34	12.85	11.59	10.52	*9.50*	*8.64*	*7.92*
35	12.95	11.65	*10.56*	*9.50*	*8.64*	*7.92*

N/I	**7%** *0.070*	**8%** *0.080*	**9%** *0.090*	**10%** *0.100*	**11%** *0.110*	**12%** *0.120*
36	13.04	11.72	*10.56*	*9.50*	*8.64*	*7.92*
37	13.12	11.78	*10.56*	*9.50*	*8.64*	*7.92*
38	13.19	11.83	*10.56*	*9.50*	*8.64*	*7.92*
39	13.26	*11.88*	*10.56*	*9.50*	*8.64*	*7.92*
40	13.33	*11.88*	*10.56*	*9.50*	*8.64*	*7.92*
41	13.39	*11.88*	*10.56*	*9.50*	*8.64*	*7.92*
42	13.45	*11.88*	*10.56*	*9.50*	*8.64*	*7.92*
43	13.51	*11.88*	*10.56*	*9.50*	*8.64*	*7.92*
44	13.56	*11.88*	*10.56*	*9.50*	*8.64*	*7.92*
45	*13.57*	*11.88*	*10.56*	*9.50*	*8.64*	*7.92*
46	*13.57*	*11.88*	*10.56*	*9.50*	*8.64*	*7.92*
47	*13.57*	*11.88*	*10.56*	*9.50*	*8.64*	*7.92*
48	*13.57*	*11.88*	*10.56*	*9.50*	*8.64*	*7.92*
49	*13.57*	*11.88*	*10.56*	*9.50*	*8.64*	*7.92*
50	*13.57*	*11.88*	*10.56*	*9.50*	*8.64*	*7.92*

INDEX

ACCEPTING HOUSES COMMITTEE 55, 58
Agency Bills 58
Assets:
  current 90–1, 106–10
  intangible 129–30, 142–3
  operational 129–30
  tangible 124, 132–6

BALANCE SHEET CASH 20
Bank Bills 58
Banking facilities 63–5
Bank of England 55, 59–62, 85
Bank rate 67, 92
Bills of exchange 56–9:
  agency 58
  bank 58
  documentary 59
  finance 59
  fine bank 58
  foreign domicile 59
  history of 56–8
  modern bills 57
  period 58
  short dated government securities 59
  sight 58
  trade 58
  Treasury 59
Bills of sale 156–7
Book value 229
Borrowing on accounts receivable 115
Break even analysis 173–6
British Bankers Association 55

CAPITAL, COST OF 160–7
Capital allowances 142
Capital debt 153–4
  avoidability and level 210–11
  convertible debentures 172–3
  cost 164–5
  level 169–73
  management 209–11
  measurement technique 170–2
  most suitable type 172–3
Capital gearing and leverage ratio 157–60
Capital reserve 153
  cost 163–4
Capital structure 8, 10, 14–15, 147–67
  and fixed assets 130–2
  assessment 157
  bills of sale 156–7
  capital debt 153–4, 164–5, 169–73
  company's objectives 168–9
  cost of capital 160–7
  debentures 154–6
  dividend policies 180–4
  loans 156
  management 156–88
  mortgages 156–7
  ordinary shares 148–50, 161–3

Capital structure—*contd*
preference shares 150–3, 163, 173–6
price/earnings multiples 186–8
reserves 153, 162–4, 176–80
rights issues 184–6
Cash 20
balances 20
budget 48–53
incurrent assets and sales 38–42
initial balance 45–6
management 35–53
net values 109–10
produce-cash cycle 31–2
reserves 36
total cash handled 38–42
Cash flows 29–31, 34, 50–2, 69–72
control of 43–5
detailed 70–2
projected 47–8
weekly 70–2
City, the 55–6, 63, 184
Close companies 192–207
and taxation 203–6, 212–17
management 223–5
Companies:
and borrowing 196
close 192–207, 212–17, 223–5
dilution of equity 196–7
overseas 203
public 192–207
value 228–30
Companies Acts 1948 and 1967 192
Convertible debentures 155–6, 172–3
Corporate structure 8, 10–11, 14–15, 191–207
borrowing 195–6
close companies 192–207, 213–15
cost of raising funds 197–201
debt 209–11
dilution of equity 196–7
economic considerations 194–201
large firms 217–21
legal environment 192–4
limited liability 192–4, 202–3
management 208–25
mergers 226–8
overseas companies 203
ownership and control 206–7, 211–12, 221–3
partnerships 192–207, 225
public companies 192–207
small firms 212–17
takeovers 227–8, 230–6
taxation 194, 205–6, 211–12
unlimited liability 192, 201–2
value of company 228–30
Corporation tax 203–5, 212
Cost of capital 160–7
capital and revenue reserves 163–4
debt 164–5
ordinary shares 161–3
preference shares 163
weighted average cost 165–7
Cost of raising funds 197–201
issuing methods 199–201
Credit sales, cost of 112–13
Current assets 23, 90–1, 106–10
accounts receivable 109
cash in 38–42
management 109–10
net cash values 109–10
Current liabilities 23–4, 91–7, 105–8
accounts payable 172–3
deferred 93
level 93–7
management 122–3
net current debt 95

DEBENTURES 154–6
convertible 155–6, 172–3
redeemable 154
Depreciation 141–2
Dilution of equity 196–7, 201
Discount houses 60–1
Discount market 59–62
"eligible papers" 61
rates 60

Dividend policies 180–4
  cash dividends 180–3
  scrip issue 180, 182–4
Documentary Bills 59

Equity, dilution of 196–7, 201
Expenditures 46–7

Factoring accounts receivable 114
Finance Act 1965 206, 213
Finance Bills 59
Financial decision making 1–16
  financial management 6–9
  financial managers 3–4
  money and finance 2–3
  planning and control 4–6
Financial management 6–9
Financial managers 3–4, 47, 213–14, 226
Financing accounts receivable 113
Fine Bank Bills 58
Fixed assets 9–10, 13–14:
  and capital structure 130–2
  definition 124, 125
  distinction between short- and long-term operations 124
  intangible assets 129–30, 142–3
  loans to other firms 126
  long-term investments 126–9
  management 124–43
  operational assets 129–30
  ownership decision 136–40
  purchase of minority interests 126–7
  sinking and reserve funds 127–8
  tangible assets 129, 132–6
  taxation 140–2
  volume decision 136
Flows:
  net cash 29–31, 34, 50–2, 69–72
  of funds 28–31, 65, 66
  planning 73–5
  short-term money 69–85
  timing 27–8
  working capital 26–8

Foreign Domicile Bills 59

Gilt edged market 63
Government securities 62–3
  National Debt 62
  short-dates 59
  Tap of Treasury Bills 62

Hire purchase 139

Initial cash balance 45–6
Insolvency, technical and legal 23
Intangible assets 129–30
  management of 142–3
Investment grants 142
Issue by introduction 200–1
Issued shares 149
Issuing houses 200
Issuing methods 199–201

Leverage ratios 157–60
Liabilities, current 91–7, 105–8, 122–3
  short-term 92–3
Limited liability 192–4, 202–3
Liquidity 21–2
  and solvency 22–5
  and working capital ratios 24–5
  operation of 38–42
Loans 156
Local Authority Boards 60
London Discount Market 59, 60
  Association 55, 58

Management of cash 35–53
  cash budget 48–53
  control of cash flows 43–5
  deposit of receipts 36–8
  initial cash balance 45–6
  operation of liquidity 38–42
  operation of solvency 43–5
  projected cash flows 47–8
  sales, receipts and expenditures 46–7
Market value 230
Mergers 226–8
  definition 226

Money 19–20
  and finance 2–3
  ready money 20
Money, cash and near cash 19–34
  cash 20
  flow of funds 28–31
  liquidity 21–2, 24–5
  money 19–20
  nearness to cash 21–2
  produce-cash cycle 31–2
  solvency 22–5
  working capital 23–8
Money flow plan 75–85
Mortgages 139–40, 156–7
Mullen's and Company 62

NATIONAL DEBT 62
Nearness to cash 21–2
  See also Liquidity
Net cash flows 29–31, 34

OPERATIONAL ASSETS 129–30
Ordinary shares 148–50
  accounting classifications 148–50
  and right to vote 150
  authorised 148–9
  contractual obligations 149–50
  cost 161–3
  issued 149
Overseas companies 203
Ownership decision 136–40
  hire purchase 139
  leasing or buying 137–9
  mortgages 139–40

PARTNERSHIPS 192–207
  and borrowing 195–6
  and taxation 203, 212–17
  dilution of equity 196
  management 225
PAYE 93, 122, 123, 305, 214
Period Bills 58
Placing of shares 200
Preference shares 150–3: and
  break even analysis 173–6
  convertible 151–2, 173
  cost 163
  redemption 175
Price/earnings multiples and ratios 186–8, 233–4
Private companies, *see* Close companies
Produce-cash cycle 31–2
Promissory notes 93
Public companies 192–207
  and borrowing 196
  and taxation 234
Public offers 199

RAW MATERIALS 120–1
  management of 119–20
Receipts 46–7
  deposit of 36–8
Receivables:
  average age 101–4
  borrowing on accounts 115
  buying accounts 115–18
  factoring accounts 114
  financing accounts 113
Reserves:
  capital 153, 163–4
  reserve funds 127–8
  retained earnings 153
  revenue 153, 163–4
Retained earnings 153, 176–80
  cost 176–9
  management 179–80
Revenue reserves 153, 176–80
  cost 163–4
Rights issues 184–6, 200

SALE BY TENDER 199–200
Sales 38, 42, 46–7
Scrip issue 180, 182–4
Share placing 200
Short-term liabilities 92–3
Short-term money markets 54–85
  banking facilities 63–5
  Bills of Exchange 56–9
  the City 55–6, 63
  discount market 59–62
  management of flows 69–85
  market for Government securities 62–3
  planning flows 73–85

Sight Bills 58
Sinking funds 127
Solvency 22–5
  operation of 43–5
Stock Exchange, the 62, 197–200
Stocks:
  average age 99–100
  types of finance 120–2

TAKEOVERS 15–16, 227–8, 230–6
  accounts receivable 231–2
  asset policies 232
  avoidance 236
  definition 227–8
  earnings growth 232–3
  method 234–6
  price/earnings ratio 233–4
  situation 231–4
  unused cash 231
  volume of debt 232
Tangible assets 129, 132–6
  management 132–6
Tap of Treasury Bills 62
Taxation 194–5, 203–6, 211–12
  and fixed assets 140–2
  capital allowances 142
  corporation tax 203–5, 212
  depreciation 141–2
  investment grants 142
  leasing and buying 142
Trade accounts 92
  average age of debts 98–9
Trade Bills 58
Treasury Bills 59, 62, 63, 65
Trustee Acts 1925 and 1961 163, 180

ULTRA VIRES RULE 194
Unlimited liability 192, 201–2

VALUE OF COMPANIES 228–30
  book value 229
  market value 230
  present value of future earnings 229–30
Volume decision 136

WORKING CAPITAL 7–9, 13, 23–8, 87–123
  borrowing on accounts receivable 115
  buying accounts receivable 115–18
  cost of credit sales 110–13
  current assets 23, 90–1, 106–10
  current liabilities 23–4, 91–7, 105–8, 122–3
  factoring accounts receivable 114
  financing accounts receivable 113
  flows 26–8
  gross 23
  long-term 105–8
  management 105–23
  net 23
  ratios 24–5
  receivables 101–4
  short-term 108–9
  stocks 99–101
  trade debts 98–9
  types of stock finance 120–2